Feeling Strangely in Mid-Century Spanish
and Latin American Women's Fiction

Contemporary Hispanic and Lusophone Cultures

Series Editors
L. Elena Delgado, University of Illinois at Urbana-Champaign
Niamh Thornton, University of Liverpool

Series Editorial Board
Jo Labanyi, New York University
Chris Perriam, University of Manchester
Paul Julian Smith, CUNY Graduate Center

This series aims to provide a forum for new research on modern and contemporary hispanic and lusophone cultures and writing. The volumes published in Contemporary Hispanic and Lusophone Cultures reflect a wide variety of critical practices and theoretical approaches, in harmony with the intellectual, cultural and social developments that have taken place over the past few decades. All manifestations of contemporary hispanic and lusophone culture and expression are considered, including literature, cinema, popular culture, theory. The volumes in the series will participate in the wider debate on key aspects of contemporary culture.

16 José Colmeiro, *Peripheral Visions/Global Sounds: From Galicia to the World*

17 Regina Galasso, *Translating New York: The City's Languages in Iberian Literatures*

18 Daniel F. Silva, *Anti-Empire: Decolonial Interventions in Lusophone Literatures*

19 Luis I. Prádanos, *Postgrowth Imaginaries: New Ecologies and Counterhegemonic Culture in Post-2008 Spain*

20 Liz Harvey-Kattou, *Contested Identities in Costa Rica: Constructions of the Tico in Literature and Film*

21 Cecilia Enjuto-Rangel, Sebastiaan Faber, Pedro García-Caro, and Robert Patrick Newcomb, eds, *Transatlantic Studies: Latin America, Iberia, and Africa*

22 Ana Paula Ferreira, *Women Writing Portuguese Colonialism in Africa*

23 Esther Gimeno Ugalde, Marta Pacheco Pinto and Ângela Fernandes, eds, *Iberian and Translation Studies: Literary Contact Zones*

24 Ben Bollig, *Moving Voices: Poetry on Screen in Argentine Cinema*

25 Daniel F. Silva, *Empire Found: Racial Identities and Coloniality in Twenty-First-Century Portuguese Popular Cultures*

26 Dean Allbritton, *Feeling Sick: The Early Years of AIDS in Spain*

27 Ana Fernandez-Cebrian, *Fables of Development: Capitalism and Social Imaginaries in Spain (1950-1967)*

28 María Chouza-Calo, Esther Fernández and Jonathan Thacker, eds, *Daring Adaptations, Creative Failures and Experimental Performances in Iberian Theatre*

29 Anna Tybinko, Lamonte Aidoo and Daniel F. Silva, eds, *Migrant Frontiers: Race and Mobility in the Luso-Hispanic World*

Feeling Strangely in Mid-Century Spanish and Latin American Women's Fiction

Gender and the Scientific Imaginary

TESS C. RANKIN

LIVERPOOL UNIVERSITY PRESS

First published 2024 by
Liverpool University Press
4 Cambridge Street
Liverpool
L69 7ZU

Copyright © 2024 Liverpool University Press

Tess C. Rankin has asserted her rights to be identified as the author
of this book in accordance with the Copyright, Designs
and Patents Act 1988.

All rights reserved. No part of this book may be reproduced,
stored in a retrieval system, or transmitted, in any form or by any means,
electronic, mechanical, photocopying, recording, or otherwise,
without the prior written permission of the publisher.

British Library Cataloguing-in-Publication data
A British Library CIP record is available

ISBN 978-1-83764-474-2 cased

Typeset in Borges by
Carnegie Book Production, Lancaster
Printed and bound by CPI Group (UK) Ltd, Croydon CR0 4YY

For Dana

Acknowledgments

I am thankful to everyone who has been a part of my life while this project was developing, and to the authors who wrote these four novels. Their work felt deeply personal, and I could not have written this book or found so much meaning in theirs if not for the people around me.

To everyone at Sweet Water Dance and Yoga for being my dance family, and especially Nyota Nayo for being a constant inspiring presence. To Valerie Deas for allowing her beautiful art to grace the cover of this book, you are missed. I am grateful to all the friends who have supported me while I wrote, revised, and ignored the book, particularly for their faith and interest in my ideas when I could summon neither. My thanks go to Sarah Poyet and Alejandra Rosenberg Navarro for their friendship over the past few years. To Irina Troconis for her impeccable close reading of my text messages. To Nora Lambrecht for more than a decade of reading, editing, and improving all of my writing, and for every chat, text, and conversation. To Elizabeth Benninger for friendship since gender class and all of the kitty support.

To Jo Labanyi for championing my work and my writing, throughout grad school and beyond. Her enthusiasm has meant so much to me. To my dissertation committee members Gabriel Giorgi and Gabriela Basterra for their early roles in shaping my project. To Chloe Johnson for her patience and guidance, and the entire editorial and production team at Liverpool University Press. To James Ryan and Kate Murphy for their work in making this manuscript a book.

To cousin-friend Robin Levine, who will always be my cool sixteen-year-old role model. To Skye Donzelli, the older sister I never had. To Kaz Uyehara for always picking up our conversations right where we left off. To Tom Chapman for every road trip in Spain and since. To Raquel del Campo González for always making our time together an adventure. To Kirin McElwain for bringing the cello back to me in a joyful way. To my grandmothers, Gramma Belle and Gramma Rankin, for expanding my childhood world. To my parents, Barbara J. Crawford and Robby Rankin, for loving me as I grow and change.

To Sirius, the truly feral cat, and Samantha, the cat who encouraged me to live in the moment and bite the things I want. To Edgardo Núñez Caballero for showing me how to embrace my feral nature. And to Dana Kaplan-Angle: you were a part of everything wonderfully strange about my childhood, you let me grow up, and our friendship taught me so much about being in the world. I love you and I miss you.

An earlier version of chapter 1 appeared in the *Journal of Spanish Cultural Studies* 22, no. 2, as "Molecular *Rareza*: Reading Science in Literature with Rosa Chacel's *Memorias de Leticia Valle*," www.tandfonline.com/toc/cjsc20/22/2?nav=tocList.

Contents

Introduction ... 1

1. ¿Qué es la materia? / What's the Matter? Material *Rareza* and *Memorias de Leticia Valle* ... 19

2. (Un)Toward Magnetism: Relational *Rareza* and *Personas en la sala* ... 63

3. Self-Centered Worlds: Perceptual *Rareza* and *Nada* ... 105

4. Difference and Desire after Darwin: Animal *Rareza* and *Perto do coração selvagem* ... 139

Conclusion ... 173

Works Cited ... 179

Index ... 189

Introduction

Que façam harpa de meus nervos quando eu morrer.
—Clarice Lispector, *Perto do coração selvagem*[1]

*M*ay they make a harp out of my nerves when I die. This sentence of Lispector's expresses a wish for bodily unraveling—and for music. I have chosen it to open this study of literary constructions of gender through the lens of scientific discourse both for its reference to nerves and for its wedding of scientific and artistic images—but mostly for its beauty: for its beautiful depiction of desire. It is desire formed in the body but not contained by its form, the desire of a living woman for a new way of being in death. In the chapters that follow, I will argue explicitly for the prominence of scientific vocabulary and ideas and their relevance for reading the construction of gender in a set of mid-twentieth-century novels. Not all of the depictions of the gendered experiences of the young protagonists in these novels are beautiful: many are even violent or painful. But they are all similarly evocative and imaginative. Undergirding my argument about how we can read these novels in the light of scientific ideas is another argument about precisely the style these authors use to construct novels about young women's experiences. That argument advocates for understanding gender through the moments in literature that resist narrative distillation. As we

---

1 Clarice Lispector, *Perto do coração selvagem* [1943] (Rio de Janeiro: Rocco, 1998), 172, [164]. All quotations in English are from Alison Entrekin's translation: *Near to the Wild Heart* (New York: New Directions, 2012). Sources date the publication of this novel to both 1943 and 1944. The English translation identifies the original copyright date as 1943, and a write-up published in *O Jornal* on December 31, 1943, suggests that the novel was already released by that time. See Adonis Filho, "Perto do coração selvagem," *O Jornal*, December 31, 1943, 7. Published translations are enclosed in quotation marks throughout with while my own translations in parentheses are not. Pagination of translated passages appears in brackets in in-text citations.

will see, Lispector's protagonist offers up many such moments, and it is her reflection above that I hope might productively set the tone for what follows. Along with *Perto do coração selvagem* from 1943, I read Rosa Chacel's *Memorias de Leticia Valle* (1945), Norah Lange's *Personas en la sala* (1950), and Carmen Laforet's *Nada* (1945).[2]

All four novels were written by women about young female protagonists. I pick up on Carmen Martín Gaite's term *chica rara* to examine the strange protagonists of these four novels.[3] It is important to situate this term historically, though I will argue that it can do important work outside of its original context and may indeed be useful for feminist thought today. Martín Gaite used chica rara to refer to the sort of protagonists that emerged in opposition to the chaste, Catholic, romantic heroines of the *novela rosa*, who were meant to become the perfect wives and mothers envisioned by Franco's regime. In *Desde la ventana*, Martín Gaite describes Carmen Laforet's protagonist Andrea, in *Nada*, as the prototypical chica rara. In *Usos amorosos de la postguerra española*, she also observes that *rara* was a term used to censure young women's nonconformist behavior or explain their social failures (remaining single, for example).[4] Though this figure is usually limited to her appearance in postwar Spain, Debra Ochoa has referred to chicas raras beyond the postwar period, and even post-Franco, to discuss female protagonists who challenge gender norms or whose femininity registers some sort of chafing strangeness of gender.[5]

In some senses, the chica rara as Martín Gaite conceived her might seem to set the bar for rareza rather low for nonconformity or strangeness. And indeed, Andrea could read as a fairly conventional protagonist with a moderate rebellious streak. I believe, however, that that is a good thing: rareza need not manifest itself in radical challenges to conventional gender roles. Rather, we will see it on a fine-grained level pervading even the smallest exchanges, perceptions, and thoughts that mark these young women and affect how they incorporate the world around them, and how the world treats them in response. Another key aspect of rareza in Martín Gaite's original

---

2 Carol Maier translated Chacel's novel as *Memoirs of Leticia Valle* in 1994; however, all translations here are my own. I will cite Charlotte Whittle's translation of Lange's *People in the Room* (Sheffield: And Other Stories, 2018) and Edith Grossman's translation of Laforet's novel, also titled *Nada* (Nothing) (New York: The Modern Library, 2007).

3 See Carmen Martín Gaite, *Desde la ventana: Enfoque femenino de la literatura española* (Madrid: Espasa-Calpe, 1987), 101.

4 Carmen Martín, *Usos amorosos de la postguerra española* [1987] (Barcelona: Anagrama, 2011).

5 Debra J. Ochoa, "Critiques of the 'Novela Rosa': Martín Gaite, Almodóvar, and Etxebarría," *Letras Femeninas* 32, no. 1 (2006): 189–203.

usage and relevant here is how it reflects observations, often by other women, about something odd going on in women and girls. She noted that women were labeled *raras* by those around them (the inescapable strangeness of certain single women captured by phrases like "Esta va para solterona" [She's going to end up an old maid]): these judgments suggest observers' (often other women's) ability to catch a glimpse of gendered strangeness—a wrong gesture or odd interest (Martín Gaite, *Usos amorosos* 38). In that sense, such judgments register and organize categories around real, material behaviors and expressions of affect. Meanwhile, scientific ideas were at work also shaping how people categorized and saw their own experiences.

The first decades of the twentieth century saw an abundance of publications describing scientific discoveries to lay audiences. Texts in French, German, and English were translated in Spanish and Portuguese, and autochthonous scientific and pseudoscientific writing spread through Spain and Latin America. Through everything from Darwinism to Umwelten to magnetism, scientists asked their readers to consider a world in which solid matter dissolved into a blur of interacting particles, our senses misled us, and the boundaries of the self and the human fell away. The dissemination of these reimaginings touched every area of human experience—from politics and governance to social mores and culture—and new scientifically inspired possibilities and anxieties seeped into all manner of social, political, and cultural formations. While some scientific-political and scientific-cultural pairings in the Spanish and Latin American contexts have been examined, in the study that follows I turn to gender, understanding it as a felt experience entrenched in everyday life and shaped by how we imagine our material and affective relations in and with the world—relations that were being fundamentally reshaped by contemporaneous scientific advancements. Guided by affect theory and new materialist theory, I consider our sensorial and affective feelings as influenced by discourses that help us understand the world, particularly oft-overlooked scientific ones, which escaped from their scholarly confines and filtered into the public imagination.

Such an interdisciplinary tendency has had its critics: Max Eastman, in *The Literary Mind: Its Place in an Age of Science* (1931), posits that the prominence of science explains "the whole contemporary agitation among critics and literary professors; it explains the present tendencies in fiction; it explains the 'modernist' poets" (whom he generally dismisses as obfuscating and unintelligible despite their attempt to "surrender themselves [...] to the mere uninterpreted qualities of experience").[6] This takedown seems to me

---

6 Max Eastman, *The Literary Mind: Its Place in an Age of Science* (New York: Scribner, 1931), 11, 85.

rather promising. The fact that the prominence of science was, in Eastman's eyes, responsible for everything he disliked about literature and literary studies among his contemporaries suggests that the 1920s, 1930s, and beyond saw the burgeoning impact of scientific ideas. But before detailing my methodology for reading literature in the age of science, I want to set out my approach to the topic I will be examining through literary and scientific lenses—gender and its construction.

As A. Finn Enke sets out succinctly on the first page of *Transfeminist Perspectives in and beyond Transgender and Gender Studies*:

> Feminist, women's, and gender studies grew partly from Simone de Beauvoir's observation that "one is not born, but rather becomes, a woman." Transgender studies extends this foundation, emphasizing that there is no natural process by which *any*one becomes woman, and also that *every*one's gender is made: Gender, and also sex, are made through complex social and technical manipulations that naturalize some while abjecting others.[7]

Gender is made, and people become women in a messy and never complete process. In what follows I will focus on femininity, rather than womanhood, treating it as an open, gendered field that may tilt subjects into becoming always-imperfect women. Judith Butler cites Aretha Franklin's singing "You make me feel like a natural woman" to discuss gender as constructed and performative.[8] I take femininity to be an exercise in *feeling like*. Feeling like means asymptotically approaching and never arriving; it speaks to the imperfect and never complete nature of gender. It sometimes means veering away from social norms into a zone of estrangement or alienation.

Gender manages to function as a category that is strictly policed while (perhaps because) its boundaries are porous and difficult to define. Even as gender is produced through a largely binary system, it not only leaves evidence of that system's constructed nature but also constantly registers its affective-material openness to other modes of being. The felt experience of gender thus includes feelings of its unsettledness. To try to speak of what individuals feel their gender to be runs us quickly into narrative and linguistic boundaries. I am grateful, then, to be able to turn to such eloquent, perplexing novels as those I study here. Novels do not necessarily mirror

---

7 A. Finn Enke, *Transfeminist Perspectives in and beyond Transgender and Gender Studies* (Philadelphia: Temple University Press, 2012), 1.

8 Judith Butler, "Imitation and Gender Insubordination," in *The Lesbian and Gay Studies Reader*, ed. Henry Abelove, Michele Aina Barale, and David M. Halperin (New York: Routledge, 1993), 317.

scientific thought, nor do they even necessarily refract it through literary language. Nonscientific writing may in fact prove to be anticipatory, pushing at the edge of a possibility or anxiety that is coming onto the horizon of the public's imagination even before its scientific theorization.

While I do note some of the "social and technical manipulations" that construct gender, I am primarily interested in how all social experience is internalized as gendered and in how those resultant *gendered feelings* can shift based on shared ways of imagining the world. Gender is everywhere: it is in the process of being formed in every action and interaction. Whereas gender *roles* may be easier to spot, I discuss *gender* as a felt experience, created in part by what society assigns as roles, certainly, but also shaped by patterns of acts, affective modes, and discourses that determine how we think about, move through, and internalize the world around us. One such discourse, largely neglected in relation to gender, is scientific discourse. While art and gender, literature and gender, politics and gender, law and gender, and many other such pairings abound in contemporary scholarship, science and gender is often circumscribed by a narrow understanding of their potential relationship, defined by scientific research on the topics of sex and gender. While biomedical science has been mined for its perspective on sex and gender—and its disciplinary control over them—other, less apparently pertinent fields are often neglected.[9] Reading early to mid-twentieth-century scientific writing for popular audiences, I draw out the trends, anxieties, possibilities, and models for understanding the world that would have reached their readers and an even wider swath of the popular imagination. Along the way, I find science and literature asking similar questions about how we sense or perceive our environments, how we delimit bodies and matter and humanness, and how we relate and communicate.

In all cases, I use *feeling* in multiple senses, informed by affect theory and new materialism, as well as by the scientific texts I study. While we might think of emotions as the socially structured and defined forms that affect takes, leaving an unincorporated, felt remainder (picking up on Brian Massumi), I tend toward an affection for the term *feelings*. Feelings hint at the importance of material sensation, and they allow us to look for insight in both pre-organized states (we can feel a rush of adrenaline, it, too, a material thing) and in the everyday expressions of emotion (I feel bored, I feel anxious) whose interrogation might yield unexpected insight into who or what we feel we are at that moment. I choose *feelings* over *emotions* in order

---

9 See chapter 1 for a discussion of early twentieth-century biomedical discourses on sex.

to sidestep the affect/emotion divide that has persisted in some affect theory and to allow for the aspect of materiality implicit in feeling.

Writing on the very process by which affect has both a social and bodily existence, Teresa Brennan uses the term "transmission of affect" "to capture a process that is social in origin but biological and physical in effect."[10] John Protevi, in *Political Affect: Connecting the Social and the Somatic*, writes that "affect is concretely the imbrication of the social and the somatic, as our bodies change in relation to the changing situations in which they find themselves."[11] Texts such as Elizabeth A. Wilson's *Gut Feminism* or Ann Cvetkovich's *Depression: A Public Feeling* explore precisely that overlap, that inextricable connection between body and society that affect theory often explores. In *Queer Phenomenology*, Sara Ahmed describes spaces as "like a second skin that unfolds in the folds of the body."[12] Thus the body is shaped by what it finds close at hand, by the motions it goes through, by what is made easeful and what is made difficult by the space it inhabits.

Jane Bennett's *Vibrant Matter* sets out a philosophical/political project to think through the commonly accepted "partition of the sensible" (via Rancière) into dull matter versus vibrant life, reworking this division in favor of vital materiality. She draws on Spinoza, Nietzsche, Thoreau, Darwin, Adorno, Deleuze, Bergson, and Driesch, contesting the idea that "materiality" should be thought of as purely Marxist and not include Foucaudian bodies and pleasures or Deleuzian assemblages.[13] Bennett's turn to sympathy picks up on the presence of affect in her work on materiality. In the chapter "Of Material Sympathies, Paracelsus, and Whitman" in *Material Ecocriticism*, Bennett attempts to extend the notion of sympathy to nonhuman and inorganic bodies, reworking it as "an impersonal ontological infrastructure, an undesigned system of affinities (which persist alongside antipathies)

---

10 Teresa Brennan, *The Transmission of Affect* (Ithaca, NY: Cornell University Press, 2004), 3. She cites processes like chemical or electrical entrainment as scientific examples of how affect is transmitted: they are processes "whereby one person's or one group's nervous and hormonal systems are brought into alignment with another's" (9). The feelings I explore in this book are sometimes shared, but other times one person's feeling is internalized in a very different form by the other. Brennan refers to feelings as "sensations that have found the right match in words" (5). My own use of *feelings* is a bit broader and includes experiences not fully expressed in language.

11 John Protevi, *Political Affect: Connecting the Social and the Somatic* (Minneapolis: University of Minnesota Press, 2009), xiv.

12 Sara Ahmed, *Queer Phenomenology: Orientations, Objects, Others* (Durham, NC: Duke University Press, 2006), 9.

13 Jane Bennett, *Vibrant Matter: A Political Ecology of Things* (Durham, NC: Duke University Press, 2010), xvi.

between and within bodies" and "a material agency, a power of bodies human and nonhuman, a mode of impersonal connection, attachment, and care that proceeds from below subjectivity and into subjectivity."[14] From this definition, sympathy becomes inclination, the gently cocked head of the nonchalant listener or the plant turned slightly toward the sun. Mimetic posture is one way into recognition that crosses into and out of the human, and that is key for Bennett's understanding of affect, highlighting again the physicality of feelings. These tendencies in recent scholarship generally orient my approach to what it means to think about gender as *felt*—as simultaneously affective and material, as relational, as incorporating human, nonhuman, organic, and inorganic bodies. My theorization of how gendered processes of feeling, relating, and desiring occur is based on scientific writing contemporary to the novels I study.

How we think and talk about ourselves shifts through metaphor, analogy, or more oblique uses of language or imagery that can arise from any number of areas. In *Becoming Insomniac: How Sleeplessness Alarmed Modernity*, Lee Scrivner describes this vividly:

> When we change the technologies or materials through which we analogize ourselves—whether we see ourselves as creatures made of clumps of earth, or of humors in and out of balance, or of temperatures and pressures of blood; whether our mental activity is conceived through the image of a filing cabinet or an Internet search engine—each respective self-imagining will suggest and then incite adjustments in our outlooks, fixations, values, and behaviors.[15]

Thus Laura Otis examines metaphor in *Membranes: Metaphors of Invasion in Nineteenth-Century Literature, Science, and Politics* (1999) as a way of tracking the possibilities opened up by scientific thought (as well as the political and social concerns that shaped scientific investigation). Otis convincingly argues for the mutual influence of scientific and literary imaginaries underlain by common political anxieties, largely in the work of literary authors who have an explicit scientific interest.

It is instructive to examine the ways in which the field of science studies has in recent years established various methodologies for considering the interaction and occasionally the blurring of science and literature.

---

14 Jane Bennett, "Of Material Sympathies, Paracelsus, and Whitman," in *Material Ecocriticism*, ed. Serenella Iovino and Serpil Oppermann (Bloomington: Indiana University Press, 2014), 239–40, 50.
15 Lee Scrivner, *Becoming Insomniac: How Sleeplessness Alarmed Modernity* (Basingstoke: Palgrave Macmillan, 2014), 24.

Sometimes science fiction joins the two fields directly, but often science is seen to pass out of a disciplinary structure, through a sociopolitical anxiety or an imaginative metaphor, and then into literary expression. Through a number of productive and creative readings of literature, critics have contributed to how we think about that middle space, and what its productive possibilities are.

In *Darwin's Plots: Evolutionary Narrative in Darwin, George Eliot and Nineteenth-Century Fiction*, Gillian Beer writes: "Most major scientific theories rebuff common sense. They call on evidence beyond the reach of our senses and overturn the observable world. They disturb assumed relationships and shift what has been substantial into metaphor. [...] When it is first advanced, theory is at its most fictive."[16] I argue that both during that period of fictiveness and during the time when once-novel scientific theory has solidified as common sense, scientific ideas do not just influence what we think and believe about the world but how we experience it and how we feel ourselves to be in it.

Beer moves deftly between scientific and literary texts when she writes on Darwin's imagination and empathy; Elizabeth Grosz structures creative genealogies that arc from Darwin to Irigaray (see chapter 4). Beer, Gross, and Otis have most provocatively shifted the ground for the study of science and literature, but they stand alongside numerous other critics who take up instances of scientific language in literary work, trace lines of influence out of the hard sciences into popular discourse and back again, and more generally track the possibilities of new scientific paradigms beyond the strictures of a single discipline.

The scientific writing I examine comes from books, magazines, and newspaper articles and is mostly aimed at a general reading public. Some of the narratives have wandered so far afield from their underpinning scientific inspiration that they become pseudoscience (see popular books on magnetism and the occult in chapter 2). In other cases, articles attest to the widespread knowledge of certain important concepts that extends beyond even a literary or literate public (as with Darwinism, examined in chapter 4). I am less interested in highly specialized scientific discourse circulated within the confines of scholarly journals, and more interested in the translations and mutations of scientific ideas out of the academy and into the popular imagination. However, the divide between the two is not entirely rigid, with scientists themselves addressing broader audiences

---

16 Gillian Beer, *Darwin's Plots: Evolutionary Narrative in Darwin, George Eliot and Nineteenth-Century Fiction* (Cambridge: Cambridge University Press, 2009), 1; emphasis in original.

in general interest publications. While my sources are textual, I highlight how certain ideas reached the public in other ways, be it through talks and museum exhibits or images in newspapers. I hope to show that these novels, despite being "high-brow" cultural products whose readership would have been limited, in part by factors like class, are a creative response to ideas that circulated more widely.

Perhaps unsurprisingly, the scientific–literary relationship is usually figured through patterns in language that make that relationship apparent. Sometimes metaphors in scientific writing make clear the sociopolitical and/or literary influences of its author; other times literary works pick up vocabulary that originated in a scientific field. It is tempting to jump at each mention of vibrations or atoms in a nonscientific text as evidence of the traffic in scientific ideas and their ability to permeate the popular imagination. Gaining access to a wider scientific repertoire allows us to be attuned to echoing implications of metaphoric structures that we might otherwise overlook: we might recognize that an allusion to evolution does not just connote change or progress but emits a static-electric anxiety that touches on the randomness of variation, the unperfected state of humanhood, and the openness of the species. Some rhetorical figures may have dulled to commonplaces with time while others might always have carried a literary burnish that obscured their scientific sides. And indeed the appearance of such words and concepts does make an argument for the ubiquity and productivity of scientific ideas outside of their original disciplines. But taking a broader view of what kind of thinking and feeling vibratory or atomic theory, for example, made possible allows us to see their presence in more abstract ways that perhaps more fundamentally shaped contemporary texts even in the absence of telltale linguistic markers.

Lisa Blackman, in *Immaterial Bodies: Affect, Embodiment, Mediation*, carefully brings scientific concepts into the realm of affect theory. While that move can be a tricky one—critics are often accused of a lack of rigor in approaching the scientific material—her reading of concepts in neuroscience, including those that have fallen out of favor, attends to the underlying debates and methodologies in the field that may prove suggestive and fruitful for affect theorists in the humanities exploring questions of consciousness and embodiment. She is also able to trace concerns that resurfaced in scientific conversations over decades and even centuries, pursuing an approach to chronology that suggests the persistence and continued relevance of ideas in scientific and nonscientific debate.[17]

---

17 See Lisa Blackman, *Immaterial Bodies: Affect, Embodiment, Mediation* (London: Sage, 2013), 181.

Regarding the timeline of the reception of scientific ideas, the editors of *Vibratory Modernism*[18]—a volume that pairs a scientific concept with a literary movement—argue convincingly, citing Michael Whitworth, that even though earlier certain concepts they examine had been discredited by the 1920s, modernist authors continued to pick up on "outdated" scientific frameworks in part because the rapidly developing science of the time was not able to offer constantly up-to-date authoritative theories of quantum physics, in part because some scientists continued to put forward older concepts, and in part because of the resonance that loosely interpreted scientific notions had found outside of the discipline.[19] This lag effect is

---

18 Something of an anomaly, Anglophone modernism with its aesthetic innovations for portraying perception and the visible and invisible world, and human consciousness—particularly works by Virginia Woolf—has attracted the attention of scholars looking at the interface of science and literature. One such exploration is Holly Henry's *Virginia Woolf and the Discourse of Science: The Aesthetics of Astronomy* (Cambridge: Cambridge University Press, 2003). While such modernism differs from Spanish-language *modernismo*, the works examined in this study might be said to be participating in an international conversation and to maintain some relationship with English-language modernism. I do not wish to position these or other Spanish and Latin American works as in any way derivative of a British or US tradition. (Apparent consonances often awaken a desire to search for influence: see chapter 4 for more on Clarice Lispector's insistence that she had not read James Joyce when a phrase from his work was suggested as the title for her own.) Rather, I believe there may be some value in considering modernism-*modernismo* writ large: Susan Kirkpatrick describes modernism as the aesthetic response to processes of modernization (see *Mujer, modernismo y vanguardia en España (1898-1931)*, translated by Jacqueline Cruz, [Madrid: Cátedra, 2003]). Jonathan Flatley uses the term to refer to the "range of practices that attempt in one way or another to respond to the gap between the social realities of modernization and the promises of the project of modernity," making modernism for him the symbolic space of contestations of modernity (*Affective Mapping: Melancholia and the Politics of Modernism* [Cambridge, MA: Harvard University Press, 2008], 32). Scientific advances indeed form part of processes of modernization, but we will see in a number of social and political contexts how those processes often entailed constraining women's possibilities. The novels in this study may be considered modern due to their aesthetic and formal innovation, but they also emerge from contexts in which women's roles in modernity are being shaped in concert with national narratives, bringing women's actions under scrutiny and increased control. The chapters that follow will explore the anxiety awakened by the need to forge women's place in modernity, a restrictive process that often called upon scientific discourse for justification. For a recent comparative study that locates Spanish modernism in a European context, see Katharine Murphy's "Spanish Modernism in Context: Failed Heroism and Cross-Cultural Encounters in Pío Baroja and Joseph Conrad," *Bulletin of Spanish Studies* 97, no. 5 (2020): 807-29.

19 Anthony Enns and Shelley Trower, eds., *Vibratory Modernism* (Basingstoke: Palgrave Macmillan, 2013), 15.

helpful to keep in mind when attempting to trace the paths that scientific thought took through time and through various disciplines.

The felt experience of gender might be defined or structured by countless categories, but here I propose just four that, broad and overlapping as they are, allow me to explore a wide range of scientific thinking that filtered into popular understanding at the time—scientific discourses and narratives, and even fragments of scientific ideas, comprising a more overlooked influence in analyses of gender in literary studies. These four categories are materiality, relation, perception, and desire. I argue that understandings of these categories shifted with emerging scientific concepts. That meant a shift in the potential ways gender was constructed through those same categories. Fascination with Darwinism, for example, rattled the human–animal division, and women—seen as serpentine, feline, or simply monstrous— could be made to answer for resultant anxieties.[20]

Atoms and molecules broke down solid matter and with it the limits of bodies and objects. These and other scientific narratives propagated for a nonspecialist audience will be explored in four chapters that each examine a different novel: ¿Qué es la materia? / What's the Matter? Material *Rareza* and *Memorias de Leticia Valle*; (Un)Toward Magnetism: Relational *Rareza* and *Personas en la sala*; Self-Centered Worlds: Perceptual *Rareza* and *Nada*; and Difference and Desire after Darwin: Animal *Rareza* and *Perto do coração selvagem*.

Published within a ten-year span, these four novels share in a specific historic moment, but from the perspective of diverse geographical locations and linguistic traditions. I am able to trace how related ideas circulated between Spain and Latin America, both through the publishing market and the effects of exile following the Spanish Civil War, resulting in shared referents on both sides of the Atlantic. I also address the distinct historical contexts affecting women, and women authors, in Spain, Argentina, and Brazil when these books were published. In all three countries, social restrictions on women were tightening after an earlier moment of expansion. I look at the specific challenges these authors faced as women writers, particularly in the creation of authorial personas that were heavily gendered

---

20 Kyla Schuller focuses on another way the human species relates to other species by looking at Lyme patients and "argu[ing] that spirochete illness exposes how the human sensory and emotional apparatus doesn't pertain to a singular subject but to a complex microbial choreography of which the human is one part." Schuller's analysis is a good example of how the scientific possibilities I raise in separate chapters—the openness of the human body in chapter 1, and the openness of the human species in chapter 4—overlap and coexist. Kyla Schuller, "The Microbial Self: Sensation and Sympoeisis," *Resilience: A Journal of the Environmental Humanities* 5, no. 3 (2018): 53.

and that they could not entirely control themselves. I do not posit these specific experiences as broadly shared even by other women within their own countries, as their identities were shaped by their race, class, relatively privileged positions, and the act of authorship itself. The social and cultural experience of something like Darwinism, which sparked so many racist and eugenicist responses, would be different for Black or Indigenous authors. I do suggest that their works register some of the cultural and philosophical questions about how we experience the world in gendered ways that cut across social sectors.

Fundamentally these authors are connected by their innovative use of language in their narratives of unusual young women. While Lispector is considered part of the *terceira fase do modernismo* in Brazil, Lange formed part of the Argentinean avant-garde, Chacel, a member of the Generación del '27, would go into exile in Latin America, and Laforet would continue to write under the dictatorship in Spain, I refer to all four as participating in the broad context of international literary modernism with works whose experimental prose styles engaged modern societal shifts, in this case with regard to gender. Not only do these authors explore the construction of gender through their young women protagonists but their use of language pushes against narrative formats. Descriptions, details, and fragments seem to collide with plot and even character development. Their prose styles are experimental in varying degrees, but in all cases their language seems to create affective confusion: readers must ask why these protagonists seem to feel as they do. And what are the pertinent details that make us understand who people are in the world and how they act? In all cases, narrative seems secondary to the creative unfolding of textual material.

I am also invested in a project of recovering women's writing and reading it seriously and imaginatively. These novels have received varying degrees of critical attention but are not generally centered in studies of the literary landscape of the period. Readings of *Memorias de Leticia Valle* are most frequently filtered through a psychoanalytic lens. Norah Lange's public role in the Argentinian avant-garde is often commented on, though her actual writing is far less so. There may be a shift toward taking her writing seriously as part of a broader artistic movement: *Personas en la sala*, translated by Charlotte Whittle, was published in English in 2018 as *People in the Room*. *Nada* is considered a classic and is a staple of Spanish literature syllabi, though critical readings are often limited in scope to reiterations of her role as a *chica rara* and to reflections on the chaotic state of postwar Spain. And while Clarice Lispector's work has been a focal point of international attention in recent years, *Perto do coração selvagem*, her earliest work, is less frequently considered than later novels and stories.

Each chapter has a roughly two-part structure, with an exploration of (pseudo)scientific ideas and a discussion of the latent anxieties and possibilities they point to preceding my analysis of the novels, which I develop in light of those scientific strains of thought. These two sections are accompanied by an overview of each novel's sociohistorical context and the critical debates that have shaped their reception when they were published and today. My hope is that readers will find the scientific ideas and language as intriguing as I have and hear their echoes in the literary language and images of these four novels. I do not seek to prove direct influence of each scientific idea on each author, but do try to evoke for readers the ideas and concerns that were part of the public imaginary while these women lived and wrote.

Chapter 1 presents my reading of materiality in relation to Rosa Chacel's 1945 novel *Memorias de Leticia Valle*. With this first pairing, I flesh out my approach to scientific ideas and literary representations of strange femininity, in preparation for how the following chapters will address the intersection of literature, science, and gender. This chapter explores scientific writing on the construction of the material world that circulated in the early twentieth century. Articles with titles like "What Is Matter?" introduced their readership to atoms, and at stake was not just where we might draw the borders of an individual object, or even of an individual person, but an understanding of how objects—and beings—might affect one another. While several of the scientific authors I cite, such as Hans Reichenbach, were not Spanish or Latin American, I track the translations of their work into Spanish and Portuguese and the publication of their studies (often across many editions) either as books or in journals such as the *Revista de Occidente*. And while I am not principally interested in science specifically on the subject of sex and gender, chapter 1 does include an introduction to biomedical approaches to sex from the early twentieth century, which serves to contextualize understandings of sex and gender in the 1940s, particularly in young people.

In exploring contemporary scientific writing on matter, I also introduce sometimes-conflicting ideas on monism and other theories of materiality. Popular understandings of matter saw the physical world as made up of such tiny parts that interactions between objects and bodies were much more complex than we might otherwise have imagined. Authors writing for a nonspecialist audience often exclaimed over the shape-shifting possibilities introduced by an atomic view of the world, even comparing physicists to alchemists. They also underscored that the organic and inorganic world, people and objects, were made up of the same stuff.

With these dynamics in mind, I turn to Rosa Chacel's novel on an "inaudita" childhood: *Memorias de Leticia Valle*. I acknowledge the readings that have been done of Leticia's gender and sexuality and Chacel's own interest in Freud. However, I aim to advance those readings by suggesting that the novel offers more than a Freudian reading of an eleven-year-old girl's attraction to and, perhaps, violation by, her much older tutor. I employ the categories of the erotic and of queer childhood to begin to understand in a new way the protagonist's rapturous emotional experiences. Leticia struggles to make sense of the (adult) world around her, and I consider what it means to "make sense" or construct a narrative in an atomic and molecular world. She expresses at one point that she is "not a little girl" and is described as being *inaudita*: unheard of and unspeakable. I read her strangeness as gendered and argue that her girlhood is constantly in question not because she acts boyishly, or in a non-girlish manner, but because her observations make fleetingly visible the blurry borders and imbricated psycho-social-corporeal worlds of those around her.

Chapter 2 examines largely pseudoscientific work on magnetism that was tangentially related to scientific discoveries regarding electromagnetism. Magnetism was discussed in terms of animal magnetism, personal magnetism, hypnotism, and sympathetic expression. Authors capitalized on public interest in self-help and occult communication to promote the idea that "magnetizers" could influence the world around them, and they couched their proposals in scientific terminology. Paul Jagot's many works, such as *Método científico de magnetismo, hipnotismo, sugestión* (translated into Spanish and published in Buenos Aires in 1938) are emblematic of this shift. Self-help publications likely found an even broader audience and addressed everything from healing oneself and others to being successful in work and love to communicating with the dead, all thanks to magnetic flows. This chapter examines the possibilities of occult communication, both as a pseudoscience based on theories of electromagnetism and as a cipher for reading invisible or imperceptible relational currents that shape gender.

In this chapter, I examine the possibility of "feeling toward others"— the directional attractions or invisible pushes and pulls that affect daily life. Norah Lange's 1950 novel, *Personas en la sala*, tells of a seventeen-year-old woman who watches three women who live across the street and might be seen as an exploration of the outcome of these sorts of magnetic feelings toward another person and the opposite: being the object of an affective pull.

As many readings of Norah Lange's texts and public life center on the role of the gaze and of performance, I provide an overview of the avant-garde cultural milieu in which she lived and worked, particularly her role as a woman in the Martín Fierro group. I then sketch out some of the readings of her work that have centered gender performativity and the role of the gaze. I also examine the role of women in occult and spiritist movements that incorporated ideas drawn from electromagnetism. My own work on magnetism as activating lines of influence and affect shares some common traits with work on the invisible but perceptible ways the male gaze affects women's experiences of themselves and of the world around them. Still, for this novel in which nearly all of the looks are exchanged among women, I take a slightly different tack, reading the complex, sometimes repetitive prose as evidencing a mode of relation determined by uncontrollable outside influences. The objects of the protagonist's gaze "invade," her, "scratch" her, and "walk all over" her (164). Instead of a narrative about a relationship, we have the textual manifestation of a form of relating among bodies, among women, that awakens intense feelings in the protagonist and that comes to define her daily life.

Chapter 3 takes up scientific observation, questions of perception and spectatorship, and Jakob von Uexküll's theory of Umwelt. Uexküll proposes that all animals, including humans, perceive their environments as suits their needs, creating an individual Umwelt for each one (translated as "self-centered worlds" in English, or "mundos circundantes" in Spanish). Uexküll's works were translated into Spanish, promoted by José Ortega y Gasset, and extensively reviewed in Spanish-language newspapers and journals. He was particularly concerned with sensory perception and how the material world stimulates the senses of each animal such that any given object becomes a different object to each species. Santiago Ramón y Cajal wrote along similar lines regarding how ants perceive their surroundings. José Ortega y Gasset's writings on *circunstancia* seem to echo Uexküll's ideas. Guided by slippages in Uexküll's own writing, I make the shift from the species-centered Umwelt to a world centered on an individual, though one conditioned by species- and society-wide concerns. I maintain that perception is tied to survival, and I ask how perception makes possible, or makes difficult, the survival of a chica rara.

Regarding the question of survival, I outline some contemporary reflections on the affective attachments of queer survival (Eve Kosofsky Sedgwick) and with that I turn to Carmen Laforet's *Nada*. First published in 1945, it positions its young female protagonist, Andrea, as a spectator observing postwar Barcelona and internalizing her chaotic surroundings psychically and physically. Laforet makes readers aware of the often violent process by which our surroundings work their way into our subjectivities and how gender inflects that process. Andrea is also the prototypical chica rara identified by Martín Gaite. I outline the postwar situation of women in Spain and the limitations and tightened restrictions on their behavior under Franco. This novel is in some ways more conventional in style than the others I read; however, I argue that Andrea's young womanhood is anything but.

I call attention to Laforet's description, in a letter to Ramón Sender, of the "secret world" that dominates women's experience, "el mundo del Gineceo," which, she says, has not found its expression in language or literature. Guided by this idea, I look to the ways that the novel describes Andrea's coming of age through how she perceives and interacts with the world around her. My close reading includes both an analysis of her visual perception of the world and how that interacts with her other senses and physical experiences, such as extreme hunger and her desire for beautiful things. Her desire for certain aesthetic experiences, which she posits as necessary to her survival, shapes how she sees and moves through the world, disregarding what her relatives and acquaintances urge her to do, and instead drawing sustenance from the cityscape of Barcelona. I also note the ways in which Andrea becomes an object in others' self-centered worlds; her family members and friends perceive her as they need and wish her to be, and she feels the effects of this process. Her strange behavior points to a mode of perception that is hidden from her family and presented only obliquely to readers, and it is there that I believe Uexküll's Umwelt and Laforet's secret world collide in this protagonist.

In Chapter 4, I take up Charles Darwin's legacy in the public imaginary. I examine his interest in creativity and aesthetics in sexual selection and the human–nonhuman continuity made available by his theory. Though Darwin died in 1882, his ideas were still being debated decades after his death, and popular and metaphorical appropriations of Darwinian concepts spread widely. Gillian Beer, Elizabeth Grosz, Travis Landry, Patience A. Schell, and others have contended with the lasting influence of Darwinian thought in literature and culture. In the first part of this chapter, I outline the central points of his work, their metamorphosis in popular literature, and the reception and propagation of Darwinian ideas in Brazil, both through the translation of his most famous works and through the appearance of Darwinian allusions in the popular press.

Reading Clarice Lispector's first novel, *Perto do coração selvagem* (1943), I trace how the protagonist's depiction as feral or otherwise nonhuman elaborates a relationship with the animal and suggests alternate genealogies and a way out of the human articulation of binary gender difference. Joana's strange femininity is not marked by masculinity but by animality. I look at this openness of the human species in light of Darwinian ideas and show how Lispector uses this view of humans to craft a literary manifestation of gendered experience outside of a narrative of binary gender difference. I also use this last chapter to return to the imbrication of desire with the categories introduced by the previous chapters, examining how materiality, relation, and perception define Joana's gendered self. Darwinism might be said to provide an alternate genealogy for the human family tree, and guided by this idea, I explore how Lispector proposes alternate genealogies for Joana. Another part of Joana's rareza is her apparent disconnection from ordinary modes of feeling emotions and her apparent estrangement from the "corpos limitados" around her; the narrator also describes her as a "living body" and "not a woman." Like the other protagonists, she feels the "wrong" emotions and desires that are not socially acceptable or even easily defined. Desire, as Darwin describes it with regard to sexual selection, is both of the body and of the species: Lispector creates a protagonist whose strange desires establish a cross-body relationship with other members of the species and other species outside of it. I look at how we can understand Joana as desiring to continually experience herself as not strictly a woman and not strictly human.

This study has two goals: with the help of scientific narratives, I aim to understand these works in a new light, and through my readings of the felt experiences of their chicas raras I aim to understand gender in a new way. Even concerns apparently remote to gender (atoms, electromagnetic waves) are being worked into experiences of gender that can only escape the heteronormative patriarchy for fleeting moments marked by strangeness, anxiety, and confusion. Alternatively, those strange moments may be terrible and even hurt us, but they leave individuals with an experience of something outside of patriarchal control, outside of the rigid binary that restricts affective possibility. They may provide new ways of relating in the future. Or a hopeful feeling in the present. Both approaches reveal my own investment in reading and interpretation: I do not wish to suggest that these fictional characters or their authors were better or worse off for having experienced gender in the wake of new scientific knowledge. I do however place value on providing a new descriptive possibility for discussing gender.

When speaking of the renovation of the categories through which gender is constructed, it is tempting to consider the radical changes as opening up endless, uncircumscribed possibilities for gender. While the feelings that are roused by gender roles or gendered acts may indeed occur outside of a binary, neither strictly male nor female nor a neat blending of the two, this unsettling of gender does not open onto an unfettered potential. Rather, the very ways that we feel, sense, and relate are structured by our understanding of the processes of feeling, sensing, and relating, and, while our understanding evolves, changing our experience of those processes, they do not possess a pregendered moment that we might access in order to entirely implode or disintegrate the experience of gender as we know it. Still, I am suggesting something more elusive and less confining than a menu of gender roles: indeed, I am suggesting that we might conform nearly perfectly to those roles and still experience gender as strange or chafing, and that feeling might be expressed through an odd perspective on the surrounding world, through difficult or uncommon relations with other humans, or through particular considerations of the body.

CHAPTER ONE

¿Qué es la materia? / What's the Matter? Material *Rareza* and *Memorias de Leticia Valle*

[E]l agua no tiene una superficie, sino sólo un límite mal determinado. Ese pilar del puente de hierro [...] manifiéstase, al considerarlo con cuidado, como una forma temblorosa, cuyas partículas se tambalean como las delicadas hojas de un ramo de flores.
—Hans Reichenbach, *Átomo y cosmos: Concepción física actual del universo*[1]

Growing up strangely in a molecular world

These passages from German empiricist philosopher Hans Reichenbach's 1930 book (Spanish translation 1931, English translation 1932) exemplify the vivid language used by science writers as they introduced paradigm-shifting ideas to nonspecialist audiences. Reichenbach connects invisibly small structures to a striking natural scene: alongside a delicately trembling branch of berries, the structures and forms that support and define daily life suddenly lose their form. This radical reimagining of everything from lakes to bridges may produce confusion and uncertainty, but for the many writers who attempted, in the first half of the twentieth century, to convey the immediacy and importance of the particulate composition of everything from elderberries to stars, the potential for revolutionary ways of relating to a world seen anew hangs heavy in their prose.

The quivering, trembling vagaries of matter do not only loosen the boundaries between bodies and objects or dissolve apparent solidity—a radical enough proposition in itself. They also call up a host of questions

---

1 *Átomo y cosmos: Concepción física actual del universo*, trans. Javier Cabrera (Madrid: Revista de Occidente, 1931), 14. "[T]here is no surface [to the lake], but only a vague frontier zone." "[The bridge] reveals itself to the closer observer as a quivering structure, whose particles tremble in confusion, like the fine ramifications of a panicle of elderberries." Hans Reichenbach, *Atom and Cosmos: The World of Modern Physics*, trans. Edward Allen (New York: Macmillan, 1957), 22.

that make materiality itself seemingly difficult to locate. The senses are quickly called into question, since what can be touched or seen may not prove materially substantial. Microscopic particles call attention to the uncertainty of the definitions of those objects that seem to impose firm borders and ignore the busyness and vibrancy inside them and permeating them. These qualities quickly introduce questions of energy, vitality, and the relation among parts and supposed wholes. Making sense of the material world becomes a particular sort of problem, and scientific discourse is poised to suggest and embrace new narratives, metaphors, and perceptual approaches.

In this chapter, I analyze a novel that is full of blurred material boundaries and interpenetrations between objects and bodies that are difficult to square with the otherwise quotidian events described in the story. Reading it in light of contemporary scientific texts on materiality provides an alternative way to understanding scenes that otherwise might seem mystical or fanciful. This alternative interpretation gives us particular insight into how materiality shapes gendered experience. Rosa Chacel's *Memorias de Leticia Valle* is a reflection by eleven-year-old Leticia on the strange feelings and events that have led up to an unnarrated incident generally read as her seduction–violation at the hands of her much older tutor, the town's archivist, Daniel.[2] Recalling her father murmuring of

---

2 Commenting in an interview with María Asunción Mateo on the inspiration for this plot, Chacel stated:

En *Memorias de Leticia Valle* se ha supuesto que era mi autobiografía, pero ya te he dicho que es un retrato, que es distinto. Recuerdo que se me ocurrió escribirla de forma casual: estando un día con Timo y Valverde —yo escribía en aquel momento *Estación. Ida y Vuelta*— me insistieron en que leyera un texto de Dostoievski, y me negué porque no tenía tiempo. Me explicaron que era una historia de un hombre mayor que seducía a una niña, y entonces me acordé de otra historia similar que sucedió en un pueblo, de un maestro de escuela que también sedujo a una niña, con el consiguiente escándalo. Pero yo, que conocía a aquel hombre, y por cierto era muy atractivo, dudé de quién había seducido a quién. Porque me puse en lugar de la niña y pensé que yo hubiera hecho lo mismo que ella por atraerlo. Les dije a mi marido y a Valverde que en la historia de Dostoievski la niña se colgaba por el ruso. Y en la historia que escribí después, Leticia seduciría al profesor, y el que acabaría colgándose sería él. Sin embargo, yo nunca tuve un profesor tan fascinante como el archivero. (Mateo 74)

(It has been assumed that *Memorias de Leticia Valle* is my autobiography, but as I've told you, it's a portrait, which is different. I remember that writing it just happened to occur to me—I was writing *Estación: Ida y vuelta* at that time—[and] they insisted that I read a text by Dostoevsky, but I refused because I didn't have time. They explained it was a story of an older man who seduced a young girl,

the episode (which ends in her being sent to live with an aunt and uncle) "¡Es inaudito, es inaudito!" she remarks that this is what she had always wanted to tell him, to name something about herself that was just that, unheard of, unspeakable, but she had not known the words to say it. Leticia conceives of porous subjectivities, describing experiences of projection—or transportation—into the subjectivities of those around her as both affective and material. The first-person narration is marked both by a unique voice that seems more mature and eloquent than an eleven-year-old protagonist might be able to muster and by attention to seemingly mundane details and daily events. Leticia seems to be able to observe ways in which the material world and people around her invade and shape her, and, moreover, she seems able to manipulate this process.

By reading the young protagonist's narration of her aesthetic and affective experiences, particularly the currents of interest and affection among her, Daniel, and Daniel's wife, Luisa (who is also Leticia's music teacher), we gain insight into ways that her self-reported strangeness reveals the construction of gender through encounters that take place on different scales—one perceptible and narratable, another that slides into the barely sensible. Society, unable to conceive of her interpenetration with the people and world around her as anything but corporeal, insists on registering her relationship with a much-older tutor not only as sexual but as culminating in a scene of seduction or rape. All the while, Leticia's gender is at stake: we have her pronouncement that "yo no era una niña," (I wasn't a little girl) while she hears from adults that "todo lo mío era inaudito" (everything about me was unheard of) (Chacel, *Memorias* 18, 7).

> and then I remembered a similar story that had taken place in a village, of a schoolteacher who also seduced a young girl, and the resulting scandal. But I knew the man, who was, by the way, very attractive, and I had my doubts about who had seduced whom. Because I put myself in that girl's place, and I thought that I would have done the same as her to attract him. I told my husband and Valverde that in Dostoevsky's story, the girl hangs herself because of the Russian man. And in the story I wrote later, Leticia would seduce the teacher, and he would be the one who would end up hanging himself. However, I never had a teacher as fascinating as the archivist.)

As the author's comments reveal, she did not set out to write a scientifically inflected novel on gender—she is interested in the narrative arc of local scandal and its echoes in a story by Dostoevsky. In this chapter and throughout, I focus not on the author's intention or her reading of scientific publications but on how scientific discourse that was popular and circulated widely can be seen as shaping literary representations of gender.

All that is unspeakable and unheard of in Leticia, I will argue, is tied to her being "not a little girl" and to her perception of the material world.

I suggest that fascination with the atomic model brought the possibility of openness between people and objects to the fore of the popular imagination, setting up a reading of material things in fiction not as carriers of fixed significance (i.e., the gift of a blanket passes on an erotic intention) but as the productive translators of uncertain meaning (i.e., Leticia feels something that is changed by seeing and feeling the blanket she will give to Luisa). The type of communication made evident by popularly propagated understandings of matter—relation and communication through material contact and invisible (e.g., vibratory) contact through objects and "ether"—suggests a blueprint for reading the flow of details in the novel that skirt narrative in favor of a nearly palpable accretion of words, gestures, glances, etc., that constructs Leticia's unheard-of non-little-girlness. In what follows, I introduce the author and the context in which she wrote and lived, including her relationship to the avant-garde and how her innovative prose style has been read, before delving into the rich and suggestive scientific discourse on materiality that circulated in the popular press. These texts explored themes including perception and the senses, permeability, and solidity in relation to the atomic or molecular composition of things. I conclude this section on science with an overview of medical science on sex and gender from this period. While the discussion in that field have different preoccupations, I show that what defined gender was very much up for debate. I then carry forward the images, portrayals of the world, anxieties, and excitement captured in the scientific works on materiality to my reading of Chacel's novel. A section on eroticism and the protagonist's non-narrative approach to "making sense" establishes parallels with these scientific texts and introduces my scientifically attuned reading of Leticia's strange childhood.

Rosa Chacel

María Asunción Mateo's biographical sketch of and interview with Chacel, *Retrato de Rosa Chacel* (Portrait of Rosa Chacel), sheds light on the movements and contacts the author felt to be central to her writing and thinking. Upon marrying Timoteo Pérez Rubio in 1922, Chacel and her husband traveled to Rome, a prelude to later European travel and to her eventual exile in Brazil and Argentina after the Spanish Civil War. In Paris, Chacel became friends with Max Ernst and Pablo Picasso, among others. In South America, she was to become friends with Norah Borges, and Victoria Ocampo would publish the first chapter of *Memorias* in *Sur* even before Chacel's arrival in Buenos Aires.³ Regarding that very first trip abroad, Mateo writes that

> [Chacel] ha contado en muchas ocasiones que para este primer viaje metió en sus maletas dos libros muy preciados y que significarían mucho a lo largo de su carrera literaria: *Retrato del artista adolescente*, de James Joyce ("Esto es la novela", diría al concluir su lectura), en traducción de Dámaso Alonso, y un tomo, el primero, de las Obras Completas de Sigmund Freud. (23)

> (Chacel has recounted on many occasions that for that first trip, she packed two treasured books that would mean a lot to her over the course of her literary career: *A Portrait of the Artist as a Young Man*, by James Joyce ["This is the novel," she would say upon finishing it] translated by Dámaso Alonso, and the first volume of the Complete Works of Sigmund Freud.)

This nod to Freud, alongside the content of Chacel's own novel, has likely led critics to focus largely on Freudian readings of young Leticia. In *Under Construction: The Body in Spanish Novels*, Elizabeth Scarlett argues that "Chacel takes on another *maestro*, Sigmund Freud, whose discovery of the unconscious mind she claims to have intuited when she was seven years old."⁴ Scarlett goes on to contrast Freud's use of "permeability of boundaries of the self to maintain that the female ego is forever incomplete" with Leticia's balance between permeability and personal autonomy (85). I argue that the narration of this permeability, when we understand it with scientific narratives on materiality, also evidences nonnormative and incompletely articulated sensibilities that skirt and run through categories such as gender and sexuality. Instead of adhering closely to Freudian concepts and categories in my reading, I trace other possible scientific genealogies of the permeable self and the unconscious mind.

Memorias de Leticia Valle allows us to delve into Chacel's focus on the generally unobserved and perhaps unobservable currents of daily experience. Interestingly, Chacel's admiration for James Joyce is less widely commented upon than is her reading of Freud, though she is quite adamant about Joyce's importance in her literary formation. She also cites surrealism, "la simultaneidad del cine" (the simultaneity of film) (Mateo 71), and her

---

3 See María A. Mateo, *Retrato de Rosa Chacel* (Barcelona: Círculo de Lectores, 1993), 25, 77-78.
4 Elizabeth A. Scarlett, *Under Construction: The Body in Spanish Novels* (Charlottesville: University Press of Virginia, 1994), 78.

"atención total al proceso de la ciencia" (complete attention to scientific progress) (Mateo 73). These varied influences reflect her broad interest in cultural developments. Chacel would define herself as "una renovadora de la forma, pero no de la lengua" (an innovator in form but not of language), and her attempt to capture lived experience through Leticia's narration results in a texture and tone that is both innovative and not unrelated to Joycean modernism (Mateo 72). This chapter contemplates both these characteristics of Chacel's prose and the unseen and often overlooked psycho-social processes taken up by the novel. However, besides sidestepping a Freudian interpretation, I also question whether sexuality is too limited a template for understanding the dynamics of the novel and if indeed setting aside the sexual in favor of less defined categories of perception and experience might shift us from understanding the novel as a relatively straightforward if surprising tale of seduction to seeing what insight it offers into how social understandings of gender, sexuality, and eroticism come to be felt by individuals. In the next section, I look at some of the scientific progress that might have interested Chacel, particularly the myriad of texts that look to explain the nature of matter to a lay audience. In breaking down matter into its smallest component parts for readers, scientific authors emphasized the lines of continuity among human and nonhuman forms, which shape our experience even if they are difficult to perceive with our senses.

¿Qué es la materia?

Numerous lectures, articles, and books published in the first decades of the twentieth century asked what precisely matter was: ¿Qué es la materia?[5] The topics of matter and materiality raised any number of questions that might seem far afield. Contained within the clarifications of atomic structure that these studies take up are questions of sameness, difference, and relation. The patterns of inquiry that emerge in popular scientific writing on matter are a reminder that the categories of materiality, perception, relation, and desire are inextricable. The insistence that we (and the stars!—recall Reichenbach's title, *Atom and Cosmos*) are all made up of the same stuff overlaps with questions of how we perceive that stuff outside of us, and what happens if it is imperceptible. These reflections on sense perception often trouble the line dividing us from what we are sensing, even as we feel its effects in our bodies. An underlying anxiety about the loss of the distinction between

---

5 See, for example, Blas Cabrera's "¿Qué es la materia?" Curso de Conferencias desarrollado en la Escuela Especial de Ingenieros Agrónomos, Sesión inaugural, 1934; or Hermann Weyl's *¿Qué es la materia?*, trans. Blas Cabrera (Madrid: Revista de Occidente, 1925).

our bodies and what they perceive also emerges in discussions of force and form—what is it that animates some matter while leaving other matter inert? And what gives it a certain shape and not another?

Materiality via monism: singular stuff

Monism—the idea of an underlying singular stuff that makes up the universe—was a widespread and oft-cited philosophical and scientific idea, with Ernst Haeckel as one of its great late nineteenth-century proponents. Much writing on monism eschews the specialized language of later texts, more along the lines of Reichenbach, that hoped to explain the world of atoms to a lay audience. Indeed, monists such as Haeckel took pains to explain to readers that their scientific ideas were in no way at odds with religious ones; this explanation animates his *El monismo como nexo entre la religión y la ciencia: Profesión de fe de un naturalista* (published in English as *Monism Connecting Religion and Science: A Man of Science*). Unlike vitalist approaches, which posited an animating force to matter, monism held that the single substance that composed the universe included both force and matter. In *El monismo como nexo*, Haeckel writes:

> Es evidente, que con esta palabra [*monismo*] expresamos nuestra convicción de que *existe un espíritu en todas las cosas*, y de que, todo el mundo cognoscible subsiste y se desarrolla bajo una ley fundamental, lo que equivale también á decir, en sentido más concreto, que admitimos la unidad esencial de la naturaleza inorgánica y de la orgánica, siendo esta última producto de la evolución lenta de la primera. (14)

> (By this we unambiguously express our conviction that there lives "one spirit in all things," and that the whole cognisable world is constituted, and has been developed, in accordance with one common fundamental law. We emphasise by it, in particular, the essential unity of inorganic and organic nature, the latter having been evolved from the former only at a relatively late period.)[6]

As this passage makes clear, monism departed from contemporary vitalism, which concerned itself with the animating force that sets organic matter apart; vitalists further set themselves against mechanists by claiming

---

6 Ernst Haeckel, *Monism as Connecting Religion and Science: A Man of Science*, trans. J. Gilchrist (Project Gutenberg, 2005), n.p., https://www.gutenberg.org/ebooks/9199. All English translations of this work are from this unpaginated public-domain edition.

that "something always escaped quantification, prediction, and control."[7] Haeckel instead posits that the material and the spiritual are one, and that the human soul is only a small part of an "alma del mundo" ("world-soul") (*El monismo como nexo* 19). Thus, while Haeckel cites Julius Robert von Mayer and Hermann von Helmholtz as the discoverers of Law of Conservation of Energy, and Lavoisier's Law of Conservation of Matter, he explains that these two laws form, to his mind, a singular law of "the conservation of substance" following the monist inseparability of force and matter.[8] The singular nature of force and matter further implies the unity of the inorganic and the organic: "tampoco podemos reconocer una absoluta diferencia entre los reinos animal y vegetal, ni aun entre el animal y el hombre" ("[nor] can [we] recognise an absolute distinction between the animal and the vegetable kingdom, or between the lower animals and man") (Haeckel, *El monismo como nexo* 14). Not only is the human soul "una parte insignificante de esa grande y comprensiva 'alma del mundo', bien así como nuestro cuerpo sólo constituye una molécula del gran mundo orgánico" ("but an insignificant part of the all-embracing 'world-soul'; just as the human body is only a small individual fraction of the great organised physical world") (Haeckel, *El monismo como nexo* 19), but all matter can also be seen to possess certain "propiedades intelectuales" (intellectual properties), cells their own "vida individual psíquica" (individual psychic life).[9] But given that cells are made up of yet smaller molecules, Haeckel is then driven to speak of this "suma de fuerzas atómicas" (sum of atomic forces) as "[el] alma del átomo" (the soul of the atom) (*La evolución* 31). Reading of the psychic life of cells and the souls of atoms, we are led to imagine ourselves along the same lines, created from the same template as the minute parts we are learning of: personification cuts both ways as the atom gains a soul and we gain an atomic nature. Haeckel might have understood these descriptions as more literal than metaphorical, though his readers likely sensed a metaphor, and that metaphor comes back for us: once we have imagined cells and atoms to behave and interact with the world as we do, even thinking and feeling as we do, their other characteristics suddenly seem as though they might govern *our* actions and experiences. If atoms are spoken of as thinking and

---

7 See Jane Bennett, *Vibrant Matter: A Political Ecology of Things* (Durham, NC: Duke University Press, 2010), 63.

8 Ernst Haeckel, *El monismo como nexo entre la religión y la ciencia: Profesión de fe de un naturalista*, trans. M. Pino G. (Madrid: Imprenta de Fernando Cao y Domingo de Val, 1893), 20. On Mayer, Helmholtz, and Lavoisier, see *El monismo como nexo* 19-20.

9 Haeckel, *La evolución y el trasformismo* (Madrid: Imprenta Rollo, 1886), 28, 29. The name of the Spanish translator is not included in this edition. All English translations from this work are mine.

feeling beings, we, thinking and feeling beings that we are, might begin to sense that we too can connect and participate in material formations much as atoms do.

Reflecting this continuity between particles and people, Haeckel writes: "El ódio ó el amor de los átomos, la atracción ó la repulsión de las moléculas, el movimiento y la sensación de las células y de los organismos celulares, la imaginación y la conciencia del hombre, son grados diversos de un mismo proceso psicológico evolutivo" (The hatred or love of atoms, the attraction or repulsion of molecules, the movement and sensation of cells and cellular organisms, the imagination and consciousness of man, are varying degrees of a single evolutionary psychological process) (*La evolución* 34). As one might expect from the affective and sensorial language he uses to speak of the lives of molecules and atoms, for Haeckel, monism immediately crosses out of the strictly scientific into a broader approach to the world: "La investigación monista de la Naturaleza como conocimiento de lo verdadero, la ética monista como educación para lo bueno, la estética monista como cultivo de lo bello, tales son los tres principales objetivos de nuestro Monismo" ("Monistic investigation of nature as knowledge of the true, monistic ethic as training for the good, monistic aesthetic as pursuit of the beautiful—these are the three great departments of our monism") (*El monismo como nexo* 49). Monist and nonmonist approaches to materiality not only brought these ethical and aesthetic concerns into view but also were related to contemporary areas of scientific investigation.

The roles of energy and vitality were chief among the list of concerns often paired with materiality as thinkers sought to understand what propelled matter, organized it, or brought it to life. There are those for whom matter and energy are enough and many for whom an élan vital, a soul, or an animating divinity must come to be mixed up in, or already reside in, the physical stuff of the universe. As early as 1869, Ludwig Büchner's 1855 book *Kraft und Stoff: empirisch-naturphilosophische Studien; in allgemein-verständlicher Darstellung* was translated into Spanish; at least eight Spanish editions were released through 1925 as *Fuerza y materia: Estudios populares de historia y filosofía naturales*.[10] Büchner exhorts readers: "¡No hay fuerza sin materia; no hay materia sin fuerza! Imposible es concebir la una sin la otra; ambas, si se las considera separadamente, no son más que abstracciones vacías de sentido" ("No force without matter—no matter without force! Neither can

---

10 See Ludwig Büchner, *Fuerza y materia: Estudios populares de historia y filosofía naturales*, trans. A. Avilés, 8th ed. (Barcelona: La Revista Blanca, 1925[?]). English translations are from: *Force and Matter: Empirico-Philosophical Studies, Intelligibly Rendered*, trans. and ed. J. Frederick Collingwood (London: Trübner and Co., 1864).

be thought of *per se*; separated, they become empty abstractions") (10, [2]). Without deviating from a discussion of matter to delve into the literature on vitalism, it may simply be helpful to know that in conversations on matter, most writers were attuned to the potential for something seemingly or temporarily inert to take on a life of its own, or to interact—in predictable or unexpected ways—with the psychic lives of the atoms or individuals around it. In all of this scientific literature, the question of matter—how it is arranged, composed, and animated—is pressing and addressed in the most vivid language, evoking a world that determines how we live and feel but that remains largely invisible.

Mutable matter

The elemental sameness at the foundation of monism survived in later texts on the material world, even when they were less concerned with positing a vital or even spiritual life of matter. That sameness was in turn highly suggestive of the possibility of transitioning between forms. Jean Thibaud, the author of *Vida y transmutaciones de los átomos* (translated by Xavier Zubiri for Espasa Calpe in 1939 from the French *Vie et transmutations des atomes*, first published in 1924 and reedited repeatedly over several decades), capitalized on fascination with this sort of shape shifting in opening the prologue to his book with a reference to alchemy: "Los físicos actuales, más afortunados que sus remotos precursores, los alquimistas de la Edad Media, han logrado transmutar la materia, es decir, provocar artificialmente la mutación de los cuerpos simples entre sí" (Modern-day physicists, more fortunate than their remote precursors, the alchemists of the Middle Ages, have managed to transform matter, that is, to artificially precipitate the mutation of simple bodies into one another).[11] In his first chapter, he goes on to explain that the apparent diversity of the world is in fact a unity that escapes our senses but that has been revealed "después de largas investigaciones acerca de la textura misma de la materia" (after extensive research regarding the very texture of matter) (Thibaud 20). Thibaud reminds his reader to think of atoms not as isolated but rather as "la individualidad necesaria del tejido material" (the necessary individuality of the fabric of matter) (21). This sort of materiality points us first to a substrate of sameness and unity before opening up the potential for new differentiations and arrangements. The *tejido material* allows for interrelation, and if atomic consistency is the unvarying warp, then its transmutable nature is the weft that allows for

---

11 Jean Thibaud, *Vida y transmutaciones de los átomos*, trans. Xavier Zubiri (Buenos Aires: Espasa-Calpe, 1939), 7. English translations mine.

new patterns and textures. This *tejido* is also very much a living tissue, open to influence and change.

According to Pedro Sala y Villaret, who in 1891 published *Materia, forma y fuerza: Diseño de una filosofía*: "[L]os mismos elementos que integran la naturaleza de un ser inorgánico componen la de un ser organizado; toda la diferencia está en los grados, en el plan, en la cantidad é intensidad" (The same elements that make up the nature of an inorganic being compose that of an organic being; the difference lies entirely in degree, order, quantity, and intensity).[12] Sala y Villaret then cites Haeckel to bolster his credibility, highlighting the consistency between his own ideas and those of the "insigne físico" (distinguished physicist)—whom he purports to have preceded in articulating them—and then proceeding to disparage the more famous man for his supposed atheism (46). While the degree, organization, quantity, and intensity of organic and inorganic matter may differ, Sala y Villaret claims, they are otherwise akin, and thus matter could potentially move between the two categories by becoming more or less organized.

A similar contemporary narrative of the nature of matter was couched in terms likely to spark the imagination of a wide public: that both stars and humans are made of the same stuff. Arthur Eddington and Reichenbach, whose books and articles were published in Spain in the 1920s and 1930s, emphasized the idea that everything from plants to humans to stars is made of the same material, and the apparent solidity of matter is understood to dissolve into undifferentiated flows. Already in 1891 Sala y Villaret was writing that astronomy and the study of stars gave us evidence that it was matter in the form of chemical elements that was a constant while larger forms shifted and changed (see Sala y Villaret 144). Not only did astronomy provide an intriguing example of arguments about matter being made in other fields, but it also suggested that while stars leave evidence—evidence that is perceptible to us—that remainder is made possible by their material composition, which we do not perceive directly.

(Im)perceptible matter

This question of what we can or cannot see or otherwise sense—while we somehow still experience the effects of that unsensed matter—brings to the fore the issue of our perceptive abilities and their limitations. In an article published in the *Revista de Occidente* in 1930, which I will discuss further below, Eddington writes of the phenomenon, and mystery, of perception:

---

12 Pedro Sala y Villaret, *Materia, forma y fuerza: Diseño de una filosofía* (Madrid: José Cruzado, 1891), 45. English translations mine.

[V]eamos cómo se alcanza nuestro supuesto conocimiento del grumo de materia. Alguna influencia de ella emanada actúa sobre la extremidad de un nervio, originando una serie de cambios físicos y químicos que se propagan a lo largo del nervio hasta una célula cerebral; allí se produce un misterio y surge en la mente una imagen o una sensación que no podemos asimilar al estímulo que la excita. Todo lo que se conoce del mundo material tiene que ser inferido, en una u otra manera, de aquellos estímulos transmitidos a lo largo de los nervios.[13]

([C]onsider how our supposed acquaintance with the lump of matter is attained. Some influence emanating from it plays on the extremity of a nerve, starting a series of physical and chemical changes which are propagated along the nerve to a brain cell; there a mystery happens, and an image or sensation arises in the mind which cannot purport to resemble the stimulus which excites it. Everything known about the material world must in one way or another have been inferred from these stimuli transmitted along the nerves.)[14]

Eddington here describes a divide between us and the matter that surrounds us, that distance standing in the way of our direct perception of it. Instead, we have only stimulus and inference—and a mystery. But the gaps in the mechanism of perception described in Eddington's account are telling. First we have "some influence" that emanates from matter, reaching our nerves, and setting off a chain of events now within our bodies. Then we have the mysterious process by which an image or sensation communicates to us something about the world outside. Eddington draws our attention to how the limits of our perception impose boundaries on our knowledge of matter. An anonymous reader commenting in the margins of a page about the form of atomic nuclei in a copy of the 1942 edition of *Vida y transmutaciones de los átomos* writes across the top of the page, "Hay condicionamiento determinado por la forma de traducir el pensamiento" (There is conditioning determined by how thought is translated) and in the left-hand margin: "Aquí debe haber una relación tamaño-espacio, que no es real, sino función de la percepción, dato previsto puesto proyección del sistema lógico perceptivo del experimentador" (Here there must be a size-space relationship that is not real, but rather is a function of perception, a predictable fact given the projection of the

---

13 Arthur Eddington, "La ciencia y el mundo invisible," *Revista de Occidente* 87 (1930): 337.
14 Arthur Eddington, "Science and the Unseen World," Google Play. Pickle Partners Publishing (2019): 18. Originally published in English in 1929.

logical-perceptive system of the experimenter).[15] Indeed, the problematic role of the experimenter will trouble scientists who speak of the "observer effect" to discuss the ways that people intervene in the systems they are trying to study.[16] But this reader of Thibaud is identifying something slightly different: how observers' perceiving minds distort their understanding of a system even if they have not physically interrupted it. Biosemiotician Jakob von Uexküll—whose work appeared in Spanish translations throughout the 1920s, 1930s, and 1940s—believed this was such a fundamental aspect of how we see the world that it was important to speak of the many different versions of the world experienced by different species.[17]

The wide range of possible perceptions of the material world and the varying interactions that result within it inform Uexküll's thesis on the existence of subjects' Umwelten—their self-centered worlds, or *mundos circundantes*. This leads him to write: "Resta tan sólo aún demostrar a la vista de los ejemplos ya citados que también la constancia de la materia es una ilusión. Las propiedades de la materia de un objeto son dependientes de las escalas sensoriales de aquel sujeto, cuyo mundo circundante es válido precisamente para nuestra investigación" (All that is left is to demonstrate,

---

15 The copy of this edition that I consulted is housed at New York University's Bobst Library.

16 The observer effect is frequently confused with the Heisenberg uncertainty principle in quantum mechanics. The uncertainty principle does not state that our being present and carrying out an experiment changes its outcome. Nor does the observer effect mean that purely by standing by and contemplating a phenomenon we necessarily intervene in it. And yet the confusion surrounding these concepts generally gives rise to the notion that our mere presence—not just physical but necessarily mental—holds some kind of sway over the material world. For more on both topics, see the *Stanford Encyclopedia of Philosophy* entries on "The Uncertainty Principle" (Jan Hilgevoord and Jos Uffink, "The Uncertainty Principle," in *The Stanford Encyclopedia of Philosophy*, ed. Edward N. Zalta, 2016, plato.stanford.edu/archives/win2016/entries/qt-uncertainty/) and "Theory and Observation in Science" (James Bogen, "Theory and Observation in Science," in *The Stanford Encyclopedia of Philosophy*, ed. Edward N. Zalta, 2017, plato.stanford.edu/archives/sum2017/entries/science-theory-observation/).

17 See, for example: Jakob von Uexküll, *Cartas biológicas a una dama* [1925], 2nd ed., trans. Manuel G. Morente (Madrid: Revista de Occidente, 1945); Uexküll, *Ideas para una concepción biológica del mundo* [1922], 2nd ed., trans. R. M. Tenreiro (Buenos Aires / Madrid: Espasa-Calpe, 1934); Uexküll, "La biología de la ostra jacobea," *Revista de Occidente* 9 (1924): 297–331. The question of how different species experience the world, viewed as a question of consciousness, would continue to be compelling, with Thomas Nagel in 1974 writing "What Is It Like to Be a Bat?," *The Philosophical Review* 83, no. 4 (1974): 435–50. However, Nagel would be interested in the gap between individual subjectivities in a way that Uexküll was not.

in view of the examples already cited, that the constancy of matter is an illusion. The material properties of an object depend on the sensory scale of the subject whose self-centered world is precisely of interest for our research) (Uexküll, *Meditaciones biológicas* 151).[18] And so, our perception introduces us to only one side of a material world that not only is in constant flux as a matter of course but also takes on different apparent forms for different (and differently invested) observers.

Which senses we might entrust with the act of perception was also up for debate. Given the ways in which vision necessarily falls short in the microscopic material world, some scientists preferred to argue for the primacy of other senses. This reshuffling of the senses raised the question of whether or not matter could be defined as something tactile, to be touched, felt, and thus observed firsthand. David Katz, in *El mundo de las sensaciones táctiles* (translated in 1930 by Manuel García Morente from the 1925 German original *Der Aufbau der Tastwelt*), argues for more weight to be given to this oft-overlooked sense, given that it has "una importancia mucho mayor que los demás sentidos en el desarrollo de la creencia en la realidad del mundo exterior" ("a far greater role than do the other senses in the development of belief in the reality of the external world").[19] Touch can disprove optical illusions and offer "proof"; yet there are those aspects of the material world that seem to escape even tactile perception.

In "La ciencia y el mundo invisible," Eddington delves into the relationship between scientific discoveries largely having to do with atoms and electrons and "the invisible world," touching on questions of religion as well as human consciousness. He traces the appearance of matter in the universe from the formation of stars to the evolution of humans, highlighting along the way scientific approaches to the material world and the questions of human consciousness and mysticism or religion that seem to edge beyond it. He, like others, is attentive to how sensory perception informs our knowledge and the tensions between firsthand observation and both the significance we draw from it and its representation in symbolic or mathematical terms. He asks us to imagine that an alien comes to earth and witnesses the time when people are observing two minutes of silence on Armistice Day, deducing that the cessation of sound is similar to a solar eclipse—the alien is right in that the silence is brought about by a changed arrangement of atoms and

---

18 English translation mine. I will return to this idea that a single material object can become multiple, differing for each perceptive individual it encounters, in chapter 3.

19 David Katz, *El mundo de las sensaciones táctiles*, trans. Manuel García Morente (Madrid: Revista de Occidente, 1930), 255. *The World of Touch*, trans. Lester E. Krueger (New York: Psychology Press, 1989), 240.

electrons but mistakes its significance (Eddington, "La ciencia" 355). People have chosen to remain silent and are not under the influence of a physical phenomenon but a cultural one. Not only might our senses mislead us, our interpretations of the world around us might be drastically limited by our social or cultural knowledge. We might be correct on one level but have profoundly missed the point on another. But the alien on Armistice Day also alerts Eddington's reader to the fact that the constant potential for misreading a world unknown to us also brings with it the possibility of rereading the one we believe ourselves to know well.

Eddington's argument is in large part about the spirit in which scientific research ought to proceed and the spirit in which it ought to be received by the public. To that end, he cites the following paragraph from the 1656 Quaker "Consejos de la Sociedad de Amigos" (Advice of the Society of Friends) as an appropriate model for the incorporation of scientific thinking:

> No exponemos estas cosas ante ti como una regla o ritual para que prescindas de ellas, sino para que todos, con una medida de la luz, que es pura y santa, puedan ser guiados; y así, caminando y perseverando en la luz, pueden realizarse aquellas cosas en el espíritu, no en la letra; pues la letra mata, pero el espíritu vivifica. (Quoted in Eddington, "La ciencia" 369)

> (These things we do not lay upon you as a rule or form to walk by; but that all with a measure of light, which is pure and holy, may be guided; and so in the light walking and abiding, these things may be fulfilled in the Spirit, not in the letter; for the letter killeth, but the Spirit giveth life). (Quoted in Eddington, "Science" 53-54)

This chapter's approach to publicly shared scientific knowledge is similar: it is a guiding spirit for my literary analysis below and understood as a light that authors walked in whether they fully perceived it or not.

When our five senses were not enough to take in information about the material world, vibratory theory stepped in: it focused on the invisible and even the wholly imperceptible, on the tiny movements of matter. Perhaps as a result, vibratory theory quickly seeped out of the realm of those who believed themselves to be real scientists giving rise to theories of the occult communication made possible by these unseen and mostly unsensed waves (interested in amplifying our understanding of the senses, Katz proposed a sixth, vibratory sense that gives us access to unseen information about the nature of objects). While there may seem to be a great distance between the earlier research on cells by those such as Santiago Ramón y Cajal and later vibratory theory and eventually quantum theory, all raised interest and concern surrounding the imperceptible structures and behavior of matter. Sala y Villaret articulated a relatively rudimentary theory of movement at the end of the nineteenth century, maintaining that higher beings of more complex and perfect organization experience faster movements, so that a hierarchy exists from undulations to oscillations to finally vibrations (see Sala y Villaret 59). That very movement, that "*palpitación* perenne" is life-sustaining: "El líquido ondula, el aire oscila. Ambas cosas se cifran en la circulación de la sangre" (Liquid undulates, air oscillates. Both are present in the circulation of blood) (Sala y Villaret 60).[20] In 1924, French physicist Louis de Broglie introduced the idea that matter could behave like waves.[21] As all of these discoveries were a matter of microscopic structures, the apparent solidity of matter and thus our relationship with no-longer-quite-solid objects came into question.

All that is solid

The disarticulation of solid matter—or rather our ability to perceive and productively discuss that fragmentation—points to the construction of the material world and communication through it, both of which take place via

---

20 This realization allows Sala y Villaret to get in a footnote jab at Haeckel: "La explicación cumplida de la sensación y demás fenómenos psicológicos es lo que no ha encontrado Haeckel ni otro alguno de los sabios, que, partiendo de principios iguales á los nuestros, han ido á parar al materialismo" (The full explanation of sensation and other psychological phenomena is what neither Haeckel nor other learned men have found, as they, working from the same premise as we do, have ended up with materialism) (Sala y Villaret 60). Sala y Villaret later proposes that we think of humans as microcosms of the universe: "Se ha dicho, y es una verdad, que el hombre es un mundo pequeño (microcosmos); todo lo del universo está representado en él, los elementos del mundo inorgánico, y las varias formas del mundo orgánico. [...] Tiene su parte sólida, líquida y flúidica; posee la gravedad, y demás condiciones de los inorgánicos de que se compone, las propiedades de la vida vegetal, de la sensitiva y de la racional: es en realidad un compendio del universo" (It has been said, and it is true, that man is a small world (a microcosm); everything in the universe is represented in him, the elements of the inorganic world, and the diverse forms of the organic world. [...] Man contains solid, liquid, and electric parts; he possesses gravity and other conditions of the inorganic substances he is made of, the properties of vegetable life, sensory life, and rational life: he is truly a compendium of the universe) (Sala y Villaret 130).

21 As Alicia Rivero explains, "electrons behave like waves in some experimental arrangements and like particles in others; this is called the 'wave-particle duality.'" Alicia Rivero, "Heisenberg's Uncertainty Principle in Contemporary Spanish American Fiction," in *Science and the Creative Imagination in Latin America*, ed. Evelyn Fishburn and Eduardo L. Ortiz (London: Institute for the Study of the Americas, 2005), 130.

processes invisible to the naked eye. Things that seem solid are no longer so. In these texts, we see matter cast as testifying to an underlying elemental consistency. This framing of the material universe held sway in even those discussions of matter that were not concerned with a monist approach. Eddington, in books such as *Stars and Atoms* (Juan Cabrera y Felipe's Spanish translation of the 1927 original, titled *Estrellas y átomos*, was published in 1928), attested to the attractive idea that we and stars were all made up of the same stuff.[22] In Eddington's writing, metaphors used to understand certain aspects of materiality flit suggestively from atomic scale to star scale to human scale:

> Una gota de agua contiene varios trillones de átomos. Cada átomo tiene, aproximadamente, una cienmillonésima de centímetro de radio. Aquí nos asombran los pequeñísimos detalles de la estructura; pero éste no es tampoco el límite. En el interior del átomo recorren sus órbitas los electrones, que son mucho más pequeños. Recorren sus órbitas como si fueran planetas alrededor del sol y en un espacio que relativamente a sus dimensiones no es menos amplio que el del sistema solar. (Eddington, *Estrellas y átomos* 18)

> (A drop of water contains several thousand million million million atoms. Each atom is about one hundred-millionth of an inch in diameter. Here we marvel at the minute delicacy of the workmanship. But this is not the limit. Within the atom are the much smaller electrons pursuing orbits, like planets round the sun, in a space which relatively to their size is no less roomy than the solar system.) (Eddington, *Stars and Atoms* 9)

He goes on: "Entre las dimensiones del átomo y las de la estrella existe otra estructura no menos maravillosa —el cuerpo humano—. El hombre se encuentra un poco más cerca del átomo que de la estrella. Aproximadamente 10^{27} átomos forman su cuerpo y unos 10^{28} cuerpos humanos constituyen material suficiente para edificar una estrella" (Nearly midway in scale between the atom and the star there is another structure no less marvellous—the human body. Man is slightly nearer to the atom than to the star. About 10^{27} atoms build his body; about 10^{28} human bodies constitute enough material to build a star) (Eddington, *Estrellas y átomoso* 18, [9]). It is not coincidental that this deft rhetorical and mathematical move brings such distant entities into relation—recall how Haeckel did something similar with the souls and

---

22 See Eddington, *Stars and Atoms* (Oxford: Oxford University Press, 1927).

psychic lives of atoms. We might not immediately perceive our relation to the vast and minuscule universes, but scientists helpfully remind us of it again and again.

Yet an idea of differentiation in form necessarily accompanies this shared material relation. What determines form? Hayles reflects on the question of form as it has to do with levels of organization: "[M]ost scientists recognise there are emergent effects that appear at different levels of organisation. Effects not noticeable at the molecular level, for example, may appear at the cellular level; effects not noticeable at the cellular level may appear at the level of the organism, and so on" (170). What makes us understand the universe-microcosm that is the human body as an individual rather than as a compilation poised to dissolve into its cosmic elements or its "propiedades de la vida vegetal" (Sala y Villaret 130)? Or if not dissolve materially, then meaningfully: Why not think about all of the carbon in a body as related (through its self-sameness) to the carbon in another body, or in many bodies? Where do we draw the lines and why? How much of what makes sense feels meaningful, and what happens when the delineations of bodies that regiment relationships among them no longer feel meaningful and can moreover be understood to no longer be quite sensible when atoms, elements, and waves have crept into our common sense? This shared mode of felt experience, an alternative "common sense"—although one that is just as ingrained and unscrutinized as ordinary common sense often is—is in fact how I look to explore gender.

The theme of a sameness underlying and defining materiality, alongside its mutability and the question of our ability to perceive this stratum of our existence, structures an understanding of the material world as a place where we make sense of things—both in our ability to reason through them and in the common sense we receive without conscious intervention. Such a world is formed in conjunction with our relation to it—we are similarly inextricable from our surroundings and unfixed, open to unsensed influences. Before turning to *Memorias de Leticia Valle*, I will provide a brief overview of the early twentieth-century scientific research on sex and gender in Spain. While this research is quite different from the scientific work on matter, it establishes gender as a slippery category, one that society must make sense of through material evidence and social means. Familiar anxieties about mutual influence and the difficulty of pinning down the material elements that could define the boundaries of bodies show up here as well.

The science of sex and gender in early twentieth-century Spain

While I consider the relation between materiality and gender to be more complex than the already complicated notion of locating maleness or femaleness in the body, it is worth outlining the pervading views on gender and sexuality as they evolved during the first half of the twentieth century, particularly as they relate to the ways that children's bodies were sexed and gendered. Sexological research met up with social discourses on gendered behavior and sexuality as scientists searched for the biologically determining site of sexual difference. In *Sex Itself: The Search for Male and Female in the Human Genome*, Sarah Richardson traces the history of the discovery and understanding of the X and Y chromosomes, which were "first called the 'odd chromosomes,' [...] discovered in 1890 and 1905," respectively, and first dubbed "sex chromosomes" in 1906.[23] It was not until 1959 that the Y chromosome was linked to determining male sex—binary sexual difference in humans was previously ascribed to the second female X—and it was then that the chromosomal diagnosis of sex overtook the hormonal one that had reigned for decades (with examination of the gonads also playing an important role) (see Richardson 83). While chromosomal sex was not generally seen as a determining factor in socially observed sex in the first half of the century, that did not stop (pseudo)scientific musing on the differences encoded in the X and Y chromosomes, frequently positing greater conservatism for females and greater variability and thus exceptionality for males (see Richardson 76–77).

What the relative fluidity of the hormonal model, the popularity of gonadal differentiation, and the later X and Y chromosomal diagnosis highlight is the uncertain location of sexual difference and the fact that the drive to uncover a definitive site or marker was coupled with, and influenced by, social concerns about gender. In *Hermaphroditism, Medical Science and Sexual Identity in Spain, 1850–1960*, Richard Cleminson and Francisco Vázquez García examine cases in which medical discourse endeavored to determine the sex of individuals through evolving styles of examination and diagnosis. They elaborate on Gregorio Marañón's theory of intersexuality, according to which "'intersexuals' were those in whom the triumph of maleness or femaleness had not been sufficiently complete to entail proper 'sexual differentiation.'"[24] Writing on the shifting definitions of (pseudo)

---

23 Sarah Richardson, *Sex Itself: The Search for Male and Female in the Human Genome* (Chicago: University of Chicago Press, 2013), 23.

24 Richard Cleminson and Francisco Vázquez García, *Hermaphroditism, Medical Science and Sexual Identity in Spain, 1850–1960* (Cardiff: University of Wales Press, 2009), 9.

hermaphroditism—but relevant, I would argue, to medico-scientific approaches to sex more generally—they note that "some doctors and social commentators wished to reassert difference between the sexes in the light of what was commonly understood as gender muddling by feminists, New Women and increasingly visible homosexuals at the time" (Cleminson and Vázquez García, *Hermaphroditism* 124). Like other scientific discourses, discussion of intersexuality reached a general public: in Carmen de Burgos's 1931 novel *Quiero vivir mi vida*, she has a Marañón-esque character lecture on intersexuality (see Cleminson and Vázquez García, *Hermaphroditism* 146). While the advent of chromosomal diagnosis served in some ways to confine the medico-scientific discussion of sex to a single site and to tamp down competing discourses on the subject, the largely prechromosomal moment of the 1940s is of interest for the heightened attention to sexual difference that comes from a confluence of social and scientific discourses.

In *"Los Invisibles"*: *A History of Male Homosexuality in Spain 1850–1939*, Cleminson and Vázquez García identify childhood sexuality and seduction as central cultural concerns. They define two periods of high panic surrounding child sexuality in Spain: the first from 1850 through the first decades of the twentieth century, "a period characterized by the explosion of the concept of 'childhood in danger' and the application of policies of child protection"; the second from the 1920s to the Civil War (1936–1939) with "the incorporation of the notion of the corruption of children as part of the burgeoning 'sexual question' with its manuals on sex education for the school and family."[25] *Memorias* was written in the 1930s and 1940s—in 1938, Victoria Ocampo asked Chacel for whatever she had written thus far and Chacel responded with the first chapter of the book—and set around when the shift identified by Cleminson and Vázquez García takes place (see Mateo 78). Both sorts of panic—over children's correct or incorrect sexuality and, importantly, their relationship with adults—produced an explosion of writing on and talking about, and sometimes to, children in relation to sex.

Alberto Mira emphasizes that while the work of Sigmund Freud was known in Spain—and certainly by Chacel—the influence of his writing was dwarfed by that of Marañón's theories. Contemporary theories of indeterminate childhood sexuality were supported by Marañón's writing on the hormones and internal secretions that would in puberty set things straight (Cleminson and Vázquez García, *"Los Invisibles"* 146). Psychoanalysis and endocrinology could in that sense cooperate: "In both the endocrinological and the psychoanalytical model, the behaviour of the

---

25 Cleminson and Vázquez García, *"Los Invisibles": A History of Male Homosexuality in Spain 1850–1939* (Cardiff: University of Wales Press, 2007), 139.

teacher or instructor could be decisive in terms of the production of the sexual differentiation sought (in Marañón's scheme); or it could produce a trauma or a communicative disorder (cf. Freud) which would favour a homosexual object choice" (Cleminson and Vázquez García, *"Los Invisibles"* 147). The talking about sexuality, whether to or on behalf of children, that these authors identify is conspicuously absent from Chacel's novel—though the role of the corrupting teacher does appear. Implicit in the polemical discussion of the time is the need to use language, either through legislation or sex education, to bridge the gap between childhood and adulthood and ostensibly to ease the transition between the two.

In order to examine the ways that infantile and childhood sexuality was addressed in Spain in the first decades of the twentieth century, Mercedes del Cura and Rafael Huertas focus primarily on pedagogy that aimed to clarify, to children and their parents, the appropriate contours of childhood sexuality and its accompanying behaviors in order to create hygienic and unneurotic children, and later adults. The authors note that despite psychoanalysis's comparatively low profile in Spain, it did exercise an influence in the debates on how, and in how much detail, to clarify children's sexuality to them through educational enterprises. Following naturally, perhaps, on the panic that centered on boys' schools and the male corruption of male minors, the "niños" spoken of—in debates over masturbation, for example—are nearly always not all children but only little boys. While discourse on same- and opposite-sex male sexuality was abundant, women and girls, outside of discussions on maternity and the family, and eventually family planning, were largely elided.[26] In *Memorias*, Leticia recalls: "Me mandaban allí [al colegio de las Carmelitas] como a curarme de algo: a que aprendiese a ser niña, decían" (They sent me to the Carmelite school as if to cure me of something: for me to learn to be a little girl, they said) (Chacel, *Memorias* 18). The schoolroom is a place where gender roles are imposed and appropriate sexual behaviors hinted at.

Despite relative silence on girls' sexuality, the space of childhood in early twentieth-century Spain was fraught with dangers that might propel a young person—biologically, psychically, or socially—onto an inescapably "incorrect" path. One of the reasons that little girls' sexuality may have remained rather unremarked upon is that it represented simply a backward extension of women's sexuality, and the same familiar concerns about

---

26 See Mercedes del Cura and Rafael Huertas, "Medicina y sexualidad infantil en la España de los años treinta del siglo XX: La aportación del psicoanálisis a la pedagogía sexual," in *La sexualidad en la España contemporánea (1800–1950)*, ed. Jean-Louis Guereña (Cádiz: Universidad de Cádiz, 2011), 189–203.

seduction, the family, and the private sphere of the home largely applied. Katherine Murphy cites debates over the New Woman to demonstrate how androgyny and women's incursions into male spheres were seen as inextricable from a slew of sexual and moral perversions. Indeed, the panic over Leticia's gender is tinged with unspoken fears of a seeping deviancy that would undoubtedly doom the social life of an adult woman, particularly in the small town where the novel is set.[27]

Already apparent in these medical and legal discussions of gender and sexuality is that both are categories created and enforced in a social setting. Doctors and others took into consideration an individual's interactions with others, be it in examining the romantic and/or sexual interests of their intersex patients or monitoring the actions of young boys and male teachers; influences outside of the body were just as vital as hormonal flows inside. This attention, which crosses from the psychic to the social to the corporeal and back again, is not so unlike crisscrossing materialist narratives that move from the souls of atoms to the bodies of humans to the stuff of stars. Yet, unlike physicists, physicians are often more concerned with finding a fixed diagnosis and thus "curing" their patients with a concrete narrative, while scientific discourse, as we have seen, may provide a more open framework for understanding gender outside of a regimen of diagnosing ills. The immediately apparent strangeness that characterizes Leticia's complex relation with femininity (or perhaps more precisely, "little-girlness") certainly evades straightforward diagnosis, but it also provides insight into how materiality shapes gendered experience.

Materiality and gender in *Memorias de Leticia Valle*

I now turn to *Memorias de Leticia Valle*, and the unusual voice and minute observations of its young narrator. I suggest analyzing the novel's narrative style to think about language through coetaneous conceptions of materiality. I allow the scientific texts above to guide my attention to material encounters of bodies and objects that come into close proximity or contact, dissolve and re-form affects and sensed experiences, and subsequently change the physical ways that individuals interact. This approach can allow us to better understand the accretion of details throughout the novel and the somewhat opaque encounters with secondary characters whose lives collide with

---

27 See Katherine Murphy, "Unspeakable Relations: Eroticism and the Seduction of Reason in Rosa Chacel's *Memorias de Leticia Valle*," *Journal of Iberian and Latin American Studies* 16, no. 1 (2010): 51–72, esp. 63.

Leticia's own when we are given only vague hints as to their psychologies or motivations.

Unheard-of erotics

Leticia's narration resists solely sexual, solely mystical, or solely Freudian interpretations, not just in the instances of her "transportation" into other bodies and objects, which I will describe at greater length below, but throughout the more quotidian events in the novel in which Chacel describes in great detail Leticia's thoughts and the way in which she observes and recalls the world around her with all five senses. She must come to terms with the fact that her projections of herself, her melding with other people— or her understanding of herself as affectively and materially interrelated with those around her—is interpreted by society as sexual. Thus, in the text, her strangeness is both gendered and sexualized while maintaining some quality that exceeds the limits of both. This leads up to the "inaudito," unheard of and unspeakable, event of her possible seduction–violation by Daniel, the unnarrated denouement around which the young girl's memoirs are structured. I am interested in reading the erotic traces in the text not as sexual or mystical but rather as an index of the instability of both the limits of the body and the borders between the corporeal, psychological, social, and sexual. We are left with evidence of society's discomfort in the face of reconfigurations of the social skin that come about through material, and yet not immediately perceptible, processes.

Much in *Memorias* might be said to be "erotic," but beyond perhaps pointing to a critical discomfort with referring to a young girl's recitation of poetry as overtly "sexual," it may be difficult to see what that pliable term is doing. I am interested in the erotic not as a more delicate way of discussing children's relation to sex, but as a way to focus on certain qualities that may accompany sex but are also seen to be present elsewhere. Georges Bataille establishes eroticism as concerned with inner life, and fundamentally with the loss of self through transgression, the violation of taboo.[28] I do not maintain the specificity of what for Bataille constitutes taboo, but the idea of transgression as crossing out of the self is helpful for thinking about Leticia's experiences and about the scientific discourse on materiality that made the limits of the self questionable to begin with. Chacel, in "Esquema de los problemas prácticos y actuales del amor" touches on the question of *eros* in an argument about the possible differences between the sexes

---

28 See Georges Bataille, *Erotism: Death and Sensuality*, trans. Mary Dalwood (San Francisco: City Light Books, 1986), 31.

and their role in cultural and intellectual life.[29] While her argument, with frequent references to Max Scheler and Georg Simmel, attempts to explain a wide array of social and cultural phenomena—and explain away erroneous ideas about the differences between men and women and their intellectual, psycho-social lives—the essay also suggests how we might read the erotic as deeply embedded in the question of being: "[S]iendo el problema del eros consustancial del problema del ser, sólo aquellas teorías que se ocupen de éste en su más estricto y riguroso sentido metafísico, tendrán con aquél legítimo parentesco" (As the problem of eros and the problem of being are consubstantial, only those theories that address the latter in its strictest and more rigorous metaphysical sense will have any meaningful tie to the former) (Chacel, "Esquema" 131).[30] This framing of the subject, and Chacel's connection of the erotic to the intellectual, psychological, and social experiences of men and women, suggest that we might read *Memorias* as taking up the imbrication of eroticism with other forms of affective life.

Audre Lorde, in "Uses of the Erotic: The Erotic as Power," distinguishes between the "superficially erotic," seemingly aligned with the pornographic, and the erotic as "that power which rises from our deepest and nonrational knowledge."[31] The erotic for Lorde is a fullness of experience that can imbue our work, despite the attempts of capitalism to undo that experience, and also a "measure between the beginnings of our sense of self and the chaos of our strongest feelings" (54). I would relate that "chaos of strong feelings" to another aspect of Lorde's erotic, which is "sharing deeply any pursuit

---

29 See Chacel, "Esquema de los problemas prácticos y actuales del amor," *Revista de Occidente* 31, no. 92 (1931): 129–80. The publication of such an article by a woman was in itself an oddity and a sign of Chacel's own strangeness within male-dominated intellectual circles: Shirley Mangini points out that with the essay, the author "enter[ed] into a dialogue [on the question of *eros*] that had previously been sustained in *Revista de Occidente* by men only" (Mangini, "Women, Eros, and Culture: The Essays of Rosa Chacel," in *Spanish Woman Writers and the Essay: Gender, Politics, and the Self*, ed. Kathleen M. Glenn and Mercedes Mazquiarán de Rodríguez [Columbia: University of Missouri Press, 1998], 129).

30 The continuation of this same passage demonstrates her distain for much contemporary theorizing on the subject: "mientras la balumba de tendencias social psicológicomorales llenas de menudas concomitancias con que en general se le acomete, formará sólo la falsa y efímera norma que constituye la desorientación y desconcierto íntimo de nuestra época" (while the bulk of social-psychological-moral trends, full of the attendant trivialities that tend to overtake it, will only lead to the false and fleeting standards that constitute the innermost disorientation and disconcertion of our era) (Chacel, "Esquema" 131).

31 Audre Lorde, "Uses of the Erotic: The Erotic as Power," in *Sister Outsider: Essays and Speeches* (Berkeley, CA: Crossing Press, 1984), 53.

with another person," particularly sharing joy (56). Looking away from the erotic, misusing it, corralling it into prescribed arenas and experiences is a misuse of feeling and leads to our using one another rather than sharing joy and feeling across our differences (see Lorde 59). From Lorde's evocative and broad descriptions of the erotic, I would like to pick up on the erotic as affect, as sharing, and as nonrational knowledge: all potential ways of crossing out of the self.[32] The confusion of the particles that make up nature and the chaos of feelings that make up the psycho-social world both find a place in my reading of *Memorias* as a text on the possibilities of the non-narrative, even nonsignifying interactions—dually affective and material—that create a self that is gendered strangely. *Memorias* is also a story of a young person coming to understand how society codifies her feelings and experiences, and it may be that childhood itself is a time when the openness of erotic possibility, which is to be quelled and translated into sexual and gendered categories, is more highly visible.

Making sense

Both scientific rethinkings of materiality and Chacel's rethinking of little girl-ness through Leticia might be understood as participating in a shift in sense making supported by aesthetic, linguistic, and scientific innovations. That is to say, a change in technical proceedings for understanding and representing or narrating to ourselves what we perceive, and a related, though not necessarily directly translated, shift in how such conclusions are absorbed into public consciousness so as to inform "common sense" interpretations of the world—how, by default, we collectively make sense of what we perceive and feel. Importantly, Chacel's "not a little girl" does not manifest these changing intellectual currents as divorced from lived experience. Rather, Leticia demonstrates just how regimes of perception, affect, interpretation, and individual bodily incorporation are vitally intertwined in daily life. This is not to say that such regimes could be lifted to reveal an underlying flow of affect as pure potential not yet channeled, formed, and actualized. It instead suggests that the sense making that goes into shaping how we feel—how we feel like women or like little girls, or not—is in flux. And the strangeness, unease, and discomfort registered by Leticia's unusual narration suggests the possibility of feeling or sensing otherwise while operating within fairly strict aesthetic or gendered boundaries: it will be the deft tailoring of a little girl's dress that leads to one of the most unsettling and erotic moments of the book, and to the novel's uncertain denouement.

---

32 For an exploration of affect as interpersonal, see Brian Massumi, *The Politics of Affect* (Cambridge: Polity, 2015).

We may be able to see aesthetic production, particularly writing, as close to the experience of gender in that an individual is trapped by the confines of a sign system but feels and experiences outside of it. Both scientific investigation and linguistic production are structured around the inaccessibility of direct knowledge or perfect meaning with the appearance of boring toward it. If science writing in the first half of the twentieth century was, like Reichenbach's, increasingly showing just how indirect and imperfect our perception of the world and our representation of it were, we might see modernist novels as registering both the attempt at expressing lived experience and the creativity and possibility of change that inhered in the distance between language and experience.

The question of gender, particularly childhood gender, as felt experience in *Memorias*—what it means to feel like or not feel like a little girl—raises questions of how feelings get into our bodies from outside stimuli and how those feelings are understood as gendered or sexed. How are moments of physical contact with, or observation and recognition of, material objects caught up in the net of femininities and masculinities? How are they coded as erotic, sexual, or gendered? The intersection of materiality and gender need not necessarily have to do with sex and its location(s) in or on the body.[33] Scientific discourses from the first half of the twentieth century introduce their own complexities by determining sex according to a host of factors including genitalia, secondary sex characteristics, hormones, social behaviors, and eventually chromosomal sex. Yet I would like to think about the materiality of gender as also about meaningfully translating countless interactions with the material world—everything from clothing, to animals, to food—into a gendered experience.[34]

---

33 Arthur Kroker suggests it is not useful to talk about a single body and proposes instead "body drift," "the fact that we no longer inhabit *a* body in any meaningful sense of the term but rather occupy a multiplicity of bodies—imaginary, sexualized, disciplined, gendered, laboring, technologically augmented bodies. Moreover, the codes governing behavior across this multiplicity of bodies have no real stability but are themselves in drift—random, fluctuating, changing" (*Body Drift: Butler, Hayles, Haraway* [Minneapolis: University of Minnesota Press, 2012], 2). I would argue that this multiplicity of bodies is nothing new and that the changing codes of shifting bodies are all experienced simultaneously. Here, I center the overlapping and interacting "imaginary, sexualized, disciplined, gendered, laboring, [and] technologically augmented bodies" around the axis of materiality.

34 N. Katherine Hayles writes on the on the way we interact with objects by responding to their relevant "allure" ("Speculative Aesthetics," *Speculations: A Journal of Speculative Realism* 5 [2014]: 172). Both this and Jakob von Uexküll's take, discussed in chapter 3, on how species are attuned to the characteristics important for their survival, making objects in nature different for each species, may be useful methods

In another respect, *Memorias* asks how to testify to those things that would seem imperceptible and immaterial—affects, feelings, and desires—and yet have material results. The potential for imperceptible things (such as molecules) to have effects perceptible to our senses is an area of attention for science writers and nonspecialist authors alike. It is one thing to say that a certain dress reinforces gender norms, but how should we think about a dress—as in Chacel's novel—that suddenly seems silly (the dark green plaid Leticia dons to visit Daniel for her first lesson) or one with the sleeves pushed up for more evocative poetic gestures (the altered first communion dress) that seems to trigger a shift in a relationship? The unabating descriptions of that sort of physicality in *Memorias* underscore the inconclusive or uncertain but fundamental and foundational nature of each brush with the physical world.[35]

The narration of the novel and its attention to affective and material details leads the reader away from metaphor as the primary template for making sense of things. The things we encounter in the novel are not symbolic objects but part and parcel of a fuzzy psychological realm indistinct from the corporeal one. This mode of sense making is instructive here: in addition to looking at scientific writing that employs metaphor when describing molecular materiality—recall the panicle of elderberries—we should pay attention to scientific discourse that is difficult to understand literally and yet is not exactly metaphorical (discourse that concerns the souls of atoms and psychic lives of cells, among other apparent personifications). Slippages that seem to break down disciplinary boundaries in this way can help us understand science writing as part of the milieu in which the construction of gender takes place—just as medico-legal discourse is often seen to be influential—not just because science writing is sometimes about sex and gender, but because as a discourse it suggests particular and novel ways of trafficking in things, feelings, and unstable linguistic signs.

Questions about what signifies gender and how those signifiers allow communication on the topic of gender, and structure gendered experience, dovetail with Leticia's confusion about how the adults around her make

---

for reading the multiple ways that humans interact with their surroundings, variously attentive to what they need or what they want.

35 I have not rigorously distinguished between materiality and physicality, though Hayles's distinction between the two may be useful to keep in mind for the attention it draws to the limits of our interactions with objects: "physicality," for Hayles, is "similar to an object's essence; potentially infinite, it is unknowable in its totality"; "materiality" is defined by "the physical qualities that present themselves to us" (172). According to such distinctions, the inconclusive nature of physicality might have to do with the inaccessible experience of the unbounded totality of physicality that is present and offers the potential for a different material interaction.

meaning. She realizes that those around her employ double meanings that render significant, rather than senseless, expressions such as the one exchanged by relatives who say that her father went to get himself killed by the Moors: "Cuando yo preguntaba, era un alzarse de hombros, un mover de cabeza con lo que me respondían, y yo sentía vergüenza, no sé si por mi padre o si por mí, por no entender, por no dar en el quid de aquello que no querían explicarme" (When I would ask, they would reply with a shrug of their shoulders or a movement of their heads, and I felt ashamed—I'm not sure if for my father or for myself—for not understanding, for not getting to the essence of what they didn't want to explain to me) (Chacel, *Memorias* 12). She could understand that her father might want to die, but certainly not in such a strange and specific way; moreover, she cannot understand the tone in which the comment is tossed around among her relatives. Her inability to grasp their meaning creates a sense of estrangement but also shame. Later she sits at the dinner table at Christmas surrounded by adults as their conversation goes over her head and she cannot figure out if they are discussing real people or fiction (see Chacel, *Memorias* 72–73). But Leticia's narration does not just express a child's frustration with adult communication—though that alone might be enough to direct us to look for other ways in which she makes sense of the world: the novel is made up of myriad details that the adult reader is similarly hard-pressed to translate into narrative. This is the flow of fleeting gestures, glances, and inflections that Leticia tracks assiduously in an *inaudito* flow of narrative material because she senses their role in creating her unheard-of way of being.

Memorias offers insight into the materiality of gender and suggests a materiality of meaning while eschewing symbolism, metaphor, and even, in some places, narrative. Understanding the ways that meaning is made in the novel is important not only for working through the implications for Leticia's inaudito gender but also because it serves as a potential model for meaning making through the scientific–literary pairings I pose in this project. While Leticia does not always understand adult conversation, stymied by its figurative language or esoteric allusions, she does sense some of the feelings that are being passed through it and the relations it develops. In sketching out the scientific ideas that permeated the popular imagination in the first decades of the twentieth century, I do not intend to propose them as metaphors or narrative keys but rather as currents of understanding and feeling that shaped the experience of everyday life. *Memorias* suggests some ways in which that can happen.

If Leticia's gender is indeed depicted as somehow unheard of or unspeakable, and I am suggesting that a fundamental aspect of gender is its non-narrative or unnarratable quality, scientific discourse also depicts the physical world in a way that breaks down apparent narratives, such as those concerning the limits of bodies or the divisions between living organisms and inanimate objects. We see instead segments of experience, and of the world, that do not have predetermined or fixed forms—that carry information but not fixed meaning.[36] Some unformed potential or other ways of being, acting, and feeling among others lingers in the flow of experience that Leticia transmits as her narration tries to evoke something that can be sensed, if only by her not-yet-twelve-year-old self, but not captured in a fixed form. She brings into focus the ways that things apparently distinct and removed from our bodies—a blanket she plans to purchase as a gift, puppies she sees being drowned—can construct and make us (Chacel, *Memorias* 62, 77). Scientists, trying to communicate to the lay public the nature of matter, again and again raised the idea that apparently clearly delineated bodies and entities are made up of smaller—molecular or atomic—parts that open up those entities to existing and signifying in a different way.

Observation and admiration: the matter of affect and relation
Leticia lives largely in a world of adults. Her mother absent or dead, she lives with her father, invalided in the colonial war in Africa, and aunt. Before being sent to school "a que aprendiese a ser niña," she is tutored by Margarita Velayos: "Cada vez que dábamos lección yo observaba su traje sastre, su sencillez, su aire varonil y pensaba: cuando yo sea como ella..." (Every time we had a lesson, I would observe her tailored suit, her simplicity, her masculine air, and I would think: when I'm like her...) (Chacel, *Memorias* 18, 51). Leticia seems to seek in adulthood a style of being that does not necessarily fit a gender binary. She relates details of her tutor's and teacher's actions that take on surprising importance. When the tutor reappears toward the end of the novel, Leticia's narration emphasizes her blend of masculine and feminine features: "[A]l mismo tiempo que [Margarita Velayos] hacía aquel ademán varonil [al tomar su copa de coñac], su cabeza tomaba una actitud tan delicada como la de una virgen" (Just as she [Margarita Velayos] made that masculine gesture [of drinking her glass of cognac], she inclined her head as delicately as a virgin) (Chacel, *Memorias* 126). She forms a special attachment to her schoolteacher upon recognizing her skill in embroidery,

---

36 Gillian Beer and others have explored this idea as the linguistic mirror of a scientific idea, as in Virginia Woolf's *The Waves*. See Beer, "Wave Theory and the Rise of Literary Modernism," in *Open Fields: Science in Cultural Encounter* (Oxford: Clarendon Press, 1996), 295–320.

and eventually will form similarly intense bonds with Luisa and Daniel.[37] She relates her response to the first lesson with Daniel, the archivist, as follows: "Eso era lo que yo llamaba estar en mi elemento: tener algo que admirar" (That's what I called being in my element: having something to admire) (Chacel, *Memorias* 48). It is this state of admiration, one that eventually falters with her other teachers, that she will try to sustain with Daniel. We may read this admiration as a way of observing some extraordinary or startling aspect of another person. Observation is simultaneously a mode of relation—recall how scientists' insights into new ways of perceiving the world were accompanied by suggestions of new ways of understanding ourselves in relation to it—and Leticia's admiration always succeeds at inviting the observed and admired subject to participate with her. It is an erotic admiration in Lorde's sense: a chaos of shared feelings. Leticia will find that others' ways of looking at her produce similarly strong effects.

Leticia recalls that one of the nuns at her school judges her using the same words as she does for another student—a girl who, "[e]n la hora de la labor se iba a un rincón y no daba una puntada: lamía la pared" (when it came time to work she would go to a corner and wouldn't make stitch: she'd lick the wall) (Chacel, *Memorias* 19). Upon reflection, Leticia declares that, despite her fears to the contrary, she is nothing like this maladapted girl and that the judgment passed by her teacher was simply cruel and her own willingness to see a similarity with that other child was "un deseo de castigo" (a desire for punishment) (Chacel, *Memorias* 18). And yet, that initial impulse to recall the nun's comment linking the wall-licker to herself may in fact point to a shared strain of strangeness running through the two young girls: a relationship with the material world that is markedly uncommon and that does not respect commonly drawn boundaries between bodies and objects nor acceptable human behavior at those frontiers.

---

37 Some might fault these unlikely role models, and the effective absence of parenting, for Leticia's violent experience. Indeed, at the conclusion of the novel, Leticia's relatives comment that living in that environment (with her mother gone and her father seemingly suffering from depression and alcoholism), some kind of crack-up was bound to happen. We might instead understand growing up as a process of learning, in which desires and attachments are prescribed and proscribed by society (see, for example, Judith Butler's *Gender Trouble: Feminism and the Subversion of Identity* [New York: Routledge, 1999]; and Butler, *The Psychic Life of Power: Theories in Subjection* [Stanford: Stanford University Press, 1997]). This novel is in some ways a case study of what happens when a regimen of proscription and prescription is not firmly in place. What does it mean for a desire to be prohibited, and how does one know that it is? Leticia, despite sensing herself to be different, clearly does not quite know.

More astute than her classmate, Leticia adeptly manipulates the affective-material world around her in at least two exemplary situations: in one, she buys Luisa a blanket as a Christmas present; in the other, she carefully prepares herself to recite a poem in public directed at Daniel. Leticia observes Luisa and imagines her feet wrapped in "esas mantas afelpadas que parecen de piel de leopardo" (these plush blankets that look like leopard skin), and she sets out to buy just that for the piano teacher (Chacel, *Memorias* 62). It marks a moment when her attentions are divided between Luisa and Daniel, and the two adults seem to compete for her affection. The gift leads Daniel to remark: "'Me parece que si tú fueras un caballerito tendrías el arte de hacer regalos a las damas, y me parece también que a ti te gustaría mucho algunas veces ser un caballerito'" ("It seems to me that if you were a young man you'd have quite a knack for giving presents to the young ladies, and it also seems to me that sometimes you'd very much like to be a young man") (Chacel, *Memorias* 74). Yet Leticia rejects the simplicity of this interpretation, and she presents the affective manipulation as one subtler than the seduction of a man's wife.

In another scene, leading to the novel's denouement, she recites a poem at a public event. In preparation for this public presentation, she alters her First Communion dress with elastic that will hold back the sleeves and facilitate the sweeping arm gestures she practices. This moment represents the height of her "seduction," and as she names the king al-Hamar, she feels Daniel's heart beating: "Y desde la tribuna misma, sentí latir su corazón. Esto no es sólo palabras: lo sentí. Por la misma razón que mis sentidos naturales estaban casi anulados; miraba y no veía" (And from the platform, I felt his heart beating. That's not just a turn of phrase: I felt it. For the same reason that my innate senses were nearly incapacitated; I was looking and I could not see) (Chacel, *Memorias* 132). The display seems to have an equally strong effect on Daniel, and when she leaves the stage he has left the room (see Chacel, *Memorias* 139). I will return to these moments of *ensueño* or *transportación*, which punctuate the novel. This one is unique because she has arranged things—what she wears, how she speaks, her gestures—to bring something about, even if she does not know exactly what. Precisely because she is a child narrating what should be a quotidian scene—memorizing a poem and dressing up for a public reading—and not an adult planning a scene of seduction, that our attention goes to the material details that create such extreme affective and relational shifts. Without the signifying codes of adulthood, we see the material divisions between bodies break down; the flow of objects, gestures, and body parts begins to resemble the interactions of atoms and molecules coming together in a multitude of ways to create new, unstable forms.

As evidenced by the remarkable effects she has on Luisa, Daniel, and others, Leticia's *inaudito* quality—the "esto que era yo" (that which I was)—is shaped by these interactions with the adults she lives among and the objects that transmit affect and significance among them. This transmission depends as much on observation, giving rise to nearly invisible connections, as on material collisions. Among the material and affective exchanges that come to define her is the following scene in which Leticia discusses Daniel's observation of her after she has seen a young woman drown a litter of puppies:

> Aunque ha pasado mucho tiempo, todavía no comprendo; tienen que pasar muchos años para que yo comprenda aquella mirada, y a veces querría que mi vida fuese larga para contemplarla toda la vida; a veces creo que por más que la contemple ya es inútil comprenderla.
>
> Alrededor de aquella mirada empezó a aparecer una sonrisa o más bien algo semejante a una sonrisa, que me exigía a mí sonreír. Era como si él estuviese viendo dentro de mis ojos el horror de lo que yo había visto. Parecía que él también estaba mirando algo monstruoso, algo que le inspirase un terror fuera de lo natural y, sin embargo, sonreía. (Chacel, *Memorias* 79)

> (Even though a long time has passed, I still don't understand it; many years will have to go by before I can understand that look, and I sometime wish that my life were long to contemplate it my whole life; I sometimes think that as much as I might contemplate it, I'll never understand it.
>
> Around his gaze a smile started to appear, or rather, something like a smile, that required me to smile. It was as though he were seeing in my eyes the horror of what I had seen. It seemed that he too was looking at something monstrous, something that filled him with an unnatural horror and, yet, he smiled.)

We can observe here the contagion of affect—the way Leticia seems to have taken on the horror of what she has seen, the way she feels Daniel's expression requiring her to smile, the play of exchanged glances. We also see that she is changed not just by the experience of observing a young woman drowning young animals—that horror captured in her eyes—but also by Daniel's catching sight of the way that experience has affected her. How he looks at and feels about her changes her. The experience and the feeling created by it become transmissible through an exchange of gazes that seems nearly palpable. Leticia is particularly attuned to the often imperceptible difference an observer makes on the scene—here, her own growing up, being formed. We can recall the observer effect and the misapprehension that the observer's intervention is purely an effect of the mind when it is in fact a material one. In the novel, observation is not passive but rather is an action that intertwines the observer and the observed—or reveals the connection or relation already in formation between them.

The queer childhood of a chica rara: not a little girl

One of the benefits of the indetermination, uncertainty, and illegibility of the novel's aesthetic and affective plot can be seen in the developments in criticism that reads the Daniel-Leticia-Luisa triangle. Rosalía Cornejo Parriego underscores Leticia's "supuesta identidad masculina" (supposedly masculine identity) as the child's expressed desire, though in the passage that she cites, the narrator does not pronounce, as Cornejo Parriego suggests, that she is a boy, but instead that she is not a girl ("yo no era una niña" [Chacel, *Memorias* 18]).[38] This line of analysis—winding through reflections on the eroticism of female friendships and the instability of the gender binary—is reflective of most of the writing on *Memorias* that ventures beyond a reading of the novel as a simple but strange tale of a young girl's seduction by her teacher (or vice versa). For Cornejo Parriego, Daniel represents an interruption of the female friendship between Luisa and Leticia; his desires and perceptions are not strange but are rather the imposition of social order (see 73). He is seen to occupy the intellectual and masculine realm to which Leticia desires access while his wife is purely and richly corporeal. Given all that, she reads Leticia's seduction of her teacher as part of a plan of intellectual affirmation and vengeance on the gendered social roles that have kept her from it, with Leticia's true affection and love reserved for Luisa (see Cornejo Parriego 74). According to this line of thought, *Memorias* demonstrates Chacel's conviction that affection, eroticism, and desire not only flow through socially determined and culturally nameable channels but that attempts to live and think about gender and sexual possibilities outside of those confines inevitably fail (see Cornejo Parriego 80). I would rather not judge whether Leticia's acts and narration successfully pull off the trick of nonnormative gender identity and dodge compulsory heterosexuality—her very survival as a queer child at the book's end seems unstable—and instead focus on her yearnings and exalted feelings as evidence of a space where the boundaries of sexuality, eroticism, and friendship dissolve into undefined currents that run between bodies.

Citing Chacel's intentions to write the account of a young girl's seduction of an older man, Katherine Murphy comes out in the affirmative in the

---

38 Rosalia Cornejo Parriego, *Entre mujeres: Política de la amistad y el deseo en la narrativa española contemporánea* (Madrid: Biblioteca Nueva, 2007), 72.

debate over whether or not Leticia physically desires Daniel, but, not unlike Cornejo Parriego, she also insists that the central importance lies with the protagonist's desire to conquer the masculine intellectual realm (see Murphy 60). For Murphy, Leticia's feelings toward Luisa are those directed to a mother figure and her feelings of union with Luisa are aimed at experiencing the woman's desire for her husband, though she also recognizes the same-sex eroticism in this relationship (see Murphy 61, 65). The young girl's sensual experience of the world is thus decoded as heterosexual desire (see Murphy 62). I argue that the text's insistence on not making such pronouncements should steer us toward readings that are open to desire among the three main characters without determining a particular hierarchy. What, then, is Leticia's gendered experience as not-a-little-girl bouncing between competitive affections of an adult couple?

Kathryn Bond Stockton, in *The Queer Child, or Growing Sideways in the Twentieth Century*, reflects on the creation of childhood as a state queered by, above all, the purported innocence we assign to it.[39] Rather than the destruction of the child via Lee Edelman's theorization of it, she seeks what is happening within the suspended space of childhood that is not, to our minds, childlike. Throughout the years that young people age, learn from their surroundings, and absorb knowledge while they are still deemed children, their engagement with what society holds to be "adult" knowledge and experiences can spook grown-ups. By reading the delays, the necessarily sideways motion, required by the delay represented by not yet "growing up" but instead inhabiting childhood space and time, she brings into focus the sexuality, aggression, and secrecy that we occult in children, queering them with the requirement of innocence, which supposedly restricts a range of feelings and experiences to adulthood, postinnocence. Stockton points out not just the untenability of such a pristine state but also the twisted outcomes of our desire for it. What we protect children from is what we fear in them. Leticia remarks on "lo que la gente llama inocencia" (what people call innocence): "¡Qué asco! Nunca me cansaré de decir el asco que me da esta enfermedad que es la infancia" (How disgusting! I'll never tire of saying how much it disgusts me this sickness that is childhood) (Chacel, *Memorias* 141). The queerness of the imposition of innocence shows up vividly in Leticia; rather than conforming neatly to her childish form, bland childlike things seem harshly at odds with the secrecy, aggression, and eroticism that we will, later in this chapter, see flowing naturally through her experience of the world. Though critics struggle with the seemingly unchildlike voice

---

39 See Kathryn Bond Stockton, *The Queer Child, or Growing Sideways in the Twentieth Century* (Durham, NC: Duke University Press, 2009).

of the young narrator, judging it to be either a flaw or a calculated—if awkward—choice by Chacel, we might instead see that voice as the literary manifestation of a sort of experience that is indeed available to children, even if the sophistication of the language may not be. The desire for a simplified childish voice may not be so different from our desire for a simple, innocent childhood. In *Memorias*, we instead witness the psychic torsion resulting from that demand for innocence. Stockton's account of queer childhood underscores how children incorporate—corporeally, but also psychically and emotionally—external narratives about themselves. That process of incorporation is not straightforward; instead, those narratives or narrative fragments that work their way into the lives of children encounter numerous obstacles in the form of lived experience that contradicts or complicates them. I argue that this twisted, queered path of incorporation does not end when adulthood commences but might be heightened or more highly visible in children.

Leticia's voice and tone are not only striking because they might seem out of place in such a young narrator: rather, while Chacel constructs a clear plot arc, both the style and the content of the writing lend the text an avant-garde, non-narrative quality. Her first novel, *Estación: Ida y vuelta* (1930), is generally cited as exemplifying the tenets of avant-garde writing and reflecting her immersion in the vanguard Spanish milieu made possible by her close working relationship with José Ortega y Gasset (see Mateo 25). Any nontraditional qualities in *Memorias*, on the other hand, are often put down to an awkward attempt to have a young girl voice sophisticated ideas while maintaining some markers of childishness. I argue that *Memorias* carried out an experiment in a non-narrative sort of sense making, which permeates its narration and plot structure. As Leticia takes on the common sense of the adult world, revealing the nonsensical, complex, and contradictory nature of adult language and actions, the novel simultaneously puts forth an alternative perspective on sense making, one that edges around or works through a linguistic system to reveal that sense is made through an accretion of words, objects, and gestures that provoke sensorial and emotional feelings.[40] We might think of *Memorias* as approaching language not as a sign system but as shiftable patterns created by this accretion. This approach brings organic and inorganic things onto one plane, and in the

---

40 Similarly focused on constituent parts rather than wholes, Elizabeth Grosz suggests that we think of oppressions such as racism or sexism not as systems whose parts make sense in relation to a larger structure but as patterns of acts, which we might more readily be able to shift through new and varied acts than through externally imposed changes to social structures. *Becoming Undone: Darwinian Reflections on Life, Politics, and Art* (Durham, NC: Duke University Press, 2011).

novel we can begin to see the human body, objects, even words participating in material formations, coming together and apart in new formations as scientists told us the stuff of the universe, us included, would.

"Con mis cinco sentidos, entraba allí"

Some of the most evocative passages reflective of how Leticia not only observes the flow of people and things around her but feels herself to be relating them are those describing her experience of transportación or ensueño. We can read these passages while remembering the view of the world presented by contemporary science, in which humans are described as being made up of atoms, and atoms are also envisioned as having souls and meeting up and combining alchemically to create new forms. When Leticia first narrates her experience of this transportation it is alongside a recumbent Christ in church: "Siempre me lo imaginaba, siempre me concentraba en la idea de que andaba por allí dentro, de que me encogía para caber en el pequeño espacio que quedaba al lado de su cuerpo, pero algunas veces no era imaginar: enteramente, con mis cinco sentidos, entraba allí" (I always imagined it, I always concentrated on the idea that I was walking around there inside, that I curled up to fit in the small space next to his body, but sometimes it wasn't my imagination: completely, with my five senses, I entered that space) (Chacel, *Memorias* 17). Critics have described this moment and similar ones as a sort of mystical transportation or mere fantasy.[41] I want to propose a way of reading Leticia's flights in a nonmystical register; I argue that, instead, the material permeability she describes points to the constantly reworked boundaries between individuals that are anything but rigid to her young eye. Recall Reichenbach's description of the surface of a lake as a "vague frontier zone": this is the sort of ill-defined border that Leticia is able to slip into. This is not to dismiss the eroticism or sexual charge of Leticia's relationships with Daniel and Luisa. Rather, it is to complicate the way that sexuality comes to be a bounded term and one that defines little girlhood, or, perhaps, its limits.

In a later scene that follows the pattern of her experience with the recumbent Christ, Leticia observes the sunlight through Daniel's shirt and loses herself "en aquel clima, entre la luz de la zona aquella que me parecía a veces una gruta, a veces una selva" (in that realm, in the light of that region that sometimes seemed to me to be a cavern, sometimes a

---

41 See, for example: Jesús Pérez-Magallón, "Leticia Valle o la indeterminación genérica," *Anales de la Literatura Española Contemporánea* 28, no. 1 (2003): 139–59; Katherine Murphy, "Monstrosity and the Modernist Consciousness: Pío Baroja versus Rosa Chacel," *Anales de la Literatura Española Contemporánea* 35, no. 1 (2010): 141–75.

jungle) (Chacel, *Memorias* 81–82). As with the scene in the church, Leticia imagines a vivid physical experience of delving into a minute and intimate space that encloses her; here the experience is transformed by this shift in scale into a vast wilderness. The visual description is microscope-like, but the affective conclusion is much more radical. Later, she compares this experience with simple observation in a scene that draws out the relational or erotic possibilities of this way of sensing the world—this time entering into Luisa's body as Daniel lifts his wife into bed after she has been injured:

> Yo había observado todo el tiempo que duró la maniobra, pero ¿cómo puedo decir que lo observé? Si lo hubiese observado, ¿quién podría darme crédito? ¿Es que yo voy a considerar que mi observación queda tan fuera de lo común, o que mis dotes son tan excepcionales que sobrepasan infaliblemente las de los demás seres humanos? No, yo no observé nada: yo me transporté —pues si acaso poseo algún don excepcional es ése únicamente—, me uní, me identifiqué con Luisa en aquel momento, recorrí su alma y sus cinco sentidos, como se recorre y se revisa una casa que nos es querida. Vi todo lo que había en su pensamiento, percibí lo que sentían sus manos, sentí el sentimiento que se imprimía en su voz. (Chacel, *Memorias* 147)

> I had observed the whole length of the maneuver, but, how can I say that I observed it? If I had observed it, who would believe me? Can I suppose that what I observed was so out of the ordinary or that my gifts are so exceptional that they are infallible and surpass those of other human beings? No, I didn't observe anything: I was transported—for if I have any exceptional gift it's only that—I joined with Luisa, I identified with her in that moment, I traversed her soul and her five senses, just as we walk through and examine a house that is dear to us. I saw everything in her thoughts, I perceived what her hands felt, I sensed the feeling etched in her voice.

She refers directly to Luisa's five senses, choosing verbs of sense perception: *ver, percibir, sentir*. The description of traveling through Luisa's soul and senses like a house casts this moment as a physical one. Leticia rejects the idea that she might have uncommonly sharp powers of observation and instead classes this experience as one of transportation, one that allows her to know what another person feels, senses, and thinks in a union in which the limits of the self fall away. But though she declares herself not particularly apt at observation—she wants to emphasize instead her experience of transportation and identification—I would argue that her ability to sense and relate these moments as she does is in fact an uncommon quality of observation, or more broadly of perception. Furthermore, she is able to recognize these moments as fitting into the array of her strangeness that triggered the story she is telling. The narrative principle of the book might be said to be just that: the young protagonist is able to sense which observations, experiences, and feelings structure the short history of her strangeness, and she relates that pattern to us, arguing that, taken as a whole, it leads to the inevitable and painful outcome at the novel's end. She argues as much in her final reflections when she says: "Describí todos mis sentimientos sublimes hasta que desembocaron en aquello, porque para eso lo hice: para que se viese dónde fueron a parar" (I described all of my sublime feelings to the point where they gave way to all that, because that's why I did it: so as to show what they led to) (Chacel, Memorias 172).

Not all that is inaudito of Leticia's young personhood seems immediately related to her gender. The strangeness she herself notes has generally to do with her sense perception of the world around her and her ways of perceiving meaning and significance. Meaning making happens in the way that Luisa addresses her—"Adiós, querida"—but also in the way Daniel looks at her or in observing the act of drowning puppies in a river (Chacel, Memorias 77). Leticia's narration calls attention to the often overlooked ways in which our relations with others and our understanding of ourselves are constructed through minuscule gestures, shifts in tone, and seemingly irrelevant actions. I suggest that her moments of ensueño or transportación manifest the strength of such encounters and their potential for blurring lines that supposedly delimit the self. Her experience alongside the recumbent Christ, within the folds of Daniel's shirt, or inside Luisa's senses and soul reveals a heightened awareness of our psycho-social-affective selves' being made up of overlapping and interacting influences.

Finally, I ask how we can relate Leticia's moments of transportation to the other strangeness that she reports, as when she says "todo lo mío era inaudito," "yo no era una niña," and refers to "esto que era yo" (Chacel, Memorias 7, 18, 51). What do these interpenetrations, that would have us reconsider the limits of the body, have to do with Leticia's negotiation of gender and of eroticism? Might Leticia be registering with her senses a state of being that is in some way atomic, or particulate? The science guides our attention to the body, to the material, away from readings of gendered subjectivity or erotic/sexual encounters that exist only in a distinct psychological realm. The extreme nature of Leticia's transportation, its materiality, offers a radical openness, not to an uncircumscribed, open potential, but instead to what she finds in the world around her—Luisa's diffuse eroticism and friendship, and Daniel's more socially sanctioned and violent paternalism and sexuality. Her experience of being a materially open psycho-corporeal subject is not just marked as impossible but as both sexual and taboo. Being a little girl means feeling certain feelings as sexual, not as something else that remains undefined, and keeping your subjectivity to yourself.

When Leticia's cousin Adriana dances both parts, male and female, of a pavane, Chacel presents Leticia's enthusiasm and Luisa's comprehension of the significance of the delicate aesthetic scene. Adriana dances alone, playing both the part of the *caballerito* and of the *dama* who dance first separately and then together: "Después se cogían de la mano y bailaban la pavana. La bailaron los dos porque se sustituían con tal ligereza que la imagen del uno no se borraba antes de que el otro estuviese presente" (Afterward they joined hands and danced the pavane. There were two of them dancing it because they replaced one another so nimbly that the image of one was not yet erased when the other appeared) (Chacel, *Memorias* 93). Leticia is captivated. Her cousin's dance breaks down the apparently solidity of her body to reveal in its wake that it can contain both parts of the dance, and Leticia is delighted to see something that is not physically present. Adriana's scene is the incarnation of Leticia's mode of viewing the world in which she is able to see the porosity of individuals and their interplay and exchange. It is this scene that Leticia feels passionately about, whereas she rejects Daniel's estimation that she would like to be a little gentleman. "Sólo doña Luisa había comprendido," Leticia reflects, "¡Qué misterio! Tengo la seguridad de que si yo hubiese explicado lo que significaba para mí Adriana, no sería ella la que mejor pudiera comprenderlo, y sin embargo le había bastado mirarme la cara unas cuantas veces cuando yo le apretaba el brazo en el comedor" (Only doña Luisa had understood. What a mystery! I am sure that if I had explained what Adriana meant to me, she would not be the person to best understand it, and yet, she had only to glance at my face a few times while I squeezed her arm in the dining room) (Chacel, *Memorias* 100–101). Just as she declares herself not to be a little girl without therefore being a little boy, Leticia's feelings and actions toward Luisa do not position her to replace Daniel, as he seems to worry she might. Instead, she is attracted to the fleeting figures of the dance, to the traces they leave behind in the air, and to the way they clasp hands, making apparent solidity questionable and of minor importance. Her emotion over Adriana's dance can only be communicated with a glance and a squeeze of Luisa's arm: any narrative of this materially open interplay of bodies would fall short.

The end

If this dance scene contains the rejection of narrative paired with an unusual gendered component and the possibility of material openness, the elided scene of violence that is read as Leticia's rape represents a moment in which the adult world—and the scholarly world—has stepped in to force a single interpretation of her manipulation of erotic flows. In that scene, she describes only her observation of Daniel, who has just called her an "artist," a sound in his throat, and then: "[E]n ese momento, yo me hundí en una inmensidad de miseria, oscura como el infierno e ilimitada como el cielo. Pero es inútil querer decir cómo fue, más bien diría que sentí de pronto que todo iba a dejar de ser" (In that moment, I sank into an immensity of misery, as dark as hell and unending as the heavens. But it's no use to describe what it was like, instead I'll say that I suddenly felt that everything was going to cease to exist) (Chacel, *Memorias* 161–62). Daniel leaves the room and then returns and says, "'¡Te voy a matar, te voy a matar!'" ("I'll kill you, I'll kill you!") (162). Leticia describes what she feels, and the violence in the text is registered as the sense that everything would stop being, stop existing as she knew it to exist. When critics read the break in the text as the outcome of a physical and mental trauma that was a perhaps unexpected effect of an otherwise willful seduction, the result is at odds with Leticia's nuanced experience of the world. This mode of observation is entirely unlike Leticia's own (in her "reading" of the pavane, for example), one that she sets out as vivid and capable of tracking feelings and influences events throughout the course of the novel. The gap in the narration, in all of its violence, must not be allowed to annul what has come before it, as simple as it might be for us to mirror Daniel's look of horror, in which Leticia sees society's horror reflected back at her. Leticia all along has insisted on telling this story of how she senses the world in order to explain it as the quality that would bring about this violent outcome.

If Leticia has revealed an alternative form of sense making, what might it be? Elisa Rosales considers the unheard-of quality that marks Leticia and her narration, contending that the term *inaudito* in *Memorias* takes on a double meaning: the more ordinary acceptation of something extraordinary and a way of describing the quotidian rhythms of life, those transactions with reality that generally go unexpressed.[42] These, as much as any secret or forbidden desire, are what move the narration of the novel. The unabating relation of small moments posits them not as symbols of or keys to understanding Leticia's affections, but as carriers of feelings that do not distinguish among modes of relation—sexual, intellectual, corporeal, affectionate, or filial. When scientists share their microscopic view of the material world, they are excited about the possibilities for connection,

---

42   Elisa Rosales, "*Memorias de Leticia Valle*: Rosa Chacel o el deletreo de lo inaudito," *Hispania* 83, no. 2 (2000): 222–31.

continuity, and new formations it presents. When Leticia observes the world around her and within her with a similar microscopic eye, we get a sense that feelings and bodies could be organized differently. But the adults in her world cannot conceive of that, and as her readers we are hard pressed to fully imagine it, to grasp the importance of the molecular details that she recounts, which all add up to a novel that is rather strange.

That sense of the importance of the imperceptible structures the novel from the very beginning: it opens with Leticia's observation of something she cannot see: the growth of the ivy outside of her window. "Su vida es tan lenta" (Its life is so slow)—much like Leticia's own (Chacel, *Memorias* 8). The plant and Leticia change constantly but imperceptibly. She concludes her story on the eve of her twelfth birthday with the words: "Miré la rama de hiedra que subía por el marco de la ventana y había crecido lo que yo tenía calculado" (I looked at the branch of ivy that climbed up the window frame and it had grown as much as I'd predicted) (Chacel, *Memorias* 174). This is both a tribute to Leticia's penetrative powers of observation and a comment that forecloses unexpected outcomes. Even the unseen follows predetermined routes, and new alchemic combinations and growths are unlikely to occur.

By the novel's end, only feeling confident that what she calls her "fuerza bruta" (brute force), "algo irracional, algo así como la salud" (something irrational, like health), remains, and convinced that she will never again feel anything like love, Leticia seems to condemn all of her previous feelings (Chacel, *Memorias* 172). The subtlety and vividness of her earlier observations and sentiments seem dulled into something almost threatening. She views herself as the outcome of her way of sensing the world. Her incongruous nature has been definitively declared to be not only incompatible with social norms but simply impossible: "[La tía] [r]epetía: 'Ya te lo dije yo desde un principio; aquello no podía ser, aquello era cosa de locos. Aquello no podía ser, no podía ser'. Y no se daban cuenta de que lo que no podía ser estaba detrás de la butaca" (My aunt kept repeating: "I told you from the beginning; it couldn't be, it was pure madness. It couldn't be, it couldn't be." And they didn't realize that that which couldn't be was behind the armchair) (Chacel, *Memorias* 173-74).

Chacel's novel explores how people relate, and how the consequences of events, movements, and configurations can be tracked. Physical things happen in the world that do not immediately seem connected to their end results, yet if Leticia possesses some power of seduction it is her ability to perceive those invisible lines and harness them: rolling up the sleeves of her dress while she recites a poem and then narrating that detail, among many others. In the imperceptible feelings and moves—those only made explicit by Leticia and glimpsed fearfully by the adults—lies another way of being a little girl, or not one, configuring sexuality and gender. This approach to gender and sexuality is connected to a view of the world that understands its edges to be wavering and its solidity to be deceptive.

Leticia proposes another way of meaning or sense making, one which recognizes the affective and materially constitutive nature of countless daily interactions—the brush of skin against cloth, the dim glow of a blueish vein, the gaze that conveys horror and attraction, the sentiment conveyed by the cut of a suit or dress, the arm lifted just so in an expressive gesture, a kiss on the cheek, and so on. It is impossible to fully narrate such a particulate mode of existence, and being narrativized as a little girl is one way to restrict and manage meaning. Leticia's transportations thus describe an intersubjective state of being that unfolds even when it is not perceived—we are constantly made up of those people and things that surround us; in an atomic world, the borders between us and them waver and dissolve—and her inaudito flow of narration makes it clear that the process of confining gender and sexuality to recognized strains of feeling and acting—such as little girlhood—is a violent one.

Moreover, non-narrative communication takes place through material encounters that come to light if we understand bounded bodies, human and nonhuman, as related through atomic or vibratory organization; the nonsymbolic dress sleeves or nonmystical transport only make sense in a regime of non-narrative, affective sense that can emerge in a highly interrelated material world run through with invisible lines of (vibratory) communication and (atomic) similarity; the novel's unsexed eroticism and nonbinary gender are bolstered by the presence of a material and energetic world that is known to be in constant, uncertain, perhaps unmotivated flux where the question of which energies animate what matter within what, if any, limits is of fundamental importance.

In this reading, gender is the internalization of a regime of sense making that then shapes our affective and material interactions with the world. Leticia simultaneously refuses certain gender narratives and makes non-narrative fragments perceptible, which suggests a mutability akin to atomic or monist understandings of the world celebrated and disseminated by scientists. The felt experience of gender results from the internalization of material interactions with organic and inorganic bodies that have an affective valence. On the other hand, scientific imaginings of materiality make possible certain ways of thinking and feeling that reveal how gender (unlike, perhaps, gender roles) picks up on openness, the potential for change, new relations—which makes being a little girl an inherently strange, shifting, a-signifying or multiply signifying thing.

The importance of reading about these porous and constantly reproduced bodily boundaries in scientific texts is not that novelists can then narrate someone being anatomically or atomically fused to another body, sharing or swapping an arm or a brain: it is that readers could conceive of some version of that and begin to imagine and feel its potential effects. How bodies are organized and delimited is what determines how we treat other bodies, how we act and feel and react. In the case of Leticia, her trust in others as evidenced by how she places her psychosomatic self in their care, caring for them in turn, and her freedom to experiment with relationships and experiences, is betrayed by harsh social delimitations. And thanks to the very same knowledge of the possibilities of material-affective imbrication and relation and change, that betrayal turns back in on her own body—indistinct, as it is, from its surroundings—so that she is made to understand that she is the seducer, she has brought this on herself.

CHAPTER TWO

(Un)Toward Magnetism: Relational *Rareza* and *Personas en la sala*

El pensamiento obra hacia el exterior.
—Paul Jagot, *Método científico de magnetismo, hipnotismo, sugestión*[1]

Watching women: power in avant-garde looking

French occultist Paul Jagot harnessed the power of scientific language and concepts to sell numerous books—published in Spanish translation from the 1920s to the 1970s—that combine the genre of self-help with popular writing on both science and the occult. Editorial Tor published these many iterations on a single theme—you can change yourself and influence those around you with the power of thought!—with colorful, captivating covers, slightly toning down the style of their fiction covers to suggest that Jagot's books were serious and, indeed, scientific.[2] In giving specific suggestions for how practitioners could, via experimentation, refine their skills of magnetism, hypnotism, and sympathetic suggestion, Jagot described magnetism as an influence, a fluid, a current, or an energy. By bringing this vaguely defined force under conscious control, he wrote, practitioners could cure physical and mental disease in themselves and others. Readers of this popular pseudoscience were made to understand that imperceptible communication—and, as a result, the potential for control—ricocheted constantly among bodies and objects. The key to self-improvement, or even talking to the dead, lay in being aware of these hidden forces and following prescribed methods for bringing them under control.

---

1 "Thought works outward" (translation mine). Paul Jagot, *Método científico de magnetismo, hipnotismo, sugestión* (Buenos Aires: Editorial Tor, 1938), 184.

2 Tor also published Norah Lange's 1933 novel *45 días y 30 marineros* (which tells the story of a lone woman who takes a cross-Atlantic trip with thirty sailors, closely mirroring a trip Lange herself took to Oslo) (see María E. Miguel, *Norah Lange: Una biografía* [Buenos Aires: Planeta, 1991], 150).

While nonspecialist readers of the texts examined in the previous chapter might have misconstrued the content of what they were reading, and while the literary styles of those popular science texts might have encouraged creative interpretations of scientific ideas and their consequences, this chapter looks at ideas and publications that we can more easily categorize as pseudoscience, with a focus on magnetism, alongside a related concept that has existed alongside and intersected with scientific discourse, sympathy. The line between science and pseudoscience is not fixed: these categories may shift over time and be defined differently in different sociocultural or geographic contexts. Pseudoscientific ideas can grow out of hard science or develop alongside them with a shared vocabulary. Authors of pseudoscientific texts often use the language of scientific research and experimentation and present their writing as rigorous scientific inquiry. Pseudoscientific writing as a genre shows how scientific ideas are transmitted and morph into cultural ideas, and I am particularly interested in the slippage between scientific concepts that highlight relation and communication between people and objects (magnetism, radio waves, sympathetic observation) and pseudoscientific ideas that turn into social phenomena. Some pseudoscience may seem so fantastical that the scientific aspect recedes into the background. This is one of the ways in which scientific ideas circulate in the popular imagination and enjoy creative and varied afterlives.

The texts I cite show us that authors like Jagot leaned heavily on the prestige of science as a discipline: they depended not just on scientific concepts but also on scientific language to persuade readers. Here the *discourse* in "scientific discourse" is just as significant as the purportedly *scientific* content.[3] "Experiments," "control," and "practice" guaranteed the successful manipulation of magnetic flows (pseudoscience promises results in a way science cannot). Following the so-called scientific method of magnetism, hypnotism, and sympathetic suggestion, Jagot and his fellows argued, readers could learn to exert control over their own lives and the lives of others. Less clearly articulated in these guides, but certainly present, is the implicit opposing and complementary threat: that the thought radiating outward from someone else may work its way into you. This same anxiety of being influenced, of imperceptible communication that has the power to

---

3 Rosa María Medina Doménech reminds us that even canonical scientific research depends on narrative formulas to present a supposedly objective and definite version of events. Her work frequently focuses on the intersection of scientific and cultural ideas. See, for example, "Ideas para perder la inocencia sobre los textos de ciencia," in *Interacciones ciencia y género: Discursos y prácticas científicas de mujeres*, ed. María José Barral, Carmen Magallón, Consuelo Miqueo, and María Dolores Sánchez (Barcelona: Icaria, 1999), 103–27.

change our bodies and minds, is prominent in Norah Lange's *Personas en la sala* and frames my reading below.

Published in 1950, *Personas* strings together the thoughts and observations of a young woman who looks out of her front window and watches three women sitting in a house across the street. She becomes more and more involved in their lives, sensing that they have a secret she must access and developing strong, contradictory feelings toward them. Eventually she arranges a meeting, crosses the street, and enters their home where she speaks with them and observes them even more closely, though the narrative remains opaque and the protagonist unable to unveil the secrets she senses they hold. Finally, at the urging of her family, she leaves the city for a short while to recuperate from the strange mood that seems to have been affecting her—one, I argue, that is constitutive of her young womanhood—and, upon her return, the women are gone. The women's influence on the protagonist is unquestionable. She cannot pull herself away from them. Yet the nature of that influence, and why and how her strange mix of feelings develops through this particularly fragmentary prose and images, is less clear. What is the intense push-pull of these other women who seem to simply sit and converse in their living room? And how is it that watching them becomes a formative experience of the narrator's young womanhood?

In this chapter, I consider the constellation of scientific and pseudoscientific thought arising around magnetism and sympathy as key to understanding how relationality plays a role in constructing gender. *Personas* is very much a book about a person drawn toward other people in a twisted, unusual way of relating. I consider relation here in part as feeling directed toward/away from others, and I also consider the experience of "feeling toward others"—a concept I will use to examine some of the distinctly untoward feelings described in *Personas*. As I noted in the introduction, I am not concerned with drawing firm lines between affect, feeling, and emotion, though generally I favor "feeling" to include a combined psychological, corporeal, and social experience. In *Personas*, a surprising combination of hatred, love, and guilt directed at the people across the street moves the protagonists physically through the world and shapes her mental life. Publications on magnetism and related subjects reveal contemporary anxieties and interests in the relational power of feeling.[4]

---

4 Interestingly, certain scientific discourse has been used as a lens for reading Lange and the dynamic gaze in her writing: specifically, Vicky Unruh devotes a chapter to "Norah Lange's Art of Anatomy," describing this effect of connection with another body through observation, noting that Lange used the language of anatomy and dissection to discuss her own textual production. Unruh extends this use of anatomy to her reading of Lange's performative *discursos* and *Cuadernos de infancia*.

In addition to discussing scientific and pseudoscientific teachings on both electromagnetism and personal and animal magnetism, I will examine discourses on sympathy. Sympathy might bring to mind cheerful or unproblematic sorts of feeling. Yet its history in science and philosophy demonstrates that it raises concerns about unwanted influence and about the limits between self and other. Beneath the pleasant patina coating sympathy and the light-hearted self-improvement techniques associated with magnetism, we find a great deal of anxiety about how other people's feelings cannot be kept at bay and may instead exert inescapable control over how we think and feel.[5]

Where Chacel's narrative is somewhat fragmentary, an accumulation of particulate detail, Lange, as we will see, creates the effect of a net or web of events, expressions, and feelings. Her narration might be described as

---

Vicky Unruh, *Performing Women and Modern Literary Culture in Latin America* (Austin: University of Texas Press, 2006), see 83, 86. This anatomical metaphor is not one I will extend here, though the anatomist doubtless possesses a particular sort of gaze that we might well see constructed in Lange's often-fragmentary prose. Instead, I turn to the language of magnetism and to the pseudoscientific cloud that spread out from it and awakened people to the possibilities of imperceptible communication between and influences on bodies across space.

5 Not dissimilar lines of argumentation and interest have been revived with recent reporting on quantum entanglement—a development that is as enticing to lay readers as it is difficult to grasp. A search for *New York Times* articles on "quantum entanglement" results in forty-some pieces, some detailing the struggle between philosophers and physicists over the term and more than a few using it as a metaphor for love or politics. One wedding announcement explains the relationship was sparked by a discussion on the topic with a headline that reads: "Celeste Abou Negm and Dvir Kafri: Entanglements, Quantum and Otherwise." Recent books such as Carlo Rovelli's *Reality Is Not What It Seems: The Journey to Quantum Gravity* (translated from Italian by Simon Carnell and Erica Segre in 2017), seek to create a popular quantum narrative for a global audience. The concept's nearly poetic incorporation into the humanities may be deserving of some critique, but we also might look for its potential benefits, turning to the similar outburst of enthusiasm that accompanied magnetism and gave rise to any number of productive currents of popular thought, some widely celebrated and debated and others snaking underground through our psychic construction of the world and ourselves—as is the case of those imaginative constructions examined here with regard to gender. For more current work relating gender and quantum physics, see Daphne Grace's *Beyond Bodies: Gender, Literature and the Enigma of Consciousness* (Amsterdam: Editions Rodopi, 2014), or Karen Barad's "Nature's Queer Performativity," in *Kvinder, Køn & Forskning* (*Women, Gender, and Research*) 1–2 (2012): 25–53. Barad, notably in their 2007 book *Meeting the Universe Halfway: Quantum Physics and the Entanglement of Matter and Meaning* (Durham, NC: Duke University Press), has embraced and run with the incorporation of scientific thinking in their philosophical and critical work, to no small amount of criticism.

itself sticky, electric, vibratory, or magnetic, with variations of phrases and descriptors repeating throughout the novel, recalling one another and allowing meaning and emotion to travel suggestively from one instance to another. This is a kind of extension or elaboration of the alternative mode of sense making that we saw in *Memorias*, one that eschews straightforward narrative and instead relies on surprising associations and reflections that dismantle ordinary patterns of cause and effect. Given Lange's innovative style, it is worth considering her place in the literary and artistic avant-garde of her time. In the following section, I provide an overview of the historical and literary context she lived and worked in and explain how interpretations of her writing became entangled with her public persona and how both were permeated by questions of gender and the gaze. Then I present some of the scientific and pseudoscientific currents that circulated in Argentina at the time and that suggest an alternate reading of the glances exchanged in her novel, suggesting a form of relationality that is less optic and more magnetic.

Norah Lange: writing and performing gender

Born in Buenos Aires on October 23, 1906, Norah Lange was the fourth daughter of a Norwegian father and Irish-Norwegian mother. As an adolescent and young adult, she was surrounded by her sisters and mother and a constant influx of young artists and writers. The *tertulias* in the house on Calle Tronador where she lived would become renowned (see Miguel 72). Lange was only fifteen when she met Jorge Luis and Norah Borges and befriended Francisco Piñero, Roberto Ortelli, Eduardo González Lanuza and others (see Miguel 71). In her preface to *Personas en la sala*, Carola Moreno describes the young Norah Lange in this setting: "Norah era la única mujer. En realidad una chica que ya desde niña había mostrado un carácter rebelde, algo 'marimacho', según la muy incorrecta terminología de la época, y 'apta' por tanto para manejarse como un compañero más entre los jóvenes vanguardistas" (Norah was the only woman. In fact a girl who since she was little had been rebellious, somewhat *marimacho* [butch], according to the very incorrect language of the time, and therefore "well suited" to handling herself as just one of the boys among that group of young avant-garde men) (Lange 9). It is telling that Moreno cannot but resort to this "very incorrect term" to describe the unusual gender role Lange fulfilled in this setting, and also telling that it would disappear as a descriptor for Lange in later years as she became known for eccentricity but also for fulfilling the typically feminine role of muse to her male companions. In 1926, her second book of poetry—which, at the urging of Guillermo de Torre, adds the final *h* to her name, previously *Nora*—was published (it was also the year she met Oliverio Girondo, whom she would marry) (see Miguel 113). Though Lange traveled throughout her life, she always returned to Argentina, where she would die in 1972.

The most frequently repeated facts of Lange's life must be that she was an intimate, or muse, of Borges and a mainstay of the Argentinian avant-garde. To study Norah Lange is to listen to men who have not read her work tell you, for instance, that she once spurned Borges at a dinner.[6] The persistence of these stories and the seeming impossibility of describing Lange without naming her as a muse of someone else extends into critical writing on her work. More thoughtful recent studies of Lange critique these descriptors, though the work often still engages, and not unproductively, with the phenomena they seem to point to: the male gaze, gender as performance, public personae, and private life. I would like to redirect this line of thought away from her potential status as a muse to instead question how, in her novel, the gazes (exchanged between women) and the affective relations that travel through them shape daily life.

Lange was one of few women in the Martín Fierro group and "one of only two women among the sixty-seven poets anthologized in the *Índice de la nueva poesía americana* (1926) edited by Alberto Hidalgo, Vicente Huidobro, and Borges and widely regarded as a foundational collection for the movements" (Unruh 73). Vicky Unruh argues that, "in the heart of the Buenos Aires literary fraternity that cast her as its muse and modern performing woman," Lange accepted these roles only to wreak havoc on them (73). Yet, unruly as her persona may have been, "critics and biographers coincide in their consecration of her status in the vanguard fraternity: 'the muse of *ultraísmo*'; the 'angel and siren' of the *ultraístas*; the 'companion' and 'mascot' of the vanguard writers; their *salonnière* and *damisela*; and 'the muse and inspiration of the vanguard Martín Fierro group, a thin, redheaded walkyrie'" (Unruh 74–75). Unruh points out that these characterizations mirror those established by Lange's contemporaries (notably Borges) who were even less restrained in their florid descriptions of her inspirational presence. From the mid-twentieth century until recently, she was defined in (subordinate) relation to the men around her.[7]

---

6 The website of And Other Stories, the UK publisher of Charlotte Whittle's 2018 English translation, notes: "Too long viewed as Borges's muse, Lange is today recognized in the Spanish-speaking world as a great writer and is here translated into English for the first time, to be read alongside Virginia Woolf, Clarice Lispector and Marguerite Duras." http://www.andotherstories.org/book/people-in-the-room/.

7 The second sentence of Carola Moreno's prologue (titled "Ver, observar, descubrir" [See, observe, discover]) to the 2011 Ediciones Barataria edition of *Personas* describes Lange as "mujer de Oliverio Girondo, musa de Jorge Luis Borges, amiga de Ramón Gómez de la Serna y de Macedonio Fernández" (wife of Oliverio

Lange's eccentric reputation was reinforced by the elaborate *discursos*, which included recitation, dance, costumes, and song, that she performed among the Martinfierristas (see Unruh 79-80). Unruh connects this "public artistic persona" to the narrative of "a lone woman's intricate survival tactics" in *45 días y 30 marineros* (79). Whereas that novel chronicles the experience of one woman alone on a ship with thirty seamen, *Personas en la sala* is notable for confining itself to an exclusively female space, in which the question of the gaze and its power retains a gendered dimension while slipping out of a masculine-feminine hierarchy.

Lange was clearly attuned to the power of gendered performance and representation, and to her ability to manipulate the very images that were projected onto her. For Unruh, Lange's performance has very much to do with public-private interplay, sight, vision, and exchanged glances, and Lange's textual production develops and complicates the themes present in her gendered public performance, though critics contemporary to Lange often looked askance at these not-appropriately-feminine narratives that seemed to them to deviate from the author's persona (see Unruh 76-77). In fact, neither Lange's public persona nor her textual production may have been as malleable and amenable to male desire as thrilled onlookers supposed.

Despite the persistence of the muse frame, much insightful work has been done considering the role of the gaze, Lange's experience as a woman writer, and gender as performance in her oeuvre. I sketch out some of those readings in what follows. Indeed, two of these vectors—gender as constructed by modes of looking and watching and gender as performative—bore deeply into the "magnetic" creation of gender that I explore below. Whereas criticism has tended to consider Lange as reflecting on the effects of the male gaze or as playing with visible and performative aspects of gender roles, magnetism and related pseudoscience drive us to consider how the act of looking, assuming a persona, or interacting with others may have deeply felt and transformative effects. And the possible results of such experiences—positive, negative, or neutral—come to the fore in popular pseudoscience of this period.

A woman frequently surrounded by men, Lange crafted a public persona through speeches and performances—not to mention her writing—that was and is widely commented on. Unruh delves into this phenomenon of gendered performance in the context of female Latin American authors including Lange in her book *Performing Women and Modern Literary Culture*

Girondo, muse of Jorge Luis Borges, friend of Ramón Gómez de la Serna and Macedonio Fernández) (Moreno, "Ver, observar, descubrir," in Lange, *Personas en la sala* [Madrid: Ediciones Barataria, 2011], 9).

in Latin America. As the title suggests, Lange is much less widely read than she is "seen," even by current critics who often echo the judgmental and rather outlandish descriptors her contemporaries used in speaking of her. It is both understandable and appropriate that criticism of Lange's written work consider it in conjunction with her speeches and public persona, and her poetry and prose often point in similar directions. However, *Personas en la sala* prompts us to think about Lange in a particular, and often overlooked, way: the glances in the novel are exchanged exclusively between women, and the narrative seems to head off some of the more overt questions of public performance and gender that Lange criticism focuses on. Indeed, the novel takes place entirely inside two neighboring homes.[8] The looking and feeling that occurs among women is rendered in prose that raises more questions than it answers. While the narrator makes many declarations of her feelings, they are not at all straightforward and occasionally seem nonsensical. It is worth taking note of the role Lange has played in narratives describing the Argentinian avant-garde—to consider how she, like her characters, exerted her gaze and was gazed upon. The relational portrayal of gender in *Personas* viewed through lenses of magnetism and sympathy can then complicate our understanding of that role.

Conscious of the demands on female authors, who were expected to express palatable and respectable versions of femininity, Lange veered away from the sorts of narratives that might have either fit into or clearly cracked such molds. Instead, she did something entirely different. As Nora Domínguez notes, "From *Cuadernos de infancia* onwards she embarked on a new literary project. She built worlds without men, where women were

---

8 It may be relevant to consider whether or not these three women really exist outside of the narrator's head and, even if they do, how many of the narrator's experiences with them are imagined or projected. Marta Sierra registers Maria Elena Lagaz's interpretation that the three women are "just shadows of the narrator" (Marta Sierra, "Oblique Views: Artistic Doubling, Ironic Mirroring and Photomontage in the Works of Norah Lange and Norah Borges," *Revista Canadiense de Estudios Hispánicos* 29, no. 3 [2005]: 571). Sierra herself writes that "we realize the neighbors are only projections of the narrator's imagination, which, throughout the novel, unravels imaginary settings and visualizes them wandering busy streets and venturing out into public places. In fact, the neighbors' house is a fantastic double" (Sierra, *Gendered Spaces in Argentine Women's Literature* [New York: Palgrave Macmillan, 2012], 32). Such an interpretation would confine the narrative to just one inside space, as well as to the ample mental space of the protagonist. My reading treats the neighboring home and the women who live there as though they do indeed exist in physical space outside of the narrator, but I do not think that this take clashes with Lagaz's or Sierra's interpretations in that all three allow for questions of occulted communication and imperceptible influence, though perhaps with slightly different twists.

shut up alone in their houses and those who wrote did so not in order to earn money but secretly, for the pleasure of it."⁹ Domínguez identifies a "macro-text" that carries out this project, encompassing Lange's works from *Cuadernos de infancia*, with its child protagonist, to *Personas en la sala*, *Antes que mueran*, and *Los dos retratos*, marked by adolescent protagonists (34). All of these, Domínguez argues, "reveal that all initiation is an initiation into writing" (34). Central to this process of growth or initiation is the division between inside and outside, each space requiring specific attitudes and actions from women in order to perpetuate a stable and coherent performance of gender (see Domínguez 34). As my work in chapter 1 reveals, I am more interested, in this study, in an idea of the initiation into *gender*, one that may begin at birth but that continues and perhaps intensifies during childhood and young adulthood. In the "world without men" of *Personas*, stability and coherence are no longer in the picture. Secrecy, pleasure—and, I would add, longing and affection—are.

Personas is defined by a young woman gazing at other women—a mode of relation so intense that she schemes her way into their lives and reflects obsessively on their lives and pasts with very little information outside of what she sees as she watches them in their sitting room. (Some readers would say that the gaze is what in fact creates the women, understanding them as figments of her imagination.) As Sylvia Molloy points out in her discussion of *Cuadernos de infancia*, "Indeed, all the memories collected in Lange's text obey the impulse of what that other *voyeur* (and at times autobiographer), Felisberto Hernández, memorably called 'the lust for looking.'"¹⁰ I will ask what the looking in *Personas* tells us about how the gaze works: how it may be invasive, relational; how it might interact with or reorganize material forms (as occurs so vividly in the novel); how looking at another body affects that body and what might ricochet back through the gaze to affect the person doing the looking.

Women's rights and the female gaze

Before moving to the pseudoscientific ideas that circulated in Lange's Argentinian context, I highlight the sociocultural and political situation women faced at the time. Not only does Lange's writing have ties to

---

9 Nora Domínguez, "Literary Constructions and Gender Performance in the Novels of Norah Lange," trans. Anny Brooksbank and Catherine Davis, in *Latin American Women's Writing: Feminist Readings in Theory and Crisis*, ed. Anny Brooksbank Jones and Catherine Davis (Oxford: Clarendon Press, 1996), 33.
10 Sylvia Molloy, *At Face Value: Autobiographical Writing in Spanish America* (Cambridge: Cambridge University Press, 1991), 130.

avant-garde and modernist literary and artistic movements,[11] it takes on gendered issues that were simultaneously national ones: the public–private distinction blurs in her work, troubling both the sanctity of domestic spaces and the gender binary that underwrites the construction of the modern nation-state.[12]

Marta Sierra concludes that Lange's writing constructs domesticity as a space in the throes of economic, cultural, and cosmopolitical change—change that often became visible in shifting and contentious gender roles:

> During the period in which Lange and Ocampo produced their works, a number of important changes in relation to women's rights and their public and private roles took place in Argentina. The first decades of the twentieth century were a period of intense debate about gender roles and their implications for the traditional family structure. In 1926, important reforms of the civil code took place that benefited women's rights in marriage and in regard to issues of property,

---

11 As I outline below, the fragmentary nature of Lange's narrative can be viewed as a literary expression of avant-garde imagery (as seen in surrealism, ultraísmo, and various modernisms). The avant-garde might also be thought of as participating in a contemporary scientific moment, and Lange's place in avant-garde circles has been widely commented on. I posit a need to rethink both these critical engagements (Lange's imagery as being explained by the avant-garde and Lange as being special but firmly positioned within an avant-garde understood not only as an aesthetic, artistic, and intellectual movement but also a social circle) through a felt experience of gender. A broader examination of vanguard artistic movements and scientific thought would be tangential to my project here but constitutes an important line of investigation. Some of this work has been done by Anthony Enns and Shelley Trower in *Vibratory Modernism* (Basingstoke: Palgrave Macmillan, 2013); Fishburn and Ortiz in *Science and the Creative Imagination in Latin America*; and Cecelia Cavanaugh in *New Lenses for Lorca: Literature, Art, and Science in the Edad de Plata* (Lewisburg, PA: Bucknell University Press, 2013).

12 In *Ficciones somáticas: Naturalismo, nacionalismo y políticas médicas del cuerpo (Argentina 1880–1910)* (Rosario, Argentina: Beatriz Viterbo Editora, 2000), Gabriela Nouzeilles reads the construction of the Argentinian nation through medico-scientific discourses and regimes of control over the body. The recurring points of anxiety that Nouzeilles and others examine include the danger of unproductive (and excessive) sexuality; the overcrowding of the city, its unsanitary conditions, and the image of urban barbarity; racial and ethnic threats, with a focus the figure of the immigrant; the nation as an ailing body; madness and criminality; and women and the family home as sites of trouble. These concerns could overlap, as with the specter of immigrants posing as door-to-door salesmen to gain access to middle-class women and children in their homes (cited by Susan Hallstead-Dabove in "Disease and Immorality: The Problem of Fashionable Dress in Buenos Aires (1862–1880)" [*Latin American Literary Review* 37, no. 73 (2009): 90–117]).

financial independence, and jurisdiction over children. For instance, married women were allowed to practice different professions and use their income freely without reporting it to their husbands. The perception that women had been denied intellectual and personal freedom informed many of the debates surrounding the new economic role of women, their juridical place within the family, and their participation in the public life of their country. An intense debate on gender, prompted by massive immigration and the alteration of a nineteenth-century understanding of national culture, shaped the feminist struggle for rights.[13]

Sierra further notes that female authors and their characters often become symbols of their nation abroad, navigating cultural encounters through their gender and their bodies. Women experienced increased freedoms but also social anxieties about those freedoms. Their experiences and behaviors were both their own and looked upon as symbols of national identity or social boons or ills. In 1947, women were given the right to vote and thus become not only the target of political discourse intended to shape the public/private place of women but also the explicit audience, in a new way, of such discourse. The feminist struggle that had for decades driven the nation toward women's suffrage was put aside when it was finally won and replaced on the national stage with the image of Eva Perón and her vision of womanhood and femininity.[14] Perón's government emphasized motherhood as a way for women to fulfill their role in the nation. This meant both support for public health initiatives and encouraging a high birth rate and further repressing abortion (see Grammático 128). Despite the rhetoric that held that women's political and social role in the public sphere was to reflect their role as wives and mothers, "from 1900 until at least 1950 there was a steady increase in the number of women who worked outside the home" (Grammático 129).

The environment was such that the Lange sisters all left the home to work as executive secretaries and translators when they were old enough and

---

13 Marta Sierra, *Gendered Spaces in Argentine Women's Literature* (New York: Palgrave Macmillan, 2012), 24. For more on contemporary Argentinian politics regarding women and the nation, see Karen Kampwirth and Kurt Weyland, eds., *Gender and Populism in Latin America: Passionate Politics* (University Park: Penn State University Press, 2010); Emilie L. Bergmann, *Women, Culture and Politics in Latin America: Seminar on Feminism and Culture in Latin America* (Berkeley: University of California Press, 1992).

14 See Karin Grammático, "Populist Continuities in 'Revolutionary' Peronism? A Comparative Analysis of the Gender Discourses of the First Peronism (1946–1955) and the Montoneros," trans. Kampwirth, in *Gender and Populism in Latin America*, 131.

money was tight—a fact that was notable but not extravagant or unheard of (Norah herself was a translator for General Motors) (see Miguel 137). Lange moved freely in largely masculine intellectual circles, but her presence was constantly surveilled and remarked upon. It is perhaps not surprising that the question of the gaze, as way of looking and relating, should be so prominent in Lange's works. The following section looks at relational discourses in scientific and pseudoscientific discourses that circulated in Argentina around the time Lange was living and writing there.

"Science"

(Pseudo)science in Argentina

In her study of *Crítica* (1913-1962) and *El Mundo* (1928-1967), Beatriz Sarlo reveals their differing approaches to similar combinations of articles on science and pseudoscience—*parapsicología, videncia, sugestión,* and more— that mixed freely on their pages.[15] Sarlo sees the fantastic potential of immaterial communication—which quickly gives way to pseudoscientific theories of the occult—as particularly stemming from the radio technology that brought voices and music from afar into people's homes:

> [La radio] [c]omo innovación realiza fantasías que no son sólo tecnológicas: la comunicación inalámbrica a distancia, la captación de ondas invisibles, la manipulación de la recepción sobre todo en los aparatos a galena, la presencia de la voz y la música sin cuerpo, que remite a la desmaterialización y al tránsito de una cultura basada en la visión no mediada a una cultura sostenida sobre la mediación. En años preocupados por las transmisiones telepáticas, el hipnotismo, la recepción de mensajes transnaturales (tal como también lo prueba la avidez de los diarios al respecto y el crecimiento de las escuelas espiritistas), la radio es una revolución cultural. (Sarlo 16-17)

> (Radio, as an innovation, fulfills fantasies that are not only technological in nature: wireless communication across distances, capturing invisible waves, manipulating reception particularly in galena [lead sulfide] devices, the presence of disembodied voices and music, which points to dematerialization and to the transition from a culture based on unmediated vision to a culture built on mediation. During a period concerned with telepathic transmissions, hypnotism, the reception of

---

15 See Beatriz Sarlo, *La imaginación técnica: Sueños modernos de la cultura argentina* (Buenos Aires: Ediciones Nueva Visión, 1992), 68.

transnatural messages (as evidenced by the eagerness of newspapers to report on the topic and the growth of spiritist schools), radio is a cultural revolution.)

Spanning several decades, with everything from the technical marvel of radio to specialized scientific writing on electromagnetism, there is a confluence of popular excitement around the possibilities of imperceptible communication. Focusing on the swift scientific advancement that secured new technologies in homes and workplaces by the 1920s, Sarlo points out that this rapid change—and often shaky understanding of its underlying mechanisms—brought a sense of the miraculous into daily life. Technical marvels did not necessarily inspire investigation into their workings but rather provoked fantasies of their expanded future potential: "porque la radio o el cine ya están aquí, también llegará cualquier otro tipo de comunicación a distancia" (because radio and cinema are already with us, some other type of long-distance communication will also arrive) (Sarlo 136). Despite finding evidence of some denunciations of fraud, Sarlo argues that pseudoscience was not generally tamped down or discouraged but rather that it found fertile ground to spread in the national imaginary. Some new ideas proved not only too suggestive to write of in strictly scientific terms but also too complicated: Albert Einstein's 1925 visit to Buenos Aires set off years of writing on relativity, and *Crítica* even bought the rights to "una serie que presenta como 'valiosa primicia', cuyos artículos sobre la teoría de la relatividad son un verdadero intríngulis terminológico pero producen el demoledor efecto de la ciencia sofisticada y moderna" (a series that it presents as "valuable and cutting edge," whose articles on the theory of relativity are a true terminological quagmire but produce the overwhelming effect of sophisticated and modern science) (Sarlo 65).[16] If the radio and telephone brought long-distance communication into

---

16 For a detailed account of that visit that takes into account Argentinian press and public record as well as Einstein's diary entries on the subject, see Eduardo L. Ortiz, "A Convergence of Interests: Einstein's Visit to Argentina in 1925," *Ibero-Amerikanisches Archiv* 21, nos. 1-2 (1995): 67-126. Perhaps because of its truly paradigm-shifting complexity, relativity gained a fuzzy sort of popularity—often with interpretations that boiled down to little more than a pithy "it's all relative"—but did not see the sort of translation for lay audiences that concepts such as atomic theory or even electromagnetism did. Much press coverage of Einstein focused on the social phenomenon of the prominent scientist but necessarily avoided explicating his findings. Diego Hurtado de Mendoza finds the coverage of relativity in the Argentinian *Revista de Filosofía* to be similarly oblique (with coverage elsewhere by actual physicists downright scarce). See Hurtado de Mendoza, "Las teorías de la relatividad y la filosofía en la Argentina (1915-1925)," in *La ciencia en la Argentina entre siglos: Textos, contextos e instituciones*, ed. Marcelo Montserrat (Buenos

everyday life, and if the public was eager to pick up and run with suggestive scientific ideas, magnetism offered a particularly fertile set of ideas to the popular imagination.

Blas Cabrera introduces *El magnetismo de la materia*, originally published in 1944 in Buenos Aires by the Institución Cultural Española, by writing, "El conjunto de fenómenos y propiedades de la materia que se agrupan en el capítulo de la Física llamado Magnetismo es quizá el más difícil de abordable por nuestro conocimiento, porque carecemos de órganos de percepción directa para los mismos y sólo por sus efectos indirectos es posible su estudio" (The set of phenomena and properties of matter that can be categorized in the area of physics known as magnetism is perhaps

---

Aires: Manantial, 2000), 35–51. In *Einstein in Spain: Relativity and the Recovery of Science* (Princeton, NJ: Princeton University Press, 1988), Thomas F. Glick documents the problem of popular access to scientific ideas, specifically relativity, in Spain. In a table, Glick breaks down the reception of scientific discourse into a number of categories, defining popular responses to Einstein as follows: articulated, attempting to engage with the science; disarticulated and impressionistic, picking up on pieces of the science; understood incorrectly or impressionistically, eliding meaning through semantic slides; through a nonscientific conceptual framework such as philosophical relativism; nonassimilation that recognizes but does not attempt to engage the science; ideological response that casts relativism as good or bad unrelated to science; a priori rejection; and finally pseudoassimilation through confusion with another philosophical or scientific idea (see 240).

Each publication had to choose how to approach material that its readers and even its reporters would likely not fully grasp. Some chose to report on the event of Einstein's lecture—his speaking style, the look of the room—without approaching the subject matter. Others chose to engage scientific specialists or nonscientists to write eruditely on the lecture's specialist content or incomprehensibility, respectively. Glick concludes that the warped, opaque, or even misleading reception still signaled an openness and indeed eagerness to engage with complex scientific thought. Blas Cabrera stated in a talk titled "La Teoría de la Relatividad," given to the Sociedad de Oceanografía de Guipúzcoa in a series of conferences organized in San Sebastián in September 1921, "Yo no conozco otro ejemplo en la historia de la Ciencia, de una teoría absolutamente desprovista de aplicación a la vida práctica, por los menos en el porvenir al alcance de nuestra previsión, y que haya conmovido tan profundamente al vulgo como la que va a ocuparnos en esta tarde: la Teoría de la Relatividad" (I know of no other example in the history of Science of a theory so entirely devoid of application to practical life, at least in the foreseeable future, and that has so deeply excited the masses as the one that will occupy us this afternoon: the Theory of Relativity) (1). In 2017 article on *LitHub*, Gabrielle Bellot asks, "How Much of Einstein's Theory of Relativity Is in the Writing of Virginia Woolf?" and cites "structural relatively" in the author's novels, while also recording Woolf's likely familiarity with Einstein alongside her proclamation that she did not understand his work. https://lithub.com/how-much-of-einsteins-theory-of-relativity-is-in-the-writing-of-virginia-woolf/.

the most difficult for us to comprehend because we do not possess sensory organs to directly perceive them and can only study them through their indirect effects).[17] This indirect nature of the observation of magnetism did not stop people from wanting to read about it and about its many pseudoscientific applications. It was not necessary to understand the mechanism of electromagnetism to read the many books that promised you could communicate with others, living and dead, as clearly and invisibly as you could transmit songs on the radio. Popular literature stepped in to spread these suggestive ideas to the masses.

Magnetism and the occult

The concepts of animal magnetism and personal magnetism borrowed vocabulary and ideas from theories of electromagnetism, and the resulting pseudoscience of magnetism was grouped together with somnambulism, hypnotism, and the occult in popular publications.[18] In the 1930s and 1940s in Buenos Aires, a great number of books on magnetism and electricity were published.[19] Some—such as those that made up the series Biblioteca

---

17 Blas Cabrera, *El magnetismo de la materia* (Buenos Aires: Institución Cultural Española, 1944), 101. Following the Spanish Civil War, Cabrera lived in Mexico in exile. For more on the influence of post–Civil War exile and Spanish–Latin American communication in the sciences, see José Maria Laso Prieto, "El exilio científico español," *Ábaco* 42 (2004): 49–59.

18 See, for example, Jagot's 1938 *Método científico moderno de magnetismo, hipnotismo, sugestión*, or Armando Baeza Salvador's *Ciencia popular: Los misterios de la ciencia (magnetismo animal, sonambulismo, hipnotismo, espiritismo, etc., etc.)* (Barcelona: Ramón Molinas, 19??). Jagot explains in the first volume of his three-volume work that "Se estudian, en física, bajo el título de *Magnetismo*, los fenómenos debido al imán. Son ellos los que, por analogía, han dado su nombre a los que vamos a estudiar aquí" (Physics includes the study of phenomena due to the magnet, known as *magnetism*. These phenomena have, by analogy, given their name to those we will study here) (24).

19 In addition to Cabrera's *El magnetismo de la materia* and Jagot's *Método científico moderno de magnetismo, hipnotismo, sugestión*, books on magnetism published in Buenos Aires include: Charles A. Culver, *Teoría y aplicaciones de electricidad y magnetismo* (Buenos Aires: Arbó, 1949); Carlos Chalita, *El origen del magnetismo* (Buenos Aires: Casilla de Correo, 1948); Harvey B. Lemon and Michael Ference, *Física experimental analítica: Magnetismo y electricidad* (Buenos Aires: Espasa Calpe, 1947); José Garay, *La física en preguntas y respuestas: Óptica, magnetismo, electricidad* (Buenos Aires: Progreso y Cultura, 1942); Arthur Schopenhauer, *Las ciencias ocultas: Magnetismo animal, el destino del individuo, ensayo sobre las apariciones del espíritus* (Buenos Aires: Kier, 1946); Jagot and Guerrero J. Perez, *Método práctico y científico de magnetismo, hipnotismo, sugestión: Curso práctico de experimentación al alcance de todos* (Buenos Aires: Joaquin Gil, 1941); and Marcel Boll, *Qué es: La energía, el vacío, el calor, la luz, el color, el sonido, la electricidad, el magnetismo, la afinidad, el azar* (Buenos Aires: Ed. Pleamar, 1948).

Conocimiento (Library of Knowledge)—were strictly scientific, though they targeted a nonspecialist audience, while others purported to explain the relationship between magnetism and the occult. Journals such as *Nosotros* and the *Revista de Filosofía* also took an interest in presenting their readers with the scientific advancements of the day. Via magnetism, the notion of communication or relation that took place imperceptibly between bodies or objects provided the explanations necessary to imagine invisible attractions so powerful they could not only make people alluring in life but also be used to communicate with the dead. Such communication and effects of attraction and repulsion are precisely the concepts that can help us read the strange feelings of *Personas en la sala*.

In Argentina, various organizations spread occult ideas: the Vanguardia Teosófica (which published *Alborea*), the Biblioteca Teosófica (which published *Evolución* and *Revista Teosófica*), and the Sociedad Teosófica Argentina (which published *Teosofía en el Plata*).[20] Daniel Santamaría notes the likely overlap of adherents and organizers of the various occult movements in Argentina: "En Buenos Aires la Rosicrucian Fraternity in America compartía su casilla de correo 2921 con la Rama Argentina y con el Círculo Exito Mental (CEM). Esta última era una asociación donde sus adherentes se comunicaba solo por correo" (In Buenos Aires, the Rosicrucian Fraternity in America shared mailbox 2921 with the Argentinian Branch and with the Mental Success Circle. The latter was an association in which members only communicated by mail) (24). This dependence on written correspondence was presumably not an impediment to their communication since they believed that men's and women's minds could join with divine law and thus operate together "por un ideal común de superación, espiritualidad y triunfo" (toward a shared ideal of self-improvement, spirituality, and triumph) (24). Santamaría distinguishes between the distinct social circles devoted to the occult and to spiritualism in Argentina, the latter lacking the focus on esoteric knowledge and initiation, having a wider self-help-style reach (27).

Susana Bianchi notes that spiritism was for some a natural and highly desirable extension of another scientific concept: evolutionary theory. It denoted even further progress beyond the mere material transformations of the species.[21] Santamaría makes a similar connection: "[E]l sesgo evolucionista del ocultismo no es un simple préstamo de la época: es un

---

20 For further exploration of why pseudoscience and the occult enjoyed the popularity they did in Argentina, see Daniel J. Santamaría, "Razones y sinrazones del ocultismo," in *Ocultismo y espiritismo en la Argentina* (Buenos Aires: Centro Editor de América Latina, 1992), 7–45, esp. 24.

21 See Susana Bianchi, "Los espiritistas argentinos (1880–1910): Religión, ciencia y política," in *Ocultismo y espiritismo en la Argentina*, 105.

verdadero proyecto. Los ocultistas pretenden dar una respuesta a la pregunta de por qué la evolución, o mejor, hacia dónde evoluciona la humanidad" (The evolutionary bias of the occult is not simply a sign of the times: it was a true undertaking. Occult practitioners aimed to respond to the question of why evolution, or rather, where human evolution was headed) (13). Where evolution might have pointed out theretofore-unseen connections between humans and animals, magnetism could elevate human connections to a state of cosmic harmony. Of course, the supposed effects of magnetism were wide ranging, and not everyone was interested in the evolutionary perfection of the species; self-help texts, for example, were more attuned to people's interest in perfecting their own lives.

In a passage from his 1891 *Materia, forma y fuerza: Diseño de una filosofía* that appears in a chapter titled "Magnetismo y espiritismo," Pedro Sala y Villaret writes:

> Cuando pensamos, producimos ciertamente una alteración orgánica más ó menos profunda, especialmente de la parte nerviosa; mas según la teoría que defendemos, la substancia fluídica, asiento de la percepción y el pensamiento, toma la forma de *vibración*. [...] Es excusado añadir con tales antecedentes la inmensa posibilidad de que dichas alteraciones, semejantes harmonías, resuenen y se trasmitan á los lugares más distantes de la creación, si hay un *medio* conductor idóneo, semejante al del mundo sensible. (138; emphasis in original)

> (When we think, we most definitely produce a more or less profound organic alteration, particularly from the nervous system; however, according to the theory defended here, the electric substance, where perception and thought are housed, takes the form of *vibration*. [...] Given this context, we might note the immense possibility that such alterations, such harmonies should resonate and be transmitted to the most distant reaches of creation if there is a well-suited conducting *medium*, similar to that of the sensible world.)

He continues: "¿hay alguna imposibilidad en que esta parte, cuasi fluídica, al desgajarse del restante organismo, pase á vivir en otro organismo? Véase que nosotros no afirmamos el hecho, sino la posibilidad" (Is it impossible that this nearly current-like part, upon detaching from the organism that is left behind, should go on to live in another organism?) (Sala y Villaret 139). Here, we observe the imaginative possibilities brought about by being conscious of our relationship to a substantive, material world—even when that world, and that relation, largely escapes our perception. We see the highly suggestive idea that some current in us—or a movement that passes through it carrying something of our perceptive and thinking selves with it—could end up leaving our own bodies and entering the bodies of others.

As seen here (and as we saw in chapter 1), vibration often emerges as something that affects us not quite on the level of perception while still producing material changes—with David Katz, in 1930, proposing a vibratory sense as a sixth sense. Katz distinguishes the vibratory sense from both touch and sound, but he suggests that vibrations produce "touch-noises" (102). He underscores that our eyes cannot penetrate objects, while the vibratory sense allows us to know their hidden, inner nature. Fans of magnetism also picked up on vibratory properties, which were easily incorporated into the pseudoscientific rhetoric that permeated these authors' writing. Jagot writes that the particular techniques used by magnetizers on their subjects take advantage of those parts of the body where the organism's output of "vibratory energy" is particularly strong (these include "los ojos, la extremidad de los dedos, el encéfalo y el aliento" [the eyes, the fingertips, the encephalon and the breath]) (1.25). Moreover, vibration is what allows our thoughts to enter the minds and bodies of others: "En principio, cada uno de nuestros pensamientos atrae pensamientos de igual naturaleza; su tono de movimientos sólo los deja asimilar por mentalidades capaces de vibrar a ese mismo tono de movimiento" (In principle, each one of our thoughts attracts thoughts of a similar nature; the rhythm of their movements only allows them to be absorbed by minds capable of vibrating at that same frequency of movement) (Jagot 3.144). Attraction between thoughts constitutes an invisible mode of relating that knowledge of magnetism reveals to those in the know.

In a book called *Ciencia popular: Los misterios de la ciencia (magnetismo animal, sonambulismo, hipnotismo, espiritismo, etc., etc.)*, Armando Baeza Salvador explains some of the scientific debates on the "fluido electromagnético animal" (animal electromagnetic current), in relation to its ability to cure disease: "Estaba reconocido por muchos hombres de ciencia que el fluido proporcionado por una máquina eléctrica puede penetrar en el cuerpo de los animales, recorrerle en todas direcciones, excitar movimientos, provocar evacuaciones y, según el grado de su intensidad, producir buenos ó malos efectos" (Many men of science recognized that the current produced by an electric machine could penetrate the body of an animal, run through it in all directions, prompt movements, provoke bowel movements, and, depending on its degree of intensity, produce good or bad effects) (248). The ability to produce curative effects was one of the main attractions of magnetism. For magnetism did not just inspire occult explorations by those inclined to experiment with *magia blanca*, it also fed into a genre of popular self-help books that would allow readers every improvement, from harnessing the power of magnetism to cure disease to enhancing their personal magnetism in order to be more successful in love and life. Editions of Jagot's books in this vein came out from the 1920s through the 1970s. In Spanish, they were featured in the Enciclopedia del Hombre Que Triunfa (Encyclopedia of Triumphant Men) series that was published in Buenos Aires alongside books from Orison Sweet Marden, a US writer offering popular "inspirational" books.[22]

In the first volume of *Método científico de magnetismo, hipnotismo, sugestión*, Jagot lays out for his reader—each one, male or female, young or old, a potential magnetizer—the origins, mechanisms, vocabulary, and finally technical procedures of magnetism. He explains that a long line of scholars, starting with Franz Mesmer, honed a scientific approach to the use of magnetism, which had in past epochs been the purview of "sacerdotes, magistrados y médicos" (priests, magistrates, and doctors) in India, Chaldea, and Egypt (Jagot 1.6). Magnetizing is that act "[de proyectar] convenientemente esa radioactividad fisiológica" ([of] conveniently [projecting] that physiological radioactivity) that is magnetism (Jagot 1.8). Somnambulism is the state in which one's perception extends to objects and people out of reach to the five senses; hypnotism is then the induced state of somnambulism, where "suggestion" is the ability to influence a person in such a state (see Jagot 1.8–9).

Jagot, having laid out the scientific background and framework of the field, explains that his goal is to make such knowledge and the resultant techniques available to his reading public for their personal advancement, through the improvement of their overall wellness and relations with those around them: "cómo, en fin, obrar en la vida íntima y en los negocios sobre las mentalidades circundantes, cómo modificar las opiniones, decisiones, emociones y sentimientos de aquéllos con quienes nos relacionamos" (in short, how to influence, in private life and in business, the minds of those around us, how to modify the opinions, decisions, emotions, and feelings of those with whom we interact) (Jagot 1.13). All are assured success in what is a safe and effective system; moreover, Jagot promises, his readers will not be susceptible to popular and deceptive tricks of supposedly communicating with the dead, nor will they confuse hallucinations with true psychic communication.

We are told that magnetism itself, that "radioactividad fisiológica," is an "influencia inherente" (inherent influence) emitted by metals, plants, and

---

22 Jagot's books in the series, among them *Autosugestión, Magnetismo, El insomnio vencido, La timidez vencida, Hipnotismo, Hipnotismo a distancia*, and *El libro renovador de los nerviosos*, offered his readers the chance to take control of their lives.

animals but that emanates most strongly from humans; its exact nature is unknown, but "[b]asándose en teorías de lal [*sic*] física general, se admite que este agente está constituído por ondas resultantes de la vibración de los átomos constitutivos de los cuerpos" (based on theories from general physics, it is recognized that this agent is made up of waves resulting from the vibration of the atoms that constitute bodies) (Jagot 1.23–24). He explains that experiments carried out to influence inert matter, rather than living organisms, through magnetization have proven suggestive though less consistently successful (see Jagot 1.39). It is likely the ability to influence other living organisms—specifically other humans—that makes magnetism so appealing to begin with.

In the first chapter of the third volume of the *Método científico*, Jagot outlines the possibilities of "psicomagnetismo" to cure disease. However, he cautions, such capacities are not within reach of every practitioner, at least not right away. This is not magic, it is science: "El experimentador debe, pues, fundar su confianza en sus experimentos y no debe entregarse a sueños místicos" (Thus the experimenter must trust in his experiments and not surrender to mystical dreams).[23] Jagot's writing on "las ciencias psíquicas" (the psychic sciences) derives from magnetism a host of conclusions about individuals' ability to control their health and happiness as well as to influence others. Even earlier books and those that did not shy away from "magic," such as Q. G. Polinntzieu's *Magia blanca moderna, ó sea magnetismo, hipnotismo, sugestión y espiritismo*, seized the opportunity to suggest to their readers a modern and scientific approach: the book's title page promises that it contains "cuanto se relaciona con la ciencia moderna psicológica y su trascendental aplicación á la adivinación, á la medicina y á las relaciones con lo suprasensible" (all things relating to modern psychological science and its transcendental application to divination, medicine, and relations with the supersensible).[24] Modern science lent the imprimatur of authority.

In an echo of those scientific publications on *fuerza, energía, y materia* that we saw in chapter 1, chapter 5 of book 6 in *Método científico* is titled

---

23 Jagot, *Método científico de magnetismo, hipnotismo, sugestión, tomo III: Cómo hacer reaccionar la actividad nerviosa sobre los órganos enfermos*, trans. Pedro Labrousse (Buenos Aires: Editorial Tor, 1963[?]), 6. Sarlo cites an example of a hypnotism manual published in *Ciencia Popular*, which not only validates the pseudoscientific method by giving it its stamp of approval as a magazine of science and technology but goes so far as to call it "una rama de la ciencia" (a branch of science) (quoted in Sarlo 138).

24 Q. G. Polinntzieu, *Magia blanca moderna, ó sea magnetismo, hipnotismo, sugestión y espiritismo* (Barcelona / Buenos Aires / Mexico City: Maucci, 1899). This author also published a book "traducido del árabe" (translated from Arabic) by "mago" (magician) Ali Abubeker, *Verdadera y transcendental magia blanca*.

"Fuerza. — Energía. — Voluntad." Chapter 6 gives a definition of personal magnetism: "De una manera general, la expresión '*Magnetismo Personal*' sirve para designar esa especie de encanto que ciertos individuos ejercen sobre sus semejantes. Sin que parezcan hacer nada para eso, dichos individuos inspiran simpatía, interés, consideración. Su presencia es agradable, y se experimenta a su vista como una necesidad de conciliarse, de conquistar su estima" (Generally speaking, the expression *personal magnetism* describes that sort of charm that certain individuals exert on those around them. Without seeming to do anything to that end, such individuals inspire sympathy, interest, regard. Their presence is agreeable, and upon seeing them one feels a need to be close to them and earn their esteem) (Jagot 3.138). According to Jagot, the internal quality of personal magnetism can be created through external training (eye and voice exercises, for example), and it seems you are only one step (and short chapter) away from using that ability to influence others beyond ordinary means of doing so: "Impresionar el subconsciente de una persona a fin de hacer predominar una idea o un estado efectivo capaz de determinarla en un sentido dado, tal es el objeto de la sugestión" (Making an impression on the subconscious of a person so as to make an idea prevail or a state that will be able to give rise to that idea in a given form, such is the aim of suggestion) (Jagot 3.148). Taken together, the writings of Jagot and others offer a host of compelling ideas about how humans can and might relate. We are all magnetizers, but some are naturally more magnetic than others. Those who do not come by enhanced personal magnetism naturally can develop it experimentally and scientifically. Our thoughts and bodies are imperceptibly interacting with the thoughts and bodies of others. All of this can be brought under control to better our own lives and potentially influence others. Magnetism understood in this sense constitutes an open channel for communication and relation between individuals that may be shaping our lives whether we know it or not. While some of the ideas proposed by pseudoscientific authors may seem unserious, the underlying concerns and the kinds of social spaces opened up by those invested in this work could have significant cultural and political repercussions.

Spiritism and women

In *Spanish Female Writers and the Freethinking Press, 1879-1926*, Christine Arkinstall identifies untraditional intellectual publishing spheres as a place for women's political engagement. In her case study of Amalia Domingo Soler, she identifies spiritism alongside feminism as nodes of freethinking.[25]

---

25 For Domingo Soler in particular, spiritism, with its exploration of animal magnetism and mesmerism, is a Christian practice, and so these practices could

As Arkinstall sets out the ties between spiritism and anarchism and Spanish republicanism, it becomes clear that the movement offered a point of entry for women into intellectual and political circles (see 34). She also examines Domingo Soler's writing as *testimonio* as follows:

> The genre of *testimonio* applied to spiritism functions in a two-way sense: it allows the dispossessed and illiterate to speak through the medium of a more educated other, and it authorizes the educated—but socially, politically, and economically disempowered—female subject to write in the public sphere, given that her words are, and are not, her own. (Arkinstall 37)

Thus, an unusually broad female community was articulated through spiritist practice. Bianchi notes that the spiritist movement in Argentina was closely tied to its counterpart in Spain: "No sólo sus primeros y más activos difusores fueron peninsulares que reanudaron prácticas ya iniciadas en su país de origen —y que habían sido incluso combinadas con activas militancias sindicales o políticas— sino que los contactos se mantuvieron a través de correspondencia y de intercambio de publicaciones" (Not only were its first and most active proponents from the Iberian Peninsula, having resumed practices they had begun in their country of origin—and that they had even combined with active labor union or political efforts—but their contacts were maintained through correspondence and the exchange of publications) (98). In Argentina, as in Spain, spiritism enjoyed high levels of participation by women, as well as by people from various economic and social sectors of society—though Bianchi points out the central role of pamphlets, tracts, and books in the movement, which meant that spiritist lessons were directed mainly at a literate audience (see 100-101). Spiritism may not have challenged some aspects of traditional femininity, but it did bring women's voices to the fore, allowing them a public voice and even one of resistance: Arkinstall suggests that "spiritism is in keeping with women's culturally sanctioned role as the spiritual repository for society and that their role as medium conformed to society's view of women as passive conduits or vessels for the projects and voices of others. At the same time, I argue, spiritism allowed women to articulate indirectly their concerns behind the mask of another's identity" (41). We might view spiritism as in fact breaking down the dichotomy between "conduit or vessel" and expressions of individual identity.

hold appeal for women with religious convictions. See Christine Arkinstall, *Spanish Female Writers and the Freethinking Press, 1879-1926* (Toronto: University of Toronto Press, 2014), 35.

For some,[26] like Domingo Soler, spiritism was a discourse that recognized the inability of matter to contain one's identity given that essence and spirit exceed the body (see Arkinstall 49). It could also point to the primacy of feeling, aligned with femininity, over rationalism (see Arkinstall 50). And feeling or sentiment was generally considered in terms of sympathy (see Arkinstall 47). Thus, spiritism had the potential both to demonstrate some very real and shocking effects of supposedly feminine qualities (such as feeling and sympathy), which were otherwise devalued, and to allow women a way out of the confines of the female body as the defining factor of their experience of the world. All of this would indicate that spiritist discourses, including magnetism and mesmerism, possess a history of offering women a widely recognized narrative through which to relate to other women politically, socially, and affectively.[27] I argue that the effects of experiments with magnetism and mesmerism were not confined to sitting rooms—nor even to the stages on which women performed to large audiences. Instead, recognition of the power of sympathetic feeling seeped out of pseudoscientific discourse into relationships among women.

Sympathy

The concepts of sympathy and empathy share a rich philosophical and critical history, with various thinkers privileging one over the other or distinguishing between the two according to the qualities they wish to highlight. Authors' uses of the terms often say something about their approach to the relation between self and other or subject and object, and whether a dissolution of that boundary is desirable, or indeed possible. According to Karsten Stueber, writing in *The Stanford Encyclopedia of Philosophy*, "[t]he psychologist Edward Titchener (1867-1927) introduced the term 'empathy' in 1909 into the English language as the translation of the German term 'Einfühlung' (or 'feeling into'), a term that by the end of the 19th century was in German philosophical circles understood as an important category in philosophical aesthetics."[28]

---

26 See, for example, Sandra Gasparini, "Dos mujeres que aterran: Magnetizadoras y asesinas en los umbrales de dos géneros modernos." Paper presented at the IV Jornadas de Reflexión: Monstruos y Monstruosidades 2010, organized by the Instituto de Estudios Interdisciplinarios de Género de la U.B.A. October 21, 22, and 23, 2010.

27 Arkinstall pays particular attention to the lengthy correspondence among freethinking women in which they hashed out disagreements and put forth their views on spiritism and the contemporary topics they saw as related to it.

28 Karsten Stueber, "Empathy," in *The Stanford Encyclopedia of Philosophy*, ed. Edward N. Zalta (2017), plato.stanford.edu/archives/spr2017/entries/empathy/.

It would be Robert Vischer and Theodor Lipps who elaborated theories of empathy. Rae Greiner writes:

> *Einfühlung*, in Vischer's view, describes the way we project emotion into aesthetic objects so as to animate our relationship to the phenomenal world. It is a "feeling into" aesthetic form by the self. For Lipps, *Einfühlung* collapses the boundary between subject and object. Lipps considered this process so essential to the human understanding of mental states that, in a remarkable twist, he presents it as the engine of self-consciousness. Self-consciousness—indeed, having a self at all—depends on my ability to humanize objects, including the object that is myself.[29]

Greiner goes on to explain that, since we cannot directly know what others' bodies are telling us and must instead read signs and carry out an act of imaginative projection, for Lipps, "empathy involves an aesthetic experience of another human" (418). She notes that in contemporary use, *empathy* seems to have come to mean a kinder, less stodgy, and less moralizing version of *sympathy*, where the latter maintains a distance between sympathizer and sympathized-with (see Greiner 418). A phrase like "You have my sympathies" might stand for this not-quite-heartfelt iteration; indeed, Greiner stresses that sympathy, in the nineteenth-century context of the realist novel, was not *felt* at all. Rather, "sympathy had for some time been considered a complex formal process, a mental exercise, but not an emotion" (Greiner 418). For Greiner, sympathy is worth rescuing—for realist novels and for her reading of them—because "it denies what empathy most highly prizes, namely the fusion of self with other" (418). Sharing qualities with the sympathy championed by Adam Smith, this imaginative or intellectual sympathy makes up "a set of formal protocols for *feeling ourselves thinking* with real people and fictional ones" (Greiner 419; emphasis in original). This involves some work and some recognition of difference.

Empathy has come under fire, as, for example, in Paul Bloom's 2016 book, *Against Empathy: The Case for Rational Compassion*, which argues that empathy may be fine in interpersonal relations but dangerous when used to guide large-scale policy decisions, since being moved by the plight of one individual on television does not mean we are informed about how to change that person's situation for the better and certainly not about how to change the lives of many people for the better.[30] Empathetically misguided

29 Rae Greiner, "Thinking of Me Thinking of You: Sympathy versus Empathy in the Realist Novel," *Victorian Studies* 53, no. 3 (2011): 417.
30 Paul Bloom, *Against Empathy: The Case for Rational Compassion* (New York: Ecco, 2016).

attempts may, he writes, do more harm than good, and how we feel empathy may be informed by a number of biases such as racism and sexism. Even in small-scale, low-stakes situations, Bloom argues, we may feel moved by signs we see in another person but misunderstand them and think we are empathizing effectively when in fact our feelings may not align at all with those of the other person.

I suggest that another anxiety that might be at work in critiques of sympathy is that it can be seen as having much in common with contagion—in both, feelings, physical or emotional, are transferred from body to body. There is a long genealogy of discourse on contagion, and just as scholarly thought on sympathy frequently takes the realist novel as its point of departure, discussion of contagion emerges with particular vigor from nineteenth-century naturalist novels.[31] Contagion was of particular concern when it came to marginalized communities such as new immigrants, sex workers, and the poor. Women's susceptibility to social contagion was of grave concern, as they were understood to be uniquely placed—in the home, with children in their care—to spread undesirable social ills. Sympathy operates within a similar paradigm of openness, and though its potential for communication and communion is generally more welcomed, the anxiety of the uncontrollable spread of outside influence hovers nearby.

The history of sympathy records not only the possibilities and dangers of using it to diagnose social ills—with the chance of catching them—but also a parallel use of the feeling to diagnose medical or bodily ills. In "Seeing the Blush: Feeling Emotions," Otniel Dror traces the history of the scientific observation of emotion.[32] He takes the blush, a physical sign of an interior emotion, one that may also register a sympathetic response to another person's experience, as a jumping-off point to discuss how emotions have been measured over time. Whereas observers are of utmost importance in some scientific studies—seeing and interpreting bodily signs such as blushes, even experiencing similar reactions themselves—technology can also step in to measure bodily signs, such as heart rate or temperature. The

---

31 For more on nineteenth-century Latin American discourse on sickness and contagion and medico-scientific influence on social mores, see Nouzeilles, *Ficciones somáticas*; Kristin Ruggiero, *Modernity in the Flesh: Medicine, Law, and Society in Turn-of-the-Century Argentina* (Stanford: Stanford University Press, 2004); J. Andrew Brown, *Test Tube Envy: Science and Power in Argentine Narrative* (Lewisburg, PA: Bucknell University Press, 2005); and Julia Rodriguez, *Civilizing Argentina: Science, Medicine, and the Modern State* (Chapel Hill: University of North Carolina Press, 2006).

32 See Otniel Dror, "Seeing the Blush: Feeling Emotions," in *Histories of Scientific Observation*, ed. Lorraine Daston and Elizabeth Lunbeck (Chicago: University of Chicago Press), 326–48.

late nineteenth and early twentieth centuries thus saw a debate over which method provided more accurate information about the subject—superficial or internal measures. Dror writes that sympathy, even induced by deliberate mimicry—grimacing as their subject grimaced—was a way for scientific observers to gain insight into the experience of their subjects (331). Dror refers to these as the "sympathetic blushes" of the observer: they are echoed in a way by sympathetic responses provoked in bioassays, a procedure in which the blood of emotionally excited animals is placed on strips of muscle from another animal, and the latter was seen to manifest the excited state of the first animal transmitted through their blood (337–38). Emotional signals read by early scientists in an act of sympathy—that is, observation and interpretation of facial expressions and more—were translated into categories rendered quantifiable by technology as it became widespread. Thus, the surface-level blush that once indicated emotion became a "visceral blush" measured by heart rate and blood flow (Dror 335). It was William James who suggested that the supposed abilities of spiritualists and psychics were likely the result of their observation of minute muscle movements (see Dror 340).[33] Sympathy, Dror records, comes to be seen as possessing special abilities linked with bodily communication, and it is moreover a *relational* feeling, an emotion that inclines an individual toward the other while leaving traces of that inclination in the body. The concept of sympathy was not only instrumental in medicine but also in what might seem to be a very different practice: that of magic.

As with magnetism, practitioners of magic share vocabularies, concerns, even practices—willingly or not—with science, and certain understandings of magical practices also hinge on the powers of sympathy. First published in 1902, Marcel Mauss's *General Theory of Magic* explains the concept of sympathetic magic, the principle by which certain magical rites are effected.[34] Sympathetic magic, Mauss writes, "covers those magical rites which follow the so-called laws of sympathy. Like produces like; contact results in contagion; the image produces the object itself; a part is seen to be the same as the whole" (15–16). When direct contact does not occur, effluvia,

---

33 Meanwhile, such skills had been traditionally associated with women, particularly with sensitives or mediums, and scientific observers saw their own "emotion-gauging machines" as debunking these feminine or feminized practices (Dror 340).

34 See Marcel Mauss, *A General Theory of Magic*, trans. Robert Brain (London: Routledge, 1972). This book does not appear to have been translated into Spanish at the time, but the author's *Magia y sacrificio en la historia de las religiones* (Henri Hubert's translation of *Mélanges d'histoire des religions*) was published in Buenos Aires by Lautaro in 1946.

"magical images," the magician's soul, or other imperceptible links may provide the connection between the two subjects (Mauss 90). "Sympathy," he asserts, "is the route along which magical powers pass: it does not provide magical power itself" (Mauss 125).

Mauss also discusses sympathy's ability to bring about true belief or experience (117). He cites accused witches testifying against their own interests and medicine men who themselves "fall prey to all kinds of illusions" (Mauss 117). Those who take part in rites that rest on sympathetic understanding have experiences based on belief in that mode of interaction. I ask whether we might be led by sympathetic magic toward a way of reading influence, psychic and otherwise, that constructs a true belief in our gender, or gender as being truly felt.[35] The feelings that make up the affective world of Lange's novel may be even less straightforward than sympathy, but this feeling serves as a useful model for how we can read the persuasive possibilities of such a feeling in sociocultural contexts and even within scientific discourse.

Finally, I would like to reflect on the gaze in light of scientifically inflected ideas of sympathy. To do that, I first turn to Max Scheler's philosophical reflections on sympathy, which reveal familiar interests and preoccupations. Translated by José Gaos from the German (*Wesen und Formen der Sympathie*), *Esencia y formas de la simpatía* was published in its third edition Buenos Aires in 1942. In the 1922 prologue by the author included in this version, we read: "La nueva edición trata también de hacer más profundamente que la primera luz en estas cuestiones [...] y por ello discute también la cuestión,

---

35 In her 1991 biography of Norah Lange, Miguel devotes about two pages to the writing and reception of *Personas en la sala*. She includes a citation of Bernardo Canal Feijóo writing in *Sur* about the novel and framing it in terms of its magical qualities:

"Tengo la impresión de encontrarme ante una novela ejemplar de misterio y de magia demoníaca en la cual —oh, prodigiosa de destreza artística—, el misterio y la magia comienzan en cierto misterioso poder de manejar la difícil materia sin emplear jamás las palabras misterio y magia, sin declarar —¡y menos declamar!— jamás el propósito final o metódico, sin decir ni una sola vez abracadabra, sin gesticulaciones ni exorcismos, sin prevenidos ceremoniales, sin preconcebidas reglas." (Quoted in Miguel 181)

("I have the impression of finding myself before an exemplary novel of mystery and diabolical magic, in which—oh, prodigy of artistic skill—the mystery and magic stem from a certain mysterious power to manipulate the difficult matter at hand without ever using the words mystery and magic, without ever declaring— and certainly without announcing—the end goal or methodical aim, without saying even once abracadabra, without gesticulations or exorcisms, without prearranged ceremonies, without preconceived rules.")

vuelta a plantear últimamente por H. Driesch, H. Bergson y E. Becher, de si y hasta qué punto los hechos de la 'simpatía' son indicio de la existencia de una *unidad supraindividual de la vida*" (The new edition also attempts to shed light on these questions more profoundly than the first [...] and therefore it also addresses the question, recently brought again to the fore by H. Driesch, H. Bergson, and E. Becher, of whether and to what degree the experience of "sympathy" is a sign of the existence of a *superindividual unity of life*).[36] We can hear in this mention of an overarching unity among all living things an echo of Sala y Villaret's writing on the vibrations of magnetic current that, if aligned correctly, tie organisms together and allow them to communicate through an invisible medium. It is telling that, as continued attention to the term indicates, getting sympathy right has proven just as tricky as getting magnetized communication to come off without a hitch. These interpersonal, relational currents are difficult to measure and their effects hard to pin down.

The avant-garde gaze, in Lange and elsewhere, might be considered through the lens of sympathy. Both sympathy and empathy involve a creation of the self in relation with feeling with—or thinking we are feeling with—another, whether that is imagining that we know the feelings of someone who is suffering (and thus we suffer in a small measure ourselves and are moved to help them) or seeing ourselves as objects, as others might see us. Critics such as Sierra, Domínguez, and Unruh have traced potential intellectual genealogies of the strange gaze in Lange's writing, tending to connect it to the Argentinian avant-garde scene, due both to vanguard textual experiments with images and ways of looking that circulated in that milieu and to Lange's experience as the object of the many male gazes that saw her as a muse. In *Gendered Spaces*, expanding on a citation from Susan Suleiman's *Subversive Intent*, Sierra writes that "the avant-garde privileged women and the feminine as the object of their representations. Modernity in general has been characterized by a 'putting into discourse of "woman,"' that is, the artistic objectification of the female body as evidenced, for instance, in surrealism" (Sierra, *Gendered Spaces* 28). Having empathized with, or felt into, such depictions of femininity, women's experience of their own gender—as well as their aesthetic depictions of it—comes away changed. The history of sympathy and empathy, which winds its way through philosophy, psychology, literary criticism, and aesthetics, exists alongside their role in scientific and occult discourses.

Any number of concerns unfold from these theories: one is the desire to be able to relate to others through the material and immaterial world while

---

36 Max Scheler, *Esencia y formas de la simpatía*, trans. José Gaos (Buenos Aires: Losada, 1942), 14; emphasis mine.

controlling, or at least being aware of, external influences. Besides the hope that science will provide a foolproof method of attraction or the possibility of speaking with a dead loved one, we see a preoccupation with the ways other beings might exercise their power over us, violating the confines of a vulnerable body and mind. Willing and eager magnetizers or sympathizers might produce unwanted effects on people who did not choose to be their subjects: surely no one is always the magnetizer/sympathizer and never the magnetized/sympathized with. Instead we are caught in flows of feeling to and from those around us. It is with this line of theorization, one that unfolds from these (pseudo)scientific ideas of the time, that I turn to the gendered gaze in Norah Lange's writing.

Personas en la sala

Personas en la sala depicts the experience of a seventeen-year-old female protagonist who sits by her window to observe the three women—sisters—who live across the street. A mix of strange feelings leads her to involve herself increasingly in their lives, eventually arranging a meeting with them and crossing the street for regular visits, until her strange mood leads her family to send her away from the city for a time and she finds their house empty upon her return. The majority of the narrative is dedicated to the protagonist's observations: both what she sees and what she intuits or imagines arising from the images she describes. The style of the narration makes it difficult to disentangle concrete, real scenes that she observes from the affective layers her imaginings wrap around the targets of her vigil and voyeurism.

The novel presents a bare storyline, but its bulk is largely non-narrative. She sees a man visit the house, imagines the neighbors harbor a dark secret, and reflects on her love and hatred for them as she wishes to see the eldest woman dead. Given the nontraditional prose style, I propose that we think of this as a text that experiments with a number of possibilities beyond a mimetic narrative: it teases out feelings of affection or desire, experiments with textual fragmentation permitting interpersonal imbrication and relation, and locates invasive and inescapable forces in the power of looking. Taken in this way, the text need not be read as a messy bildungsroman or unsatisfying mystery story; instead, we watch as it makes visible the unseen paths of communication that in daily life are most often shut down or constrained, while pointing to the vital importance of such quotidian interactions and the manner in which they make their way inside of us and determine how we can or cannot feel toward others. If those overlooked lines of influence and interaction were manipulated (perhaps not overlooked by magnetizers or those interested in sympathetic communication), we could be constituted differently from how we are and we could experience the world in a different way. Whereas pseudoscientific authors argue that knowledge of the magnetic flows among us is the first step toward manipulating them to a more healthful, pleasurable end, *Personas* does not necessarily suggest that young women could have happier experiences of their gender—but it does suggest that being aware of these relational flows can provide insight into the construction of a gendered experience. The protagonist is unusual both in her attention to these exchanges in an otherwise ordinary, non-spiritist, setting and her willingness to explore and manipulate them.

Much of her exploration is visual. The gaze possesses special powers in the realms of hypnotism and suggestion: while magnetism may reside in the entire body, the special influence of staring deep into a subject's eyes remains a strong element in its practical manipulation (see Jagot 1.94). Scientific observers note the importance of seeing, and it may even have an affective or emotional component, as with the sympathetic gaze explored by Dror, a case where affective involvement via the gaze is seen to be productive and even necessary. (In a not dissimilar reckoning with the age of the microscope, Santiago Ramón y Cajal esteemed the scientist's artistic hand in bringing images of neurons to colleagues and the public: drawing and drawing beautifully are key.)[37] Vision, the gaze, and glances exchanged and avoided constitute a network of influence—as we saw in the contemporaneous (pseudo)scientific discourse detailed above—and it is the network most obviously at work in *Personas*. The influential flows, revealed by writing on magnetism and sympathy, play out powerfully as Lange sends something through the much written-of gaze in her text; she magnetizes it, makes it do new kinds of work, rather than the objectifying kind we are used to. This gaze makes visible the invisible forces that flit between people and objects, through gestures and glances, much like spiritists promised they could. And what is revealed is not a clear narrative (of curing disease or talking to someone distant) but a fragmented chaos that could be rearranged in a new way. Lange's description of a young woman watching her neighbors constitutes a space to see how such ordinarily imperceptible influence might be at work in daily life. The

---

[37] An exhibition at the Grey Art Gallery at NYU, *The Beautiful Brain: The Drawings of Santiago Ramón y Cajal*, January 9 through March 31, 2018, featured a number of his sketches of neural structures. See the exhibition catalog, Larry W. Swanson, et al., *The Beautiful Brain: The Drawings of Santiago Ramón y Cajal* (New York: Abrams Books, 2018).

narrator's gaze is a relational one: desiring, directional, and affective. The mode of relation in Lange's novel—a chaotic mix of love, hate, attraction, and repulsion—leads us to the flows of influence that run beneath and through it.

If literature on magnetism tells us that our character and even our physical selves change based on how we are looked upon by others, we might read Lange criticism that focuses on her conscious gender performance in that light as suggesting that the gaze of her milieu created learned patterns of feeling and performative response. (These learned patterns of feeling bring us back to the importance thinkers have placed on figuring out how to empathize or sympathize "correctly," to the best social or individual end.) *Personas*, however, takes us out of the milieu of the Argentinian avant-garde, removes men almost entirely from the picture and, in doing so, lets a woman look at other women with no mediation. A male character does make an appearance in the house across the street, and his unknown identity awakens the protagonist's reflections on hatred, but his presence largely points up the absence and invisibility of men in the novel. (Lange's *45 días y 30 marineros*, in which the young protagonist is the only women among a boatload of men, may represent another approach to upending conventional gender arrangements and the ways of looking and feeling that come with them.)

In *Personas*, the narrator has the power of looking, and the book explores magnet-like attraction and repulsion. The narrator is unable to resist the pull of the women across the street and they work their way into her. On the book's first pages she refers to the women across the street as "tres rostros claros que parecían vivir a gusto" ("three pale faces that appeared to be living at ease") and then as the "invisibles moradores [de la casa de enfrente]" ("invisible occupants [of the house across the way]") (13, 14, [21], [22]). These faces, standing in for inaccessible and invisible women, drive the narrator's reflections. Moreover, though she eventually will cross the street, the faces first come to her: "sus rostros cruzaban la calle" ("their faces crossed the street") (30, [37]). And this is what sets off her vigil. "Tal vez no las comprendí," the narrator says of the titular characters, "pero las miré, Dios sabe que las miré hasta que me invadieron a pedacitos, raspándome, caminándome" ("Perhaps I didn't understand them, but I watched them, God knows I watched them until piece by piece they invaded me, scratching at me, walking through me") (Lange 164, [160]). Although the figures she observes may not at first return her gaze, her vigilance implies a certain degree of communication that is somehow bodily: her gaze is neither suspended in midair nor does it sink into the figures on which it is fixed altering or distorting them. Rather, the gaze causes its object, the three women, to return, somehow materially, to the psycho-corporeal framework of the protagonist. The entire novel might be framed as the narrator's description of being invaded by invisible forces that emanate from figures she does not understand.

Attempts at understanding the women by creating a narrative fall short. The narrator wants to suss out their secret (with hints at a tragic love story, a conventional narrative that never materializes), but they in turn become her secret, indeed the secret that constitutes her: "[L]o hermoso sería que ocultasen algo o que recordaran algo terrible, preciso e inagotable, y me pareció que, para gustarme, ese algo... debía ser algo aún no castigado..." ("[I]t would be beautiful for them to be hiding something, or remembering something dreadful, inevitable, endless; and it seemed that to please me, that something... should be some still-unpunished deed") (20, [28]). Instead of a concrete story about the neighbors, we get reflections on what the narrator imagines to be pleasurable—she desires that they should have a secret. She imagines scenarios that never come to pass, such as how she would tell them about when she first started watching them: "[C]omencé a mirarlas porque siempre me gustaron las mujeres de treinta años. [...] Alguien me dijo una vez, o quizá lo leí, que muy pocas mujeres se suicidan pasada esa edad. Entonces las vi a ustedes tres, a cubierto de muertes subrepticias, de copas con su resto blanquecino, de venas abiertas..." ("I began to watch you, because I've always been fond of women of thirty. [...] Someone once told me, or perhaps I read somewhere, that very few women kill themselves after that age. Then I saw the three of you, sheltered from surreptitious deaths, glasses coated with a chalky residue, slit wrists") (23, [31]). And she imagines that they will smile at her and her death-tinged view of them, somehow understanding her attraction to their imagined suicides. These sorts of imaginings that the three faces bring forth for the narrator make up the bulk of the text and as a result the bulk of what we can understand to be her psychic self.

The wending and redoubling reflections in the novel have been read, as in critical texts by Sierra, as a textual manifestation of collage or montage, or of projections and reproductions.[38] This line of analysis tacks toward the

---

[38] Sierra reads the strange effects of Lange's writing as textual manifestations of collage, photomontage, mirroring, projections, and reproductions, suggesting that both Lange and Norah Borges use "techniques of image manipulation such as artistic doubling, ironic mirroring and photomontage that originated in the photographic endeavors of the Avant-garde." This, she says, is a creative response to their marginalization as women in their intellectual and artistic circle. The distorted visual effects permit "an oblique perception of reality" and an acknowledgment that their reality was quite different from that of the men they worked alongside (Sierra, "Oblique Views" 564).

visual and the photographic; I believe that in these same strange doubles and overlapping images—often images of death along the lines of what we have above—we might read Lange as positing the elaboration of mutually constitutive identities. The novel's strange gaze paradoxically shows us a range of affective-sensorial experiences that cannot be seen, and maybe not even sensed with the five senses, but are nonetheless felt and thus become in some way corporeal. These imperceptible forces with real mental and emotional effects are reminiscent of those unleashed by magnetizers. As the narrator watches a thunderstorm, she says that she "recogía la mayor cantidad posible de relámpagos para que durasen unos segundos más detrás de mis ojos" ("I collected as many flashes as I could, so they would last a few seconds longer behind my eyes") (Lange 17, [25]); similarly, watching the three women, she says, "[yo] recogía sus rostros durante horas" ("I spent hours on end collecting their faces") (Lange 30, [37]), in the very mode of vigilance that meant that "las tres caras se instala[ran] adentro de la mía" ("the three faces settled into my own") (Lange 43, [49]). But, she supposes to herself, if they had seen her while she collected those bolts of lightning, "[T]al vez me habrían dicho que era inútil luchar contra el destino, porque al rato, alguien me preguntó si me animaba a cerrar las persianas que daban a la calle. Yo me levanté irritada" ("[P]erhaps they would have told me it was useless to resist fate, since soon someone asked me if I wouldn't mind closing the shutters on the drawing-room window facing the street. I stood up vexed") (Lange 17, [25]). The destiny of closed blinds, of shutting out the lightning bolts that she was storing up, is precisely what she struggles against. What might her alternate destiny of an unobstructed gaze mean, and why does she seem to yearn for it? We can observe in her gaze a mode of receiving and projecting affection that is non-narrative and does not occur through direct contact. Not only does her gaze involve others, it creates a two-way flow through which the people and objects she looks upon come back into her (recall sympathy as troubling the subject-object distinction). Her feeling toward the neighboring sisters, a sentimental pull, tugs in fragments of feeling that swirl in the protagonist. Moments later, she reveals that she does not know why it is she wants what she wants, or where these feelings come from: "Ignoro por qué me gustó ese espectáculo de mí misma reflejada en el espejo, arrojada al espejo por un relámpago" ("I don't know why I was entranced by the sight of my own reflection flung into the mirror by the lightening") (Lange 17–18, [26]). But as she continues to watch that same storm, the protagonist remarks: "Mi árbol preferido se agitaba y me pareció menos árbol. Ya iba a estirar el brazo para cerrar la persiana cuando me atrajo una ventana iluminada en la casa de enfrente" ("My favorite tree was shaking, and seemed to me like less of a tree. I was about to reach out to close the shutters when I was drawn to a window with a light on in the house across the way") (Lange 18, [26]). And thus begins her vigil of the three women. It is when the tree is imbued with movement, agitation, vibration that she sees it as capable of being other than it is, less tree. But it is not any tree; it is her favorite tree. How she looks reveals what she feels, likes, and wants. And Lange creates the strange environment, like one long, strange storm, so that the protagonist's affectionate gaze pouring into the house across the street and over the three women might see things in a state of agitation. Ordinary gestures become less ordinary and more energized by feelings that create the conditions for her imbricated identity. I propose that we understand this as a form of the magnetic gaze, one capable of shaping relationships with other people.

The women are on the surface quite ordinary: they have drinks, smoke cigarettes, chat. For all of the ways that the novel bucks textual convention, the social interactions Lange portrays are mundane though heightened to the point of appearing uncanny. They reveal exchanges of self-making bits of feeling through words and glances just as in daily life. How radical to have a young women make it all so vivid, so vitally important, and on her own terms—which may indeed be the danger, the reason she is sent away, though as we will see her family largely fails to notice her entire adventure, noting only her *rareza*. Readers who say the whole scene must be imaginary may think that nothing so strange could be real. But that interpretation may really be registering the socially accepted limitations of a young woman's ability to engage in the exchange of world- and self-making influential glances on her own terms. It must—readers diagnose—be all in her head. The real world is Lange's mother dressing her up as a boy (Miguel 37), or critics treating her like an inexperienced young girl, or an entire artistic movement that seemed to want just to look at her and use her as a talismanic object. But in the novel itself, the narrator makes up and arrays all of the objects and affects herself.

The danger posed by/to women on the threshold of the home (answering the door, going to the window) is traditionally thought about more or less in terms of sexual contagion brought about by contact: men will be able to talk to women, arouse them, sell them frivolous and addicting commodities (see footnote 31 in this chapter); women will be able to talk back, walk out, see something untoward. *Personas* largely consists of an extended scene in which a young woman apparently has no objectionable contact and does only the proper thing while she sits on the threshold of the family home watching an anodyne sitting-room scene through the window and reading a book (though reading might in other contexts be considered an inappropriate feminine activity). And yet *Personas* unravels this scene and reveals it to be shot through with shocking feelings, observations, images, and thoughts. The psychic and emotional influence of unseen radio waves, sympathetic glances, or magnetizing currents cast lights on the construction of gendered experience when narratives of contagion through contact fall short.[39]

Sight is not the only sense that gives rise to the narrator's reflections; Lange details a scene in which hearing works in a similar way. The protagonist recognizes her own voice in the voice of one of the women who asks for a telegram form at the post office:

> No puedo darme vuelta para averiguar quién usa mi voz, o si yo soy otra persona, o si yo no soy yo y estoy equivocada y quiero enviar un telegrama en vez de esperar. [...] Recogí las monedas sin saber hacia qué lado dirigirme para no toparme con mi voz, la voz mía, yo, repetida. Recuerdo haber pensado que nadie puede reconocer su voz ni oír cómo es su propia voz para los demás. [...] Y si no era mi voz, ¿cómo podían equivocarse mi piel, mis nervios, cuando no esperaban un miedo de esa clase? (Lange 34-35)

> (I can't turn around to find out who's using my voice, or if I'm someone else, or if I'm not myself and I am mistaken, and what I really want isn't to wait, but to send a telegram. [...] I picked up the coins, not knowing which way to turn to avoid confronting my voice, my own voice, myself repeated. I remember thinking no one could identify their own voice, or hear how it sounded to others. [...] And if it wasn't my voice, then why had I suddenly felt that fear in my skin, my nerves?) (41)

She not only hears something strange, she feels the eerie quality in her body; her skin and nerves sense it. They are alive to this confusion between self and other. The voice and the gaze enter into the vibratory or magnetic effluvium that belies the apparent divisions among individuals; they create external signs there, but the effects ricochet through body and mind. Wracked with fear, she decides not to repeat the phrase she heard her voice say in case the post office employee should not recognize her as a different person,

> porque significaría que yo persistía en otra voz, que otra voz me llevaba por calles desconocidas, por muertos sin retratos, sobre una cuna, conociendo cocinas llenas de humo, y olor a grasa, cubiertas de barcos, pidiendo perdón sin que yo lo supiera o sabiendo que detestaba pedir perdón; inventándome sitios nuevos, descuidados y

---

39 There are those narratives of contagion, such as miasma theory, that do not require direct contact.

hermosos, escuchando música desesperada y nerviosa, o pronunciando innumerables "te quiero" y quizás aunque no me importaba tanto, un "ojalá te mueras." (Lange 35)

(since it would mean that I endured in another voice, that another voice was leading me down unfamiliar streets, past the portrait-less dead, over a cradle, entering smoky kitchens smelling of fat, boarding ships, saying sorry without my knowledge or knowing I hated to say sorry; imagining new places for me, derelict and beautiful, hearing desperate, anxious music, or uttering countless "I love you"s, and perhaps, though I minded less, a single "I hope you die.") (41)

The vibration of the uncannily shared voice might transfer her into another set of surroundings and move her to say things she does not mean or really understand. If the voices of the dead may be heard through the bodies of mediums, this is a sort of twist: her voice would stay the same but her physical world would change.

In another scene, she watches the women across the street but is only partially able to make them out. Where in the post office scene hearing is paramount, here *not* seeing is vital. She describes the outlines of their gestures: "Me fue imposible verificar si comían algo; sólo alcancé a percibir las partes claras, que eran sus manos acercándose a la boca. Hasta el no verlas comer me entusiasmó; me pareció un signo, la contraseña pasiva de sus tardes sin episodios" ("It was impossible to tell whether they were eating anything; I could only see the lighter parts—their hands moving towards their mouths. It was even intriguing not to see them eat; it seemed like a sign, the quiet key to their uneventful evenings") (Lange 21–22, [30]). What is invisible in the image is what makes it important to her. Shortly hereafter she will declare these moments the time when "me las adjudiqué como una pertenencia..." ("I claimed them like a possession...") (Lange 22, [30]). In another moment of being attuned to the traces of what she cannot see, she describes the youngest sister's hand: "la mano que había sido tan largamente besada la tarde anterior y que parecía vivir besada, como si la piel viviera conmemorando el beso" ("the hand kissed so slowly the night before, which seemed to still live in that kiss, as if her skin hadn't ceased to remember it") (Lange 70, [73]). The drawn-out aftereffects of moments she has glimpsed—or past scenes she has imagined—are indeed what fascinate this narrator. While she does not reveal a conventional secret that would explain the lives of the women across the street, she does seem to see the secret effects and lingering impact of otherwise unremarkable actions. Lange makes those effects not just psychic or social but material and corporeal: the skin of the woman's hand incorporates the having been kissed. In this, we can see echoes of the magnetizing forces that supposedly cure sick bodies as well as the more abstract interest in how we are invisibly impacted by forces and people around us.

Sometimes the influences explored by the narrator are directly related to the occult. She overhears part of a conversation in which the women discuss communicating with the dead: "Es lo mismo comunicarse con un espíritu, por medio de la mesa, que pensarlo o necesitarlo constantemente. También puede molestarle la insistencia del recuerdo" ("Tapping the table to communicate with a spirit is no different from always thinking about it, or longing for it. They might be just as troubled by the persistence of a memory") (Lange 82, [84]). Here Lange brings spiritist practices into the realm of everyday, nonoccult life. The narrator supposes that here the women are alluding to an earlier time when they carried out such experiments and begins to imagine them at a later date: "También pensé que una tarde en que se quedaran muy quietas, descubriría los primeros hilos de una telaraña, que se extenderían desde los ojos al pecho, o a las manos, sin que ellas lo advirtiesen, persuadidas de que era una manera distinta de tener sueño, porque las pestañas se volvían pesadas por los pequeños tirones elásticos de la araña" ("I imagined, too, that one evening when they were very quiet, I would discovered the first threads of a spider's web, spun from their eyes to their chests or hands without their noticing, convinced as they were that it was just another way of being tired, since their lashes felt heavy, weighed down by the spider pulling on its tiny elastic threads") (Lange 83, [85]). In the first quote, one of the women posits that thinking of or needing a spirit exerts as strong a pull as a séance. In the second, the narrator creates the image of a spider web appearing on the women's bodies and pulling them into a new sort of sleepiness with its barely present silken threads. This image makes visible the potential of heretofore unknown and unseen causes and effects. It gives material form to the ubiquitous, imperceptible, and unexpected communicative and relational forces that have the potential to agitate daily life, creating different ways of feeling.

The affective world of the novel's protagonist is one of attraction and repulsion, of a strange mix of *amor*, *odio*, *dicha*, and *culpa* (love, hate, joy, and guilt). Of feeling toward others. The descriptions of the women's faces invading the protagonist's body are of a piece with her fervent declarations of love and hate: Lange creates a language of suppositions and projections that thicken and gain substance so that the affective and the material, the psychic and the sensorial cannot be disentangled. This constant flow of relation sometimes takes apparently contradictory turns. One of the repeated phrases in the novel is the narrator's reflection on how she would like to see the oldest sister dead: "[P]ensé [...] que me gustaría verla muerta" ("I thought [...] that I would like to see her dead") (Lange 20, [28]); "[S]i alguna vez sentí deseos de verla muerta era porque me gustaba y siempre imaginaba muertas a las personas que me gustaban" ("[I]f I had once felt a desire to see her dead, it was because I was fond of her, and when I was fond of people, I always imagined them dead") (Lange 159, [156]). This is just the strange kind of relation that propels her feelings into the house across the street. It may also suggest the limits of life as she experiences it; she instead is seeking a return to the corporeal, indeed to a corpse from which social constraints fall away.

Sitting with her family in her dining room, the narrator feels a fleeting desire to "concederles un poco del misterio que flotaba en torno mío; hasta de prestarles, un instante, las tres caras que les faltaban por no ser pacientes" ("bestow upon the others some of the mystery floating all around me, and even to briefly lend them the three faces that their own impatience had prevented them from seeing") (Lange 50, [55]). She thinks her relation with the three women could perhaps be extended to her family, with the right words or gesture. But instead, with a typically odd mix of feelings, she unfolds her napkin with a sad gesture, though, she notes, she was happy (see Lange 50). No one notes anything strange. And she reflects that the vital, life-giving nature of her watching of the women is such that they could, in all their power, take her very life away from her, and no one would notice the state of imminent danger she was in:

> Me dio un poco de tristeza pensar que [...] mi vida podía cambiar, sufrir verdaderas alteraciones, pasar del amor al odio, que las caras me obsesionaran y cayese en manos de tres aventureras que me gritarían las líneas de mi mano, obligándome a extenderlas, diariamente, para anunciar que la línea de mi vida podía abreviarse si no las complacía, sin que nadie adivinara ni sospechara el peligro. (Lange 50)

> (It saddened me a little to think [...] that my life could change, suffer real disturbances, swing from love to hate, that I might become obsessed with the faces, and fall into the hands of three wayward women, who would cry out the lines of my palm, forcing me to hold it out to them daily, threatening that if I didn't obey them, my life line might be cut short, and no one would ever guess, or suspect I was in danger.) (55)

She imagines that the three faces could make her ill, yet no one would know the cause of her illness (Lange 50). She is also terrified that if she gives too much away, her family will try to take the three faces from her. During this meal—which occurs after she has intercepted a telegram meant for the three women and then delivered it to their house, bringing them together for the first time—her family's conversation floats on without her while she is preoccupied by feverish imaginings: "[Y]o pensaba en una señora desconocida que dejaba bajo la puerta una tarjeta donde se destacaban dos palabras: 'tu madre', y eso significaba que no yo era hija de mi madre y que esa señora misteriosa cuyo nombre desconocía, deseaba mi muerte frente a un retrato mío que colocaba hacia abajo" ("I imagined a stranger sliding a card under my door; the card bore the words, 'Your mother,' which meant I wasn't my mother's daughter, and that the mysterious woman, whose name I didn't know, was wishing me dead in front of my portrait, which she turned to face the wall") (Lange 50, [56]). In this scene, she would exist in a portrait, as the object of the gaze of others, and another woman would desire her death just as she desires the death of her neighbor. She would be dislodged from her current family and given another set of relations that would define her. Lange uses the narrator's flights of imagination to explore the, here frightening, possibility of real changes that could triggered by this mysterious exchange of relational forces.

The narrator's feelings, including hatred, move and flow through space like a magnetic current. When a man makes a visit to the house across the street, she reflects: "Mi odio se movía todo el tiempo, ocupaba sitios inesperados y, para no odiarlo más, miraba el caballo, su piel espesa y lustrosa que a veces tenía temblores repentinos y entonces algunas gotas caían sin salpicar" ("My hatred kept shifting, occupying unexpected places, and so as to not hate him more, I watched the horse with its thick, shiny coat, which from time to time suddenly flinched, causing droplets of water to roll gently off its back") (Lange 57, [61]). It is raining when she goes out to observe the man more closely: "Las gotas que caían de los árboles parecían atenuar mi odio sin disiparlo del todo" ("The raindrops falling from the trees seemed to lessen my hatred, but didn't dispel it completely") (Lange 57, [62]). In this uncertain relationship between raindrops and hatred, feelings take on material dimensions. They also spring from unlikely sources: "Me disgustaban tantas cosas, que las que me atraían más constituían una obsesión, como las personas que me contaban largas enfermedades, la madera al ser cepillada, el terciopelo negro" ("[S]o many things troubled me that the things to which I was most drawn became obsessions, like people who told of long illnesses, like freshly planed wood, black velvet") (Lange 15, [23]). These are strange sources of attraction, and we might recall the mutual constitution of material things from chapter 1, which here passes not through atoms or molecules but through an affective relationship of attraction, a pull, which, much like magnetism, has no readily apparent or visible cause.

In addition to hatred, disgust, and attraction, an obsessive sense of guilt also enters the narration early on: "Ya sé que la culpa fue mía. Yo siempre fui culpable de todo" ("I know it was my fault. I was always to blame for everything") (Lange 33, [39]). She frequently repeats this same phrase of undefined guilt and responsibility. But she is not the only person or thing that is culpable: "Me parecía que sus vestidos podían ser culpables de muchas cosas que decían o, por lo menos, que variaban su contenido" ("I thought their dresses might be to blame for many things they said, [or they at least changed the content]")[40] (Lange 109, [110]). In light of this quote, we can read her pronouncements of guilt as registering influence where we ordinarily see none. The narrator makes us aware of the otherwise imperceptible effects she has on the world and that the world has on her: she sees the rippling effects of her own presence, and this strange, seemingly misplaced guilt is one sign of this mode of relating to her surroundings.

The protagonist is a desiring being, yet it is unclear what exactly she wants or if she gets it. But the novel is a portrait of young womanhood as shaped by the possibilities of imagining and manifesting desires, principally through a powerful gaze. She also takes risks to meet the elusive neighbors. She would be shaped by them whether or not she could meet them—whether or not they really exist. The fragmentation of bodies and objects that make of the individual an amalgam of her surroundings is perhaps the recurring element in Lange's works that has attracted the most critical attention. It is what evokes comparisons to surrealism and to studies of anatomy. Some figures in *Personas*, such as the spider, the sky-blue dress, and the open vein, recur throughout the narration, becoming charged with the protagonist's desire. She never quite makes out the hidden past of the women she watches. Nor do these images provide clues to a narrative whole; they are neither metonymic nor metaphoric. Instead, they anchor the verbose narration by appearing again and again throughout the text; the nervous repetition, long strung-out sentences, and supplicating tone of the narration contrast with the weight the unusual images carry by virtue of their reiteration. Unlike the non-narrative style in *Memorias de Leticia Valle*, the accumulation in *Personas* is not of experiential fragments; instead, it is of suppositions, projections, imaginings, and attractions that channel unseen forces and becomes embedded in the characters. The constant interplay of conditional and subjunctive expressions repeats unceasingly until the suppositions that hang off of the unusual images (the spider web, the dead horse, the white

---

40 Adapted from Whittle's translation, which has "or that they at least were a change of topic"—I understand *variar* to suggest that the dresses effect a change on the content or meaning of the conversation.

gloves, etc.) gain substance and weight, becoming the (counter)narrative material of the novel.

Conclusion

The anticlimactic ending of the book—she is sent away, she returns, the neighbors are gone—indicates that some feelings, imaginings, and ways of being or becoming a woman are simply too strange to be reckoned with. And yet the forces at play around her, the things she has seen and the way she has felt herself to have been seen, are embedded in her gendered self. A family member, prior to her time away, diagnoses the protagonist's behavior and pronounces, "Se sentía rara, y ya lo hemos observado. Lo interesante sería conocer los motivos de esa rareza" ("She was feeling strange, just as we thought. And it would be interesting to know why") (Lange 125, [123]). It is not that she has behaved strangely but that she has been feeling strange, and they could tell. Her strange feelings have manifested in the novel's strange textual practices—they are what have allowed us to visualize a network of affects, objects, and bodies that would have otherwise exerted their influence imperceptible and unremarked upon. Terrified at being discovered, the narrator says, "[S]i fuesen pacientes, si fuesen pacientes, Dios mío, debían de mirarme y advertir las tres caras adentro de la mía, intactas, perfectas, llevaderas, atrozmente llevaderas" ("[I]f they were patient, if they were patient, my God, they should stare at me, and detect the three faces inside my own, intact, perfect, easy to bear, so terribly easy to bear") (Lange 125, [124]). But they are not patient and instead decide on the books that she holds in her lap while looking out the window as the likely bad influence.

If we think of gender as constructed in part through relation, texts on magnetism point out that relation includes perceptible and imperceptible influence. On an individual level, we are shaped by how people feel toward us, and gendered feeling is about socially determined limits of feeling that become embedded in people's bodies and minds so that they are part of their gender identity. That feeling is communicated in many nearly imperceptible ways, and the gaze is a strong example of it. So might be the objects, words, and gestures we exchange. The "people" of the title are three women, and the narrator is a woman, but with so little overt reference to gender in the novel, why read this text as describing a felt experience that is gendered? Because this is about a girl's gaze—one that does not objectify (like the male gaze, not even to creatively rework objects, like the male surrealists' gaze), one that is relational, that goes unnoticed (her family thinks she is reading her book by the window), one that registers a wild range of feelings and does not claim to be dispassionate. It does not create narratives or objects; it reveals unseen affective flows and fragmentation that shows that other ways of being are possible. She imagines them and to some extent lives them. The narrator is shaped not by how men view her but by her own experience of looking at other women, women who seem to ricochet back at her, into her, through her own gaze.

Lange's novel suggests that our thoughts and feelings work on one another (and one another's bodies) in ways we often do not perceive. The result is that there are not just "correct" ways of acting but "correct" ways of feeling and desiring (and perhaps little we can do to escape them). "Magnetizers" told us that we could harness forces that we already had to change others or communicate psychically, secretly. All women, not just mediums, could be said to be experts on what is communicated silently through glances and the feeling of being looked upon. Perhaps what is truly surprising in *Personas* is that the narrator loves/hates/desires so actively because she is doing the looking—yet she cannot escape the power of those she looks at. For her, it is attractive, necessary, not threatening, and yet it must come to an end. Lange creates a world in which the imperceptible flows of influence become visible, and a woman works to manipulate them driven by her own inexplicable feelings. She registers their influence as both a threat and as a thrilling possibility. Even if the narrator's experience is cut short, Lange's portrayal of these relational forces or ways of feeling toward others points toward the possibilities that arise from an openness to the subtle relational feelings that lie outside of gender narratives.

CHAPTER THREE

Self-Centered Worlds: Perceptual *Rareza* and *Nada*

Nos vemos rodeados de pronto de una abrumadora plétora de mundos nuevos que no constituyen el producto muerto de una máquina sin vida, sino que son el resultado orgánico de las calidades vivas de los sentidos.
—Jakob von Uexküll, *Teoría de la vida*[1]

Sensing to stay alive

In this passage from Jakob von Uexküll's *Teoría de la vida*, published in Madrid in 1944, the author offers a vivid description of the plethora of worlds created by the many and varied perceptive capacities of individual species—worlds that are reflections of the distinct ways that animals, including humans, interact with their environments in order to survive and thrive. He calls these worlds *Umwelten*, usually translated into English as "self-centered worlds," and into Spanish as "mundos circundantes."[2] His idea of multiple, harmonious worlds caught on, and his publications were widely translated and published in the decades after he wrote them. Uexküll's work persists in offering contemporary scholars a way to look at perception, sense making, and survival that emerges from a mode of thought in which the animal realm firmly includes humans; his work has been taken up by thinkers, such as Giorgio Agamben, whose work is founded on that premise.

---

1 Jakob von Uexküll, *Teoría de la vida* (Madrid: Editorial Summa, 1944), 128. (We suddenly see that we are surrounded by an overwhelming plethora of new worlds that are not the dead product of a lifeless machine but rather the organic result of the living qualities of the senses.)
2 The 1944 translation cited above actually refers to "mundos visibles," as in the title of chapter 4: "El mundo visible de los seres vivos" (The visible world of living beings). A footnote on the first page of that chapter explains: "*Umwelt*, en el original, mundo en torno, mundo visible" (*Umwelt*, in the original, surrounding world, visible world). This is a less-than-ideal translation given that the worlds Uexküll describes are not only, or even primarily, perceived visually.

Carmen Laforet's novel *Nada* might be said to be a story precisely about perception, sense making, and survival. In *Nada*, first published in 1945, a young woman named Andrea observes her chaotic surroundings in postwar Barcelona and emerges from scenes of violence and obscure emotions to walk away at the end of the novel declaring that she believed herself to be taking nothing with her from that time and place in her life. While the character is clearly looking for a narrative fresh start in the next stage of her life, I argue that Laforet in fact creates layers of sensory details that structure Andrea's urban life and that her perception of seemingly unusual or minor objects and moments are what allow for the persistence of her unconventional young femininity.

Shortly after the end of the Civil War, Andrea, whose parents have died, travels from the small town where she was living to Barcelona to stay with extended family and study at the university. Her grandmother, uncles (Román and Juan), aunts (Angustias and Juan's wife, Gloria), a young cousin, and a cook (Antonia) all live in a falling-down apartment of a piece with the chaotic state of their lives. Brothers Román and Juan fight violently. Román, who lives upstairs from the family in an attic room, seems to derive pleasure from tormenting all the members of the household. Antonia is particularly obsessed with him and listens in from the hallway to his apartment. Andrea's grandmother is frail and despairing of the unrest in her home, barely sleeping and sometimes confused. Angustias makes a show of her religious devotion and suffering while she has fallen in love with her married boss. Juan is a frustrated painter who cannot make money to support his young son and his wife whom he abuses. Gloria sneaks out to gamble and sell her husband's canvases as scrap to make ends meet.

Furniture piles up in crowded rooms of the apartment while other rooms are emptied and closed up. Food and money are scarce, and mealtimes are scenes of familial conflict. Andrea arrives on this chaotic scene late one night and throughout the novel tries to find a way to cope, eat enough, and perhaps enjoy her new life in Barcelona. She meets rich and artistic friends through her university classes, including the blond and glamorous Ena and a fleeting love interest, Pons, and glimpses the possibilities of another life. Still, she must return every night to the site of confusion and violence that is her home. In the end, she is extracted abruptly with a job offer in Madrid from Ena's father.

Andrea is also the prototype of what Carmen Martín Gaite would call the *chica rara*—the unconventional young women in novels juxtaposed to the traditional protagonists of the postwar *novelas rosa*. She is disappointed with the young men she meets and in many ways with the comfortable life she brushes up against. Her happiness and ability to survive in a harsh and unpredictable environment do not hinge on love, marriage, family, religion, or even her university studies. It is in fact hard to make out what drives Andrea. I argue that theorizations of queerness, particularly queer survival, can productively enter into dialogue an analysis of rareza and of this strange young Spanish woman in particular. In understanding Andrea not as queer but as a chica rara (building on Martín Gaite's definition), as having a strange experience of gender, one shaped by how she perceives and internalizes the world around her, I frame her rareza viewed through a scientific lens as a productive theoretical contribution to discussions of gender and queerness today. Before expanding on Uexküll's scientific ideas about perception and their popular reception, I introduce Laforet's literary approach to gendered writing and women's experience and the social context of Spanish women following the Civil War.

Secret worlds

At the novel's end, the narrator declares from an unknown point in the future: "De la casa de la calle de Aribau no me llevaba nada. Al menos, así creía yo entonces" ("I was taking nothing from the house on Calle de Aribau. At least, that's what I thought then") (Laforet 213, [244]). Is it possible that she leaves behind the confines that defined her in Barcelona? Will a new job, a new home, and a new city, Madrid, offer the freedom, or even perhaps the adventure, she sought at the beginning of the novel? In a letter dated February 10, 1967, decades after the publication of *Nada*, Laforet writes to Ramón Sender of her desire to write the secret of women's language and experience:

> Quisiera escribir una novela (pero no antes de dos años o cosa así) sobre un mundo que no se conoce más que por fuera porque no ha encontrado su lenguaje... El mundo del Gineceo. [...] En verdad, es el mundo que <u>domina secretamente</u> la vida. Secretamente. Instintivamente la mujer se adapta y organiza unas leyes inflexibles, hipócritas en muchas situaciones para un dominio terrible... Las pobres escritoras no hemos contado nunca la verdad, aunque queramos. La literatura la inventó el varón y seguimos empleando el mismo enfoque para las cosas. Yo quisiera intentar una <u>traición</u> para dar algo de ese secreto, para que poco a poco vaya dejando de existir esa fuerza de dominio, y hombres y mujeres nos entendamos mejor, sin sometimientos, ni aparentes ni reales, de unos a otros... tiene que llover mucho para eso.[3]

---

3 Carmen Laforet and Ramón J. Sender, *Puedo contar contigo: Correspondencia*, ed. Israel Rolón Barada (Barcelona: Ediciones Destino, 2003), 97.

(I'd like to write a novel (but in two years or so, at the earliest) about a world that is unknown, except from the outside, because it hasn't found its language... The world of the Gynaeceum. [...] In truth, it's the world that <u>secretly controls</u> life. Secretly. Instinctively women adapt and they set up inflexible laws that are often hypocritical, for a horrible control... Us poor women writers have never told the truth, even if we want to. Men invented literature, and we continue to use the same lens for things. I'd like to attempt a <u>betrayal</u> to put forth part of that secret, so that little by little that controlling force ceases to exist, and men and women can understand one another better, without apparent or real subjugation of one another... a lot has to happen for that to be possible.)

Here Laforet describes a way that women experience the world that is defined by patriarchy but that exceeds a simple narrative that sets out gender roles and gendered restrictions. Instead, this is a secret world that cannot be expressed through language. I consider the felt experience of gender to arise in just such a world—one that shapes our insight and our language and even our feeling. By Laforet's own judgment, *Nada* is a novel that remains firmly inscribed in a masculine tradition. Still, its young female protagonist and the novel's description of her strangely broken family through her eyes mark a certain departure from traditional narratives. I argue that Laforet does in fact write a marginal experience—one that in its subtle social critique hints at a language of resistance, albeit one that is necessarily occluded. Andrea's narration may indeed participate in a tradition that limits the expression of gendered feelings; however, I argue that if we understand the details of *Nada*'s narration and the observations the narrator includes as reflecting her particular way of perceiving her surroundings, her own Umwelt, we may gain insight into an experiential world that is at once largely unexpressed and deeply necessary for her survival within, around, and out of the constriction of gender. Renee Congdon proposes that Laforet uses the senses in *Nada*, with an emphasis on smell and hearing, so that Andrea may communicate "a través de este exceso de información sensorial lo que no se atreve a comunicarnos directamente" (through this excess of sensorial information what she does not dare to tell us directly).[4] If Laforet

---

4 Renee Congdon, "Olores y sonidos de la postguerra española: Un análisis sensorial de *Nada* de Carmen Laforet," in *Carmen Laforet: Después de "Nada", mucho*, ed. Mark Del Mastro and Caragh Wells (Valencia: Albatros Ediciones, 2022), 137. Congdon explores how hearing and smell are tied memory and affected by trauma; she cites both the terrible odors of the house and the smells that attract Andrea like the smell of the sea (145). Teresa Brennan notes smell, alongside "various forms

did not fully manifest the secret world on the pages of *Nada*, by approaching the text with an eye to Andrea's sensory perceptions and the strange mode of survival she portrays, we glimpse some of the workings of that world.

Postwar women

Nada sends its protagonist out into the streets of Barcelona at a time when city and country were reeling from the effects of the Civil War. Women who had found their way out of the home during the fighting or the comparative freedom of Republican Spain were being compelled to find their way back in under Francisco Franco's dictatorship. Yet in the novel's moment there is still considerable freedom to be found in the streets for working women, students, the poor, and those who disregard propriety.[5] While Andrea's aunt Angustias does all she can to control her orphaned niece, Andrea refuses to desist from her wandering search for something, rather than nothing, in the streets of Barcelona. In the bizarre ancestral home on Calle de Aribau, she finds "todas las tensiones sociales y toda especie de violencia de la posguerra; la angustia del hambre, la locura derivada de las frustraciones amorosas o profesionales, los resentimientos sociales y las prácticas marginales del juego y del contrabando" (all of the social tensions and all sorts of violence of the postwar period; the anguish of hunger, the madness arising from amorous and professional frustrations, social resentment, and the marginal practices of gambling and smuggling)[6] as Valeria de Marco puts it. And so, although Andrea's experience may seem to be a particular and peculiar one, it might in fact have quite a bit in common with those of all the women not living out novela rosa–like happy endings.

Under Franco, those freedoms that had been legally gained and socially experienced under the Republic vanished, and requirements for proper womanhood included marriage and motherhood, domesticity, and Catholicism—all upheld as coherent with true femininity, often described

---

of neuronal communication" as "not such respecters of persons" in comparison to sight, which "appears to leave the boundaries of discrete individuals relatively intact." Brennan, *Transmission of Affect* (Ithaca, NY: Cornell University Press, 2004), 10.

5 Marta E. Altisent writes of the perceived fluidity between the figure of the prostitute and the working woman in postwar era: given the poverty and the "sordid character of post-war Barcelona [...] spinsters live a double life, out-of-town students and impecunious single ladies find themselves on the fringes of prostitution, while prostitutes assume decorous and bourgeois façades." Altisent, "Images of Barcelona," in *A Companion to the Twentieth-Century Spanish Novel*, ed. Altisent (Woodbridge: Tamesis, 2008), 146-47.

6 Valeria de Marco, "'Nada': El espacio transparente y opaco a la vez," *Revista Hispánica Moderna* 49, no. 1 (1996): 74-75.

as reflecting their "natural inclination" and true essence.⁷ The *perfecta casada* and *ángel del hogar* was expected to dedicate herself to the "science of motherhood," the only science that should concern her (Kebadze 15). The home was to be the extension and natural ambition of women, and filling it with children was rewarded with *premios de natalidad* (birth prizes; see Kebadze 16, 18). Female state employees were required to leave their jobs when they married and were compensated with a *dote* (dowry) from the government (see Kebadze 18). These and other policies aligned national interests with women's comportment in society. Yet economic need forced many women to work outside of the home, and the Sección Femenina, the fascist women's organization that modeled prescribed women's roles, offered another version of official femininity that might be seen to be navigate around state-imposed gender norms by offering women active public-facing roles. Nino Kebadze's against-the-grain readings of several novelas rosa demonstrate that even those texts that conformed to norms of female writing (or were lumped into the genre for their apparent concordance with it—or due to the expectation that that was where female authors would naturally fit) register the incongruities and fault lines of hegemonic gender expectations.

Until 1973, the age of maturity for women—the time when they could leave their birth family without entering into marriage or a convent—was twenty-five.⁸ Examining literary production within this repressive environment, Patricia O'Byrne takes women's fiction (specifically neorealist and testimonial novels) from 1940 to 1960 as a source of historical memory, one allowing particular insight into private spaces and personal experiences. She cites Laforet's success at such a young age (and her winning of the Premio Nadal) as "the single most influential factor in stimulating women to write novels" (O'Byrne, *Post-War* 31). O'Byrne underscores the fact that writing was considered an appropriate profession for women, with women's writing even encouraged by the Sección Femenina (see *Post-War* 32–33).

Laforet wrote *Nada* from the age of twenty-two to twenty-four. Like the protagonist of *Nada*, she arrived in Barcelona at eighteen to stay with her

---

7 Nino Kebadze, *Romance and Exemplarity in Post-War Spanish Women's Narratives: Fictions of Surrender* (Suffolk: Tamesis, 2009), 12. For more on the way the Sección Femenina navigated the limits of women's roles and potentially exceeded them, see Jo Labanyi, "Resemanticizing Feminine Surrender: Cross-Gender Identifications in the Writings of Spanish Female Fascist Activists," chapter 5 in *Women's Narrative and Film in 20th-Century Spain*, ed. Ofelia Ferrán and Kathleen Gleen (London: Routledge, 2002), 75–92.

8 See Patricia O'Byrne, *Post-War Spanish Women Novelists and the Recuperation of Historical Memory* (Suffolk: Tamesis, 2014), 121.

extended family in a chaotic, repressive environment on Calle de Aribau where she felt trapped inside and nearly always hungry.[9] Many of her acquaintances and friends would have their calques in *Nada*. Laforet met Xavier Zubiri, translator of Jean Thibaud's *Vida y transmutación de los átomos*, and became friends with his wife, Carmen Castro Madinabeitia in 1940 (Caballé and Rolón Barada 116). Like her protagonist Andrea, she would leave Barcelona for Madrid. Though she was far less of a public figure than Norah Lange, her treatment by the press was not so different. In the prologue to their biography of Laforet, Anna Caballé and Israel Rolón Barada note: "No hay entrevista de los años cuarenta o cincuenta que no pondere el hermoso rostro de la escritora, su melena rubio oscuro, su expresiva mirada, su belleza singular y modernísima" (Not a single interview from the '40s or '50s fails to reflect on the writer's lovely face, her dark blond mane, her expressive gaze, her singular and ever so modern beauty) (17). Throughout her life, she avoided interviews and public appearances, and was judged to be *una mujer rara* for her rejection of public life: "Ella, en fuga permanente, no hizo más que acrecentar su leyenda de mujer enigmática. Así la consideraba Josep Vergés y así se lo dijo al periodista Lluís Permanyer cuando éste le pidió su dirección para remitirle el 'Cuestionario Proust' que publicaba semanalmente en la revista *Destino*: 'Ni lo intentes, es una mujer muy rara. A todo dice que no'" (Her permanent state of flight only made her more legendary as an enigmatic women. That was the view Josep Vergés offered to journalist Lluís Permanyer when he asked for her address to send her the "Proust Questionnaire" that he published weekly in the magazine *Destino*: "Don't even try it, she's a very strange woman. She says no to everything") (Caballé and Rolón Barada 20). Before turning to her also strange protagonist, the prototypical chica rara, I outline some of the scientific ideas surrounding perception that circulated at the time, particularly Uexküll's, which were promoted widely in Spain.

Perception

To think about perception as an experience that shapes gender, and gendered survival in particular, I look to Jakob von Uexküll's biosemiotic theories. His works were translated into Spanish, promoted by José Ortega y Gasset, and extensively reviewed in Spanish-language newspapers and journals. He wrote for scientists and lay readers alike. According to Uexküll, each creature experiences life from its particular Umwelt, internalizing the elements of its environment necessary to its survival. Uexküll applies this rule to all

---

9 Anna Caballé and Israel Rolón Barada, *Carmen Laforet: Una mujer en fuga* (Barcelona: RBA, 2010), 105.

animal species, including humans, positing a divinely ordered harmony of Umwelten whose coordination means that all individuals of all species can exist in their distinct worlds side by side. Uexküll's theory got at the way that individuals interact with their environments through all five senses, bringing to the fore questions of what we need to perceive to survive and what possibilities of perception are foreclosed by our position as a certain kind of subject.[10]

Uexküll's works published in Spain include *Cartas biológicas a una dama* (Biological letters to a lady, 1925, published as part of the Nuevos Hechos, Nuevas Ideas [New facts, new ideas] series by Revista de Occidente) and *Ideas para una concepción biológica del mundo* (Ideas for a biological conception of the world, first published by Espasa-Calpe in 1922), as well as shorter pieces published in the *Revista de Occidente* and elsewhere.[11] As scientist Teófilo Ortega observed in the *Revista del Ateneo* in 1930, "Las ideas para una concepción biológica del mundo, de von Uexküll, son tan corrientes y familiares para cualquier curioso lector, que nadie puede atribuir a simulación de autoridad científica el hecho de hacerle concurrir a este enjambre de simples observaciones" (Von Uexküll's ideas for a biological view of the world are so widespread and familiar to any curious reader that no one can be accused of feigning scientific expertise for citing this set of simple observations).[12] This is to say that this scientific and philosophical concept reached a wide range of lay readers and thinkers and might productively be incorporated into discourses on public and private space and the importance of how individuals interact with their environments: a concern of pedagogues, physicians, politicians, and others—a concern with gendered inflections that women in public, urban space are often made to embody.

---

10 A very different scientific concept, the Heisenberg uncertainty principle, introduced in 1927, also brings the question of observation to the fore. It explains that the more precisely we know the position of a particle, the less precisely we can know its momentum. However, much like the theory of relativity (see chapter 2), the Heisenberg uncertainty principle seems to have been too technically complex to have rooted itself in the popular imagination with quite as much vigor as Umwelten. It may have helped that readers did not need to depend on scientists, journalists, or others to translate Uexküll's ideas for a lay audience: he himself wrote quite consciously for those without training in scientific disciplines.

11 See Uexküll, *Cartas biológicas a una dama*, trans. Manuel G. Morente (Madrid: Revista de Occidente, 1945); Uexküll, *Ideas para una concepción biológica del mundo*, trans. R. M. Tenreiro (Buenos Aires / Madrid: Espasa-Calpe, 1934); and Uexküll, "La biología de la ostra jacobea," *Revista de Occidente* 9 (1924): 291–331.

12 Teófilo Ortega, "El espejo y el camino," *Revista del Ateneo* 54 (1930): 128.

Mundos circundantes: Uexküll on mind and matter

As microscopic discoveries broke down matter into cellular units and knowledge of atomic theory became commonplace, the place of humans alongside inorganic matter and within the universe came into question. Rather suddenly, people were circulating as organized groups of atoms, whose organization (man rather than monkey, man rather than plant or lamppost) might seem random or unstable. Evolution and natural selection arising from random mutation similarly disturbed settled orders and provoked rethinkings of people's relation to their environment, as we will see in chapter 4. Uexküll was particularly put off by the randomness he saw in Darwinism, of which he had once been a proponent, preferring instead the idea of "coordination," which comes close to a divine order that makes possible the harmonious coexistence of the many Umwelten, or "mundos circundantes." As he puts it, "En estos últimos decenios hanse persuadido los hombres, de manera fantástica, que no existe coordinación en el mundo y que el mundo es el ciego juego de átomos inánimes" (In recent decades, men have convinced themselves, in a fantastical manner, that there is no coordination in the world and that it is a blind game of lifeless atoms), claiming that "[l]a salvación se encuentra en la biología exacta, que devuelve al individuo su más peculiar propiedad: su mundo circundante" (salvation is to be found in exact biology, which returns to individuals their most particular property: their self-centered world) (Uexküll, *Cartas* 149–50).[13] While the existence and nature of atoms might have been a settled matter among scientists, the implications of an atomic worldview were clearly not.

In *Cartas biológicas a una dama*, Uexküll explains to the lay reader—the lady reader, in fact—the tenets of his theory through sections on sounds, colors, time, space, shape, the self-centered world, origin, species, the family, the state, coordination, and spirit. He insists on the perfect harmony of nature, extending a music metaphor to explain the beautiful melody of biological coordination, with every being perfectly adapted to its environment. In his famous example of the tick, later taken up by Agamben, Uexküll explains that the tick's survival depends on its perception of its surrounding environment, specifically on its ability to sense the exact temperature of the blood of mammals. This arrangement means that the tick's world

---

13 Originally published in German in 1920, this work has not been translated into English; all translations are mine. One of the results of this drive to discover an organized scheme was the success of pieces such as those by Eddington and Scheler, who were also translated and published in Spanish and appeared repeatedly in the *Revista de Occidente*—works I have discussed in previous chapters.

is entirely different from that of the deer or dog it may land on. It has different needs and so it senses differently and is differently oriented toward its surroundings. The many self-centered worlds are different perceptual universes, each one allowing for a species' perfect relationship with its environment and thus its ability to survive.

Man—in addition to animals—"está situado dentro de un mundo perceptible correspondiente a sus capacidades" (is situated within a sensory world corresponding to his abilities) (Uexküll, *Ideas* 116). According to Uexküll, this is what defines a creature's understanding of the world through the internalization of stimuli and resultant production of a model of the world that necessarily varies by species. Yet all of these internalized worlds fit together in perfect harmony, which is for him proof of divine coordination. In *Cartas biológicas a una dama*, this all leads up to the question: "¿[E]s realmente esta época apta para buscar en la coordinación la esencia de lo viviente?" (Is this epoch truly apt for seeking in coordination the essence of the living?) (Uexküll, *Cartas* 159). His affirmative answer indicates his philosophical orientation toward a harmonious spirit of coordination that not only sets each animal in perfect congruence with its self-centered world but also synchronizes all of the Umwelten of all creatures in the universe. Uexküll considers his work philosophically important not because of the mode of relation between humans and the objects that surround them—though that is something that I want to consider here—but because knowledge of the Umwelten of animals, to which we must, he believes, grant equal legitimacy, makes it impossible to consider the universe only as humans perceive it (see Uexküll, "La biología" 330–31). Instead, we must confront a multiplicity of spaces, times, and objects that define our shared world, which must "constituir una nueva base para la filosofía" (constitute a new basis for philosophy) (Uexküll, "La biología" 331).

Uexküll focuses on sensory perception to describe the way that creatures interact with their Umwelten. A particularly illustrative example is that of color: "El sujeto recibe estímulos, a los que responde con sensaciones de color. Traslada estas sensaciones hacia afuera, y viste el objeto con cualidades de color" (The subject receives stimuli, which it responds to with sensations of color. It transfers these sensations outward, and it dresses the object with the attributes of color) (Uexküll, *Cartas* 27). This dressing of the world describes roughly how the mechanism of Umwelten functions, with an emphasis on the active construction of the self-centered world. "La Naturaleza consiste en objetos, y cada objeto tanto es un producto de nuestra vida anímica como también la causa de esta producción. Como recordamos, son puros grupos de estímulos materiales los que actúan sobre nosotros. Son convertidos por nosotros en objetos, y estos objetos son concebidos como causas de estímulos situados fuera de nosotros" (Nature consists of objects, and each object is both a product of our psychic life and the cause of that production. As we can recall, what acts on us are purely groupings of material stimuli. They are converted by us into objects, and those objects are understood as causes of stimuli situated outside of us) (Uexküll, *Ideas* 119–20). In *Cartas biológicas a una dama*, Uexküll explains in great detail how this material stimulation works upon us to produce the objects we seem to observe passively such that we are "creando sin cesar unidades con que poblamos el mundo" (endlessly creating units with which we populate the world) (65). That species create objects and entities out of groups of stimuli means that objects are different for each species: "Gracias a ello, la misma cosa se convierte en dos cosas diferentes" (Due to which the same thing becomes two different things) (Uexküll, *Teoría de la vida* 154). This understanding of the world as made up of groupings of stimuli that result in different objects depending on the observer will allow for an opening through which the chica rara's oblique mode of observation may allow her to create unexpected objects for her survival. My interest in the psycho-social implications of Uexküll's biological theory is not at odds with how contemporaries read his work; indeed, Uexküll himself ventured views on the nonbiological effects of humans' surroundings.

While Uexküll's view is not anthropocentric, he does reflect on the specificity of human experience. Though humans do not passively internalize the objects around them, Uexküll still views changes to their environment as potentially threatening, and the city is a particular concern of his. He speaks quite literally of the horizon as circumscribing the Umwelt of humans— we perceive our world only so far as the eye can see. He points out that technologies such as the microscope have shifted the boundaries of our self-centered worlds; he must also have had in mind that the urban landscape changes them radically. If our view of the horizon is cut off by a tall building, our world might seem to have shrunk, and yet urban experience confirms that the cityscape continues always just around the corner. This creates a clash between what we perceive and what we know to be true and useful to survival. Uexküll notes the potential danger of the passive self in the world, which he says is a particularly urban threat: "Aun es más peligroso cuando se abandona la propia formación de objetos y nos contentamos con el resonar de los esquemas" (It is even more dangerous when the formation of objects itself is left behind and we content ourselves with the echo of schema) (*Ideas* 129). This impoverishment of our surroundings runs counter to the mutually constructive interaction we naturally have with the objects around us.

Uexküll's preoccupation with the atrophying of humans' productive relationship with objects is telling. To him, the inorganic objects that distinguish the city are mere shadows of their country cousins. However, it is not that inorganic objects are of a different nature; after all, sensory perception should handle them identically, and Uexküll lists them side by side when naming the few things a city dweller apparently comes in contact with: "El mundo que logran ver en un paseo sólo se componen de tres o cuatro objetos: camino, árbol, casa, perro" (The world that they manage to see during a stroll is made up of three or four objects: path, tree, house, dog) (*Ideas* 130). Instead, explaining the impoverishment of the object-life of urban centers, Uexküll comments on flashy advertisements as signs of our weakened capacity for interacting with objects (reduced as we are to recognizing their outlines as calls to buy) and writes of city inhabitants and their surroundings: "Ya no se llega, en modo alguno, a la plena formación de cada objeto. Tan pronto como suena un esquema, ya no se preocupan más del objeto, sino que pasan inmediatamente al pensar abstracto" (The full formation of objects is no longer achieved. As soon as a schema is familiar, they no longer concern themselves with the object but instead move on immediately to abstract thought) (*Ideas* 130). In his view, abstract thought is in some way inferior to the psycho-sensorial engagement that results in individuals' perceiving objects in their surroundings. He sets up a visceral experience of the material world that is more in tune with truth and beauty, as we will see below, but also one that is closer to the way that other species' experience their surroundings. These reflections on humans' propensity for abstraction moves his argument about perception away from the purely biological and its sets the stage for philosophical reflections on how humans relate to their surroundings.

In *Ideas para una concepción biológica del mundo*, Uexküll directly addresses Ernst Haeckel's monism—which we saw in chapter 1—decrying its approach to the material world as the arbiter of the spiritual one.[14] If, he claims, we follow such a tack, "muy pronto queda finiquitado lo 'verdadero, bello y bueno'" (the "true, beautiful, and good" will be soon wiped out) (Uexküll,

---

14 Uexküll couches his critique of Haeckel in the strongest of terms and in personal attacks: "Haeckel quiere suplantar esta concepción [biológica] del mundo con sus galimatías de célula de alma y alma de célula, y cree aniquilar con sus salidas de chicuelo al gigantesco Kant. Las palabras de Chamberlain sobre el haeckelianismo: 'No es ni poesía, ni ciencia, ni filosofía, sino un bastardo de las tres, nacido muerto', están grabados en el alma de todo hombre ilustrado" (Haeckel wants to replace this [biological] conception of the world with his gibberish about the cell of the soul and the soul of the cell, and he thinks his boyish quips can wipe out someone of the gigantic stature of Kant. Chamberlain's words on Haeckelism—"It is not poetry, science, or philosophy, but rather a still-born bastard of all three"—are etched in the soul of all educated men) (*Ideas* 128).

Ideas 109). According to him, the divine soul as organizing principle is forced to cede to the mechanized reign of material things, which takes the spiritual as yet another moving part it has produced. It is doubtful that Haeckel would agree with Uexküll's characterization of his work, though it is true that he followed the path of Darwin. Nonetheless, Uexküll's critique of monism is useful for understanding that what was at stake for him was not just how animals sensed their environments but how and to what end the material world was organized—and the complications that human perception introduce.

The idea of worlds specific to a species is not limited to Uexküll. Santiago Ramón y Cajal, writing on "Las sensaciones de las hormigas" (The sensations of ants) in an article published in the *Archivos de Neurobiología* in December 1921, refers to the world as perceived by ants as "un mundo aparte, específico, fundamentalmente diverso del nuestro, salvo la comunidad de ciertas propiedades geométricas y de determinadas emanaciones materiales" (a world apart, a specific world that is fundamentally distinct from our own, except for the commonality of certain geometrical properties and certain material emanations).[15] These separate worlds—of ants, ticks, men, and women—are tailored not to the individual but to the species. Neither Uexküll nor Ramón y Cajal would argue that one ant's sense of vision or touch differs from that of another ant with the goal of providing each one with a greater chance of psycho-social survival given its specific circumstance. For someone like Uexküll, the divine and spiritual are likely meant to attend to any needs unmet by securing shelter and a food source. Yet his reflections on the particularity of urban environments and the shifting meanings of objects for humans can lead us to reflect further on how individuals survive. He notes that an object, such as a stone, has no single *significación* but rather changes based on its relation with a subject: if someone picks up a stone from the road to throw at a dog that stands threateningly in his path, the stone's significance changes—it is no longer a part of the road but instead becomes a projectile.[16] And it is certainly a different kind of object for the dog from the kind it is for the stone thrower. Similarly, the urban landscape of a novel like *Nada*—or a cultural object that becomes imbued with significance for a queer community, as in Eve Kosofsky Sedgwick's work, which I will discuss below—might point to modes of perception, of sensing, that are available to individuals and that shape their survival within the species.

---

15 Santiago Ramón y Cajal, "Las sensaciones de las hormigas," *Archivos de Neurobiología* 2, no. 4 (1921), 15–16.
16 Jakob von Uexküll, *Meditaciones biológicas: La teoría de la significación*, trans. José M. Sacristán (Madrid: Revista de Occidente, 1942).

Not only did Uexküll posit that considering the world from a nonhuman perspective was key, but he also suggested that it should constitute a new basis for philosophy. As Agamben notes: "Uexküll's investigations into the animal environment are contemporary with both quantum physics and the artistic avant-gardes. And like them, they express the unreserved abandonment of every anthropocentric perspective in the life sciences and the radical dehumanization of the image of nature."[17] Dehumanizing the image of nature, or rather how we imagine it, may require quite a bit of discursive work, however: Agamben notes that the drawings with which Uexküll illustrates his books depicting the perceptual worlds of other species are fruitfully disorienting, but he particularly values the scientist's lengthy description of the tick's world, a description that Agamben argues "certainly constitutes a high point of modern antihumanism" (45). But despite Uexküll's ability to describe the mechanisms of the tick's world, it remains impossible for us to experience those other worlds.

Our inability to know other Umwelten veils the world around us. Teófilo Ortega writes in the *Revista del Ateneo*: "En torno nuestro y sobre nuestras cabezas, hay algo que desconocemos, que no podemos ni siquiera expresar. [...] ¿Hasta dónde llegaría su pensamiento si desde tan encumbrada posición apunta?" (Around us and above our heads, there is something that we are ignorant of, that we cannot even express. [...] Where might his thought reach if it aims from such lofty heights?) (129). Ortega cites Uexküll at length as he wonders what the world might be like considered though the rich accumulation of all its many Umwelten. He urges readers to examine their own self-centered worlds but also consider the existence of the unknowable world around them. Agamben also picks up on this unknowability, noting: "Though the spider can in no way see the *Umwelt* of the fly (Uexküll affirms—and thus formulates a principle that would have some success—that 'no animal can enter into relation with an object as such,' but only with its own carriers of significance), the web expresses the paradoxical coincidence of this reciprocal blindness" (42). Thus while creatures sense and interact with stimuli to the degree that they can perceive them out of a need to survive, they are cut off from perceiving those same external things as other creatures do. I would read this unknowability structuring Umwelten as echoed by the unseen power of the secret language of women's experience noted by Laforet. If we consider this secret world as a sort of women's Umwelt, Laforet not only posits that men cannot access it

---

17 Giorgio Agamben, *The Open: Man and Animal*, trans. Kevin Attell (Stanford: Stanford University Press, 2004), 39. We might recall the avant-garde experimentation of Lange's writing and milieu explored in chapter 2.

but also raises the question of whether women can speak of or even fully sense the way that they must interact with the external world. Indeed, Uexküll might alert us to the existence of a human Umwelt, but he can only describe its processes and results; our creation of it is an activity that goes largely unsensed. The narrator of *Nada* struggles to sense and express the way she is internalizing and creating the world around her, but she invites the reader to do the interpretive work of reading the accumulated stimuli she encounters to try to understand her perceptual world even when she declares that she carried nothing of that world with her, and then relenting: "así creía yo entonces."

I am thus dually concerned with Andrea's remarks on her sensorial perception of the material world around her, which I interpret as a sort of individualized Umwelt (rather than one common to the species), and with how her observations in the narrative point to the effects of living at the center of a secret, not exclusively material, gendered world that she neither sees nor knowingly articulates. This extrapolation based on Uexküll's suggestive work is not unprecedented: José Ortega y Gasset not only promoted Uexküll's writing in Spanish translation, he cited its influence on his own work.

Reading Umwelten

It seems entirely plausible that José Ortega y Gasset's reflections on *circunstancia* in his 1914 *Meditaciones del Quijote* are inspired in part by his knowledge of Uexküll's *mundo circundante*. An August 4, 1925, book review on page 2 of *El Sol* (signed G. C.) of *Ideas para una concepción biológica del mundo* notes that any reader of Ortega y Gasset will be familiar with Uexküll's name and that Ortega y Gasset "llegó a confesar que una gran copia de sus ideas se debe a la sugestión de este germánico biólogo" (even confessed that a great many of his ideas are due to the influence of this German biologist). In the passages on circunstancia, Ortega y Gasset cites biology as now studying "el organismo vivo como una unidad compuesta del cuerpo y su medio particular" (the living organism as a unit composed of the body and its particular surroundings).[18] Thus, he explains, life is not just a question of the body adapting to its environment but of the environment adapting to a body (see Ortega y Gasset 43). He goes on: "La mano procura amoldarse al objeto material a fin de apresarlo bien; pero, a la vez, cada objeto material oculta una previa afinidad con una mano determinada. Yo soy yo y mi circunstancia, y si no la salvo a ella no me salvo yo" (The hand seeks to mold

---

18 José Ortega y Gasset, *Meditaciones del Quijote* (Madrid: Residencia de Estudiantes, 1914), 43.

itself to the material object so as to grasp it firmly; but, at the same time, each material object conceals a previous affinity for a specific hand. I am myself and my circumstance, and if I do not save it, I do not save myself) (43–44). Paying attention to our surroundings, to the things around us, so that we might take them in and absorb them is an urgent matter for Ortega y Gasset not just because "[e]l hombre rinde el máximo de su capacidad cuando adquiere la plena conciencia de sus circunstancias" (man makes the most of his abilities when he is fully aware of his circumstances), but because he believes that "uno de los cambios más hondos del siglo actual con respecto al siglo XIX, va a consistir en la mutación de nuestra sensibilidad para las circunstancias" (one of the most profound changes of the current century in comparison to the nineteenth century is going to consist in the shift in our sensitivity toward our circumstances) (34–35, 37). Where for Uexküll our self-centered worlds operate equally whether we consider them as such or not, for Ortega y Gasset, attention to our surrounding objects and the knowledge that our lives are molded by the specificity of our worlds may indeed result in a better and more conscientious life.

He further maintains that it is important to reflect on what we find around us while being careful to "no confundir lo grande y lo pequeño" (not confuse the great and the small) and maintaining a sense of hierarchy so as not to descend into chaos (34).[19] I argue that what might be thought of as the minutiae of our surroundings looms much larger if we base our understanding of hierarchy on Uexküll's nonanthropocentric vision. Skin temperature might seem a small thing, and might not enter at all into Ortega y Gasset's understanding of our surroundings, but for the tick Uexküll studies it is a matter of survival and even more immediately determines the tick's movements through the world. Accepting and even seeking a chaos of details may draw us to otherwise overlooked objects and moments that orient lives and permit survival. This is the mutation of our readerly sensibility that I argue should drive us in considering Andrea and other chicas raras.

Uexküll's tone is frequently celebratory: it is a beautiful, divinely ordained system that allows all creatures to live in harmony. This attitude is not unlike Ortega y Gasset's inclination that we can live better if properly attuned to our circumstance. Survival seems to carry with it the implicit assumption of happiness: an alive tick is a happy tick. Or perhaps what comes through

---

19 Ortega y Gasset was largely responsible for Uexküll's Peninsular presence. For an extensive look at Ortega y Gasset's relationship with Uexküll's thought and other contemporary science, see Manuel Benavides Lucas's *De la ameba al monstruo propicio: Raíces naturalistas del pensamiento de Ortega y Gasset* (Madrid: University Autónoma de Madrid, 1988).

in Uexküll's texts is not the happiness of all animals but his own: he seems pleased with the whole arrangement and it is a contagious sort of pleasure, making it easy to imagine that ticks and spiders and humans are best off and therefore content in this way. Yet despite his insistence that humans are just one more species in this global network, his concerns about urban living do something to belie this view. Uexküll is concerned that, overstimulated in cities, we do not fully form objects based on the stimuli we receive, as we should. Instead, we jump to abstract ideas, which place us in impoverished worlds. Let us recall that for Uexküll a nonanthropocentric view of the world should form the basis of a new philosophy and *we* receive "groupings of material stimuli" that *we* "convert into objects" with which *we* populate the world. I take his comments on our poor object formation in cities as a point of departure for thinking about Umwelt and Andrea's strange, gendered perceptual world in *Nada*.

Are all Umwelten successful Umwelten? Are all successful Umwelten happy Umwelten? In this chapter, I use Umwelt to focus on the role of perception in the construction of gender and to contemplate gendered survival, but I might have used it to frame everything that I am calling "the felt experience of gender." Which then might raise the question of whether that experience is to be understood as affective/social/political/bodily success or failure. As optimistic or pessimistic? As disorienting? As queer? Robyn Wiegman's "The Times We're In: Queer Feminist Criticism and the 'Reparative' Turn" considers queer feminist engagements with Sedgwick's categories of paranoid and reparative reading as reflective of critics' drive to establish value for their interpretive work.[20] For Wiegman, the paranoid and the reparative are twinned rather than estranged (with contemporary practices of both carried out by Judith Butler and Eve Kosofsky Sedgwick in the mid-1990s), and the constant in the many different affective and theoretical approaches to objects is the value we place on that very relationship: reading cultural objects (be they novels or ephemeral performances) is important. As Wiegman puts it, paranoid and reparative reading share "an emphatic and [...] empathetic attachment to *interpretation* as a self and world enhancing necessity" (18–19; emphasis in original). She writes of such reading as motivated by her relationship with her mother, who was diagnosed as bipolar. I too have an investment in interpretation, a drive to queer feminist reading practices. I take from Wiegman that there is productive work to be done in examining our connection to objects whether or not the resultant relationship seems to be a successful one or not.

20 Robyn Wiegman, "The Times We're In: Queer Feminist Criticism and the 'Reparative' Turn," *Feminist Theory* 15, no. 1 (2014): 7.

As to how that connection is formed in light of Uexküll's thought, I would like to underscore a series of concerns he raises. From Uexküll's music metaphors and his language of coordination, harmony, and beauty, we must consider aesthetics as related to survival. From his treatment of the urban environment, we see that humans face specific challenges that may inhibit a deep and meaningful interaction with their surroundings: in this, he views humans as special (ants or other creatures living in the city do not seem to face the same issue). We also see that he privileges immediate, sensory perception, which allows us to form the objects that permit our survival, over abstract thought that may unfold from our perceptions. While humans are unique, they also share in and benefit from a visceral experience of the world.

A single thing—a grouping of stimuli—can become multiple different things depending on how it is perceived and used by different species. We are surrounded by meaning that escapes us, that is meant for other species' survival but not our own. Moreover, sensory perception creates a link between subject and object, which raises the question of how we become objects for others. Uexküll offers a disorienting view in that we are effectively excluded from the worlds of others, and so while the net effect of many worlds may be harmony, the immediate result is utter unknowability and estrangement from others' worlds. This experience of mutual exclusion may be a productive framing for Laforet's conception of a secret women's language and experience, one contained in a shared world but separate from it and inaccessible from outside of it, with literature and language tethered to that outside.

In *Nada* we find an individual who seems to see things in a way that others do not and who must figure out how others see her and how she is affected by becoming an object in their worlds. I am also interested in how she perceives objects that change her world and maybe change her significance or meaning in the worlds of others. I suggest that she perceives her surroundings in such a way that they allow her to survive in her rareza. Before delving more deeply into the novel, I turn to what makes Andrea a chica rara and what that has to do with her construction of a self-centered world that can sustain her.

Rareza and queer survival

Martín Gaite acknowledged the novelty of Laforet's portrayal of Andrea, calling her—and the female authors of novels that broke with the novela rosa tradition—chicas raras.[21] While the novela rosa, romantic genre fiction

---

21 See Carmen Martín Gaite, *Desde la ventana: Enfoque femenino de la literatura española* (Madrid: Espasa-Calpe, 1987).

aimed at a female audience, enjoyed huge popular success in postwar Spain, a new tradition of unconventional protagonists would take off: "De ahora en adelante, las nuevas protagonistas de la novela femenina, capitaneadas por el ejemplo de Andrea, se atreverán a desafinar, a instalarse en la marginación y a pensar desde ella" (Henceforth, the new protagonists of women's novels, led by the example of Andrea, would dare to be off key, to live in marginalization and think from there) (Martín Gaite 100). While a few scholars have demonstrated with against-the-grain readings of novelas rosa their potential for subverting traditional gender norms, the out-of-step, marginal existence of the chicas raras brought any such rebellion into much sharper relief.[22] I suggest that we think of the chica rara as living in and thinking from the margin, and as experiencing a strange femininity in the process. I am not interested in declaring Andrea a queer protagonist per se, but I do think that certain concepts that have emerged out of queer theory are helpful for analyzing gender in *Nada*. Indeed, the concept of rareza in general alongside the chicas raras whose strangeness is gendered in particular might provide an antidote to the slide toward declaring everything and everyone potentially queer with a flattening of difference and dissidence in the process. When I discuss queer survival below, I am acknowledging an overlap and potential relationship between queerness and rareza: femininity experienced as strange may sometimes be queer, but it may also exceed understandings of queerness and even suggest new directions that contemporary theorizations of gender and sexuality might take.

Keeping in mind the formative nature of Umwelten, I suggest that strange femininity arises from how we interact with the world around us—any negative valence, the shiver caused by strangeness, might be said to result from the ways that these young women conflict with gendered expectations. As readers, we perceive one thing when we were expecting something else. One such clash has to do with women's surroundings: it was Martín Gaite who observed how these peripheral young women relate to the spaces they find themselves in, citing as a common characteristic of chicas raras the inability to remain enclosed in private, indoor spaces typically thought of as safe for or assigned to women (see Martín Gaite 101–102). The street becomes highly attractive, whether the chicas raras are able to walk along it or must content themselves with looking at it through a window (as is the case for what Martín Gaite terms the "mujer ventanera"—*Personas en la sala* might

---

22 For more on the novela rosa as an overlooked genre marked by subversive possibility, see Patricia O'Byrne, "Popular Fiction in Postwar Spain: The Soothing, Subversive *Novela Rosa*," *Journal of Romance Studies* 8, no. 2 (2008): 37–57.

be said to present a very peculiar *mujer ventanera*) (102). Aunt Angustias sets out a gendered expectation when she warns Andrea that "[u]na joven en Barcelona debe ser como una fortaleza" ("a young girl in Barcelona must be like a fortress") (Laforet 23, [15]). And yet a strange frisson makes itself felt when Andrea and the reader find that safe, protective enclosed spaces and subjectivities are nowhere to be found in the novel—certainly not in the old family home—and this projection of a guarded femininity ensuring survival with strong, high walls dissolves against the reality Andrea faces. And so, *Nada* leads us to question the strict division between house and street, between public and private, and between masculine and feminine. That said, instead of examining such binaries—or even their collapse—I am more interested in looking at how strange young women become strange young women through their perception of the multiple spaces and objects around them.

For another approach to what is "queer" or strange about *Nada* and its chica rara protagonist, it may be helpful to recall my discussion in chapter 1 of Katherine Bond Stockton's description of childhood as a space queered by expectations of innocence. The imposition of gender narratives, and that of femininity in particular, might be seen to effect a similar queerness particularly for those individuals who find that their gendered experiences run up violently against those expectations. At the same time, I look to Laforet's letter to Sender on her desire for a language that would express the unspoken phenomenon of women's experience. I would like to add to this reflection on queer and strange femininity the question of survival, as taken up by Eve Kosofsky Sedgwick, and contemplate Umwelt as a way of reading survival via our perception of our surroundings.

Queer survival

In "Queer and Now,"[23] Eve Kosofsky Sedgwick looks at queer survival and how it is made possible by affective attachments to objects read queerly, perceived in such a way that they take on special significance for queer individuals or communities. Citing the incredibly high rates of suicide attempts in the late 1980s among LGBTQ youth, Sedgwick explains that queer survival means "surviving *into* threat, stigma, the spiraling violence of gay- and lesbian-bashing, and (in the AIDS emergency) the omnipresence of somatic fear and wrenching loss. It is also to have survived into a moment of unprecedented cultural richness, cohesion, and assertiveness for many lesbian and gay adults" (3). She writes that

---

23 Eve Kosofsky Sedgwick, "Queer and Now," in *Tendencies* (London: Routledge, 1994), 1–19.

it was in many cases attachments to cultural objects—"objects whose meaning seemed mysterious, excessive, or oblique in relation to the codes most readily available to us"—that permitted queer children and youth to survive into adulthood (Sedgwick 3). She explains that interest in, love of, fascination with, and attention to certain objects can facilitate survival. I build on Sedgwick's argument by focusing on the role of perception: this affective investment requires perceiving objects in a particular way, seeing that they offer something that normative readings of that same object do not reveal.

Andrea, the young protagonist of *Nada*, supposes that she was born for "un pequeño y ruin papel de espectadora" ("a small, miserable role as spectator") (163, [184]). I will argue that what her spectatorship allows her is to perceive her surroundings in an unusual way, creating affective investments that permit her to develop a femininity that does not conform to contemporary gender roles. While Laforet wrote that she failed in creating a language that would reflect the "mundo del Gineceo"—the truth of women's social experience that could not find expression in the borrowed language of men—I will look to the language of the novel as giving us a glimpse into this perceptual world that is ordinarily occluded. I will explore how the net effect of affective illegibility arises from a confusion of physical and psychological elements and drives (from hunger to beauty to ghostly furniture to the street), and how Andrea's role as spectator defines her femininity, how her watching in turn defines the objects and relations around her, and how they become the "notas" or "marks" (to use Uexküll's term) that define her psychic world. The novel deals with Andrea's struggles to find the intellectual, emotional, and social experiences to help her survive in a family that seems intent on sapping her of food, warmth, and reason. She struggles, not unlike the scientific observer, to make sense of chaotic surroundings. It is not enough to say that she is shaped by her environment, a diagnosis that might have fit in earlier naturalist novels; instead, Laforet insists on making us aware of how our surroundings work their way into our subjectivities and how our choices, or gendered limitations—not being allowed to walk alone in the street at night, for example—inflect that process. I also ask how the novel treats people as objects of significance and meaning for other people. I propose that Andrea's mode of perception creates attachments to her urban environment that ultimately allow for her survival into chaos, violence, and limitation.

Andrea in the self-centered city

Laforet opens her novel with an epigraph, a fragment of a poem by Juan Ramón Jiménez: "A veces un gusto amargo, / Un olor malo, una rara / Luz, un tono desacorde, / Un contacto que desgana, / Como realidades fijas / Nuestros sentidos alcanzan / Y nos parece que son / La verdad no sospechada..." ("Sometimes a bitter taste / A foul smell, a strange / Light, a discordant tone, / A disinterested touch / Come to our five senses / Like fixed realities / And they seem to us to be / The unsuspected truth..."). The poem touches on each of the five senses: where it might first appear that there is "nothing" of note, or where our senses receive a strange, unsettling, unpleasant stimulus, we may find the unexpected truth of things. While Laforet declared herself unable to elaborate a feminine language to speak of the secret truth of women's experiences, I read her book as guiding her readers to moments of sensing and perception that might seem to lack importance but in fact contain the truths of a young woman's world in construction. While *Nada* has much more of a plot than *Personas*, for example, and there is some mystery regarding the family members' pasts that propels the story forward, the bulk of the textual material exceeds the narrative. The text itself is strange: Laforet creates a quotidian flow of dialogue that includes fragments, interruptions, and interjections. Where narrative falls short, descriptions evoke Andrea's sensorial world to try to get at the ways in which strangely felt moments are not incidental but instead pivotal in orienting us in the world as gendered beings.

Andrea arrives in Barcelona to stay with extended family and attend university. Coming from a small town, she hopes the city will provide freedom and excitement but also a warm welcome in the family home she only vaguely recalls from her childhood. Throughout her year in the postwar city, she will take on the role of spectator and sometimes mediator, both in the streets and among her family and newfound friends—her mere presence subtly altering the way of things in an urban experience that seems far removed from the liberating possibilities she had hoped for. What emerges in the text alongside a record of privation and confusion is a parallel narrative documenting her desirous, dreamlike experience of the city, which more closely approximates what she hoped for upon her arrival in Barcelona. In scenes of household chaos and of urban wandering, she becomes a piece of something larger, from the very moment of her arrival at the train station where she is "una gota entre la corriente" ("a drop in the current") (Laforet 13, [3]). Not only does she become an element of this urban experience, but her own *significación* also shifts as she becomes an object in relation to the city, the street, and the members of her extended family. In the process, the dichotomy of public and private will become confused, with the city providing the solace that the dysfunctional, violent family home precludes, and the realms of house and street will break down and their characters, sounds, and sentiments will bleed into one another.[24]

While many readings of *Nada* have tended to emphasize the distinction between interior spaces and the city, the house and the street, Valeria de Marco resists this division in her 1996 article, "'Nada': El espacio transparente y opaco a la vez." Just as the apparently impulsive and desirous Andrea and the apparently observant, reserved Andrea emerge as an integrated personality from her year in Barcelona, the public/private city spaces, according to De Marco, merge into an indistinguishable whole. At first reading, there is a stark contrast between the delight and desire of the street and the coffin-like depressive darkness and weight of the house (with its "fantasmas," "brujas," "calaveras," [ghosts, witches, skulls] and constant mourning); however, closer attention will break down this apparent divide (quoted in De Marco 62, 74, 62). De Marco reads two strands in the narrative: one that relates Andrea's past to the reader and another that reflects on it (see 62). The result is a past that is not packed away but is instead an ever-present source of anxieties and contradictions that obviate a clear divide between outside and inside, public and private, street and home.

> La tensión narrativa se expresa en múltiples relaciones cambiantes entre opacidad y transparencia: a Andrea le tocaba darse cuenta de que tras la transparencia de las luces de Barcelona también hay muerte y degradación; tras los fantasmas y calaveras del piso hay también huellas de vitalidad; y, sobre todo, le tocaba convivir con la imposibilidad de que el mundo se presentara transparente a su mirada observadora y al lenguaje analítico de la narradora. Le tocaba convivir con la opacidad de las relaciones existentes entre el piso y la ciudad. Por eso la narración consiste en plasmar el lento recorrido de Andrea hacia el descubrimiento de la contigüidad entre los dos espacios y del hecho de que cada uno de ellos late según el ritmo del otro. (De Marco 62)

---

24 Walter Benjamin tells us that the urban street can harbor danger and criminality (as in the detective novel) but also love (as in Baudelaire's "A une passante") and the possibility for art. Early on, he breaks down the binary of inner sanctuary and public threat that so many interpretations of street and city life rush to restore. See Benjamin, *The Writer of Modern Life: Essays on Charles Baudelaire*, ed. Michael W. Jennings, trans. Howard Eiland et al. (Cambridge, MA: Harvard University Press, 2006), 77.

(The narrative tension is expressed in multiple, shifting relationships between opacity and transparency: Andrea must realize that behind the transparency of the lights of Barcelona there is also death and degradation; behind the ghosts and skulls of the apartment, there are also traces of vitality; and, above all, she must live with the fact that the world will not appear transparent before her observing gaze and analytical language. She must live with the opacity of the relationships that exist between the apartment and the city. Therefore, the narration consists of reflecting Andrea's slow path toward discovering the contiguity between those two spaces and the fact that each one pulses with the rhythm of the other.)

What De Marco describes as "opaque" relationships between the house and the city, and more broadly as an opaque world that Andrea finds herself in, I would like to approach as self-centered worlds where expected meanings—transparency associated with vitality—have mutated and objects must be rediscovered in their new forms. Where De Marco refers to the limits that Andrea's observation and analytical language run up against, I focus on her perception and non-narrative sense making. De Marco concludes that the feminine, domestic perspective that shapes the novel contradicts the Francoist conception of the home as the "ambiente Cristiano, sano y armonioso" (Christian, healthy, and harmonious environment) that should represent Spanish society and reveals it instead as an ear (much like Angustias's bedroom) that captures, and re-presents, the tensions of postwar Spanish society (75). The supposedly sacrosanct feminine space of the home is deeply unsettled and seems, as a result, to produce new versions of femininity, but it does so in conjunction with Andrea's role as an observer who sees and relates things in an oblique, novel light.

The marked strangeness of the house and its inhabitants, rather than being distinct from the city, could be said to be "the metonymic expression of Spain."[25] Andrea's aunt, Angustias, provides her anxious religion-laced take on the national situation when she says, "La ciudad, hija mía, es un infierno. Y en toda España no hay una ciudad que se parezca más al infierno que Barcelona" ("Cities, my child, are hell. And in all of Spain no city resembles hell more than Barcelona") (Laforet 22, [14]). Laforet, in letters to Sender, reiterated her preoccupation with this national strangeness—which she stopped short of calling hellish—that she felt paralyzed her work.[26]

---

25 Mirella D'Ambrosio Servodidio, "Spatiality in *Nada*," *Anales de la Narrativa Española Contemporánea* 5 (1980): 59.

26 "Estos días en España son rarísimos. Uno se disuelve como un terrón de azúcar en un vaso de agua. No se hace nada de provecho" (These days in Spain are so strange. One dissolves like a sugar cube in a glass of water. One does nothing of any

Thus, just as *Nada* delves into the coming-of-age tale of a young woman, it depicts a moment of change in Spanish society. One when making sense of one's surroundings and using language to narrate that experience was challenging and potentially dangerous. Alongside the particular strangeness of Andrea's home and family, we may read the more general strangeness and chaos of a postwar society.

One of the most apparent ways to explore Andrea's relationship with the city is to turn to her constant hunger and search for food. After many insufferable meals with her extended family, Andrea chooses to stop contributing money from her allowance to the food budget and instead eat all her meals outside of the house. While this decision allows her a certain freedom, it also inaugurates her most agitated experience of the city. At the beginning of each month, she splurges on flowers for her friend Ena and meals in cheap restaurants for herself. She delights in being able to give something away and spend carelessly—an experience reserved for a select few, particularly after the war. However, she spends much of the month famished and irritable. Food in her world comes to signify only the money it eats up and is stripped of any sustaining quality. She prefers to spend that money on flowers and other gifts. When she has spent all of her allowance on treats for her friends, she leaves the house to sit alone: "[L]a hora del mediodía es la más hermosa en invierno. Una hora buena para pasarla al sol en un parque o en la Plaza de Cataluña" ("Midday is the most beautiful time in winter. A good time to sit in the sun in the park or on the Plaza de Cataluña") (Laforet 93, [100–101]). She seems to be sustained not by the meager food she is able to get but by the affective experience of giving gifts to Ena—a chica rara in her own right—and the aesthetic and sensory one of sitting alone in the city. While Uexküll fretted about humans' jump to abstraction, Andrea makes more extreme leaps as she transforms food and gifts into objects that have unexpected significance.

After one of many fights in the house, Andrea looks out at the street and notes: "Aquel día de Navidad, la calle tenía aspecto de una inmensa

use) (Laforet and Sender 41). "Todas estas cosas que le cuento un poco deslavazadas son para explicarle por qué no puedo hacerle una promesa fija y seria de un viaje. Los viajes, las distancias, desde España son muy largas; parecen grandes cosas llenas de inconvenientes. Algo absurdo. El tiempo también como una cosa a saltos —unas veces da para muchísimo, otras se va sin sentir— y todo es una confusión..." (Everything I'm telling you a bit disjointedly is to explain why I can't make you a serious and certain promise of a trip. Trips, distances, from Spain are very long; they seem like huge things filled with inconveniences. Something ridiculous. Time also goes in leaps—sometimes there's time for so much, other times it slips away without your noticing—and everything is confusion) (Laforet and Sender 60).

pastelería dorada, llena de cosas apetecibles" ("On that Christmas Day the street looked like an immense golden pastry shop full of delicious things") (Laforet 56, [56]). Not only does this observation reflect her yearning to consume the city—traces of which remain until she escapes with Ena's family to Madrid after a year—but it also converts the street into a source of aesthetic sustenance. Andrea does not waste her income on pastries because she particularly likes sweets; she instead likes the feeling of purchasing something frivolous and beautiful. Yet just as her indulgences are necessarily rare—she supplements her meager diet with the tepid leftover water that has been used to boil vegetables—she comes to realize that if her relation with the city is "iluminado por una chispa de belleza" ("illuminated by a spark of beauty"), as when she imagines the squalor of the Barrio Chino, that spark will quickly burn out (Laforet 46, [43]). And in that dim and depressing atmosphere, even her long walks come at a cost: during her wanderings she feels compelled by the old beggar on her street to turn over the few coins and the little food she sometimes has—as she is implicated in a relationship with the other figures in the street, she must pay for it.

It becomes clear that Andrea desires not just adventure and freedom in the city but also beauty, an aesthetic experience that allows her to thrive. After a party at Ena's house, Andrea finds herself feeling at last free in the city and seeking in her slightly drunken nighttime flight through the streets an aesthetic and spiritual beauty that has eluded her in a disappointingly dirty and pedestrian Barcelona: "Yo de pronto me encontré en la calle. Casi había huido impelida por una inquietud tan fuerte y tan inconcreta como todas las que me atormentaban en aquella edad. [...] Aún no estaba segura de lo que podría calmar mejor aquella casi angustiosa *sed de belleza* que me había dejado escuchar a la madre de Ena" ("Suddenly I found myself on the street. I'd almost fled, impelled by a restlessness as strong and unspecified as all the others tormenting me at that age. [...] I still wasn't sure what would do more to calm the almost agonizing *thirst for beauty* that listening to Ena's mother had left in me") (Laforet 85, [92]; emphasis mine). It is only the cathedral that can "calm" and "amaze" her imagination, and, raising her eyes to the façade of the building's impressive architecture, she feels the "peace" and "clarity" of the architecture wash over her. She is captivated by the spell cast by the silent stones of the cathedral until, turning to go, she is surprised by Gerardo, an acquaintance. He chides her for walking the streets late at night alone, and she thinks to herself: "¡Maldito! [...] me has quitado toda la felicidad que me iba a llevar de aquí" ("Damn you! [...] You've robbed me of all the happiness I was going to take away from here") (Laforet 87, [94]). In contrast, when she returns home, she finds a pile of old chairs stacked in her bedroom and signs that her bed has been slept in. As she falls asleep that night, Andrea recounts, "En la agradable confusión de ideas que precede al sueño se fueron calmando mis temores para ser sustituidos por vagas imágenes de calles en la noche. El alto sueño de la Catedral volvió a invadirme" ("In the agreeable confusion of ideas that precedes sleep my fears were abating, replaced by vague images of empty streets at night. The lofty dream of the Cathedral invaded me again") (Laforet 91, [99]). Where her aunt and even her peers view the streets as a danger for a woman alone, she sees something in them that she needs more than even food. There is a push and pull of what people tell her the city is about and what it will do to her, and how she perceives in it. Survival is not just about possessing senses that allow us to find food but about seeking out the affective experience that makes sustaining life possible and worthwhile: the thrill of buying flowers versus the need to drink tepid vegetable water.

The novel's most striking street scene is a nocturnal flight through the city when Andrea chases an enraged Juan through the Barrio Chino as he searches for his wife who has been maintaining both of them by sneaking out to cheat at cards in her sister's bar. It is a hallucinatory journey: Juan seems not to see Andrea even as he doubles back on his path and brushes by her, he brawls with a stranger as the neighborhood cheers them on, and the chase ends at the door of Gloria's sister's bar, where Andrea drops to the sidewalk in exhaustion. This is Andrea's introduction to the Barrio Chino, and it further collapses the distinct realms that seem to structure the spaces of the novel: the very same descriptors that mark the house as decaying, dark, and ghostly, filled with shouting arguments and physical violence, reappear in this scene to indicate part of the breakdown between public and private spaces that the novel elaborates (see De Marco 74). Over the course of the novel, Andrea's expectations shift, so that, finally, after Román's suicide, Andrea returns again to the streets, seeking not their beauty but the comfort of their run-down decadence:

> Para ahuyentar a los fantasmas, salía mucho a la calle. Corría por la ciudad debilitándome inútilmente. Iba vestida con mi traje negro encogido por el tinte y que cada vez se me quedaba más ancho. Corría instintivamente, con el pudor de mi atavío demasiado miserable, huyendo de los barrios lujosos y bien tenidos de la ciudad. Conocí los suburbios con su tristeza de cosa mal acabada y polvorienta. Me atraían más las calles viejas. (Laforet 208)

> (To drive away the ghosts, I went out a great deal. I wandered the city, uselessly wearing myself out. I wore my black dress that the dye had shrunk and that kept getting bigger on me. I wandered instinctively,

embarrassed by my shabby clothing, avoiding the expensive well-tended neighborhoods in the city. I came to know the suburbs with their sadness of poorly made, dusty things. The old streets attracted me more.) (237–38)

Andrea here seeks out something new in the architecture of the city and its streetscapes. And while she supposes herself to be a detached spectator—with the added help of narrating the story at a temporal remove—I maintain that we can observe not just the merging of the public and private realms but also the collapse of the distinction between observation and attachment. Andrea's Umwelt is constructed in the streets where her needs form the objects she perceives around her in concordance with the needs that drive her. In no sense is this how young women are supposed to move through the city.

At the beginning of Andrea's time in Barcelona, her aunt warns her, "No vuelvas la cabeza. […] No mires así a la gente" ("Don't turn your head. […] Don't look at people like that") (Laforet 27, [21]). However, Andrea will inevitably not only observe those around her but also allow this observation to implicate her in the lives that that explode in chaos in the house on Calle de Aribau—we might think of chapter 2's magnetic relation between people, she is pulled in. This is both the wrong type of looking, excessive, excessively involved, and the only kind she is capable of. Women have typically been associated with the dangers of urban contamination and the hysteria of crowds.[27] The typical (male) flâneur is divorced from the crowd, in it but not of it. He is able to draw on the energy of the street and its particular characters as inspiration for his art, but he is simultaneously a site of tension and evidence of the commodification of the labor of the masses that crowd the street: while occupying a somewhat privileged position in relation to the crowd, he too must sell his art. (This stands of course in sharp contrast to Juan, whose wife secretly sells his paintings to the ragman to get money for the canvas—but then he only leaves the closed-up world of the apartment to earn money at odd jobs.) Andrea, on the other hand, feels deeply involved in her surroundings. On the street, she feels attracted by passersby: "Alguna vez veía un hombre, una mujer, que tenían en su aspecto un algo interesante, indefinible, que se llevaba detrás mi fantasía hasta el punto de tener ganas de volverme y seguirles" ("Sometimes I'd see a man, a woman, who had something interesting, indefinable in their appearance, and who carried my imagination away with them until I wanted to turn

---

27 See Elizabeth Wilson, *The Sphinx in the City: Urban Life, the Control of Disorder, and Women* (Berkeley: University of California Press, 1991).

and follow them") (Laforet 27, [21]). And as time passes, she finds herself consumed by life in the apartment: "[S]e iba agigantando cada gesto de Gloria, cada palabra oculta, cada reticencia de Román" ("[E]ach of Gloria's expressions, each hidden word, each of Román's insinuations, grew to gigantic proportions") (Laforet 35, [31]). She is able to observe, and relate to the reader, the distortion not just of physical objects and their meaning but of gestures, words, and appearances.

Andrea's spectatorship is not confined to the walls of the family home. Attending a dance at the home of Pons, an admirer, she finds herself alone against a wall in her shabby dress and shoes observing the dancing and chatter of the wealthy young people she feels so removed from. When Pons discovers her hours later, she excuses herself and flees from the opulence of the house (so distinct from the decay and rot of her own) to the street: "Me parecía que de nada vale correr si siempre ha de irse por el mismo camino, cerrado, de nuestra personalidad. Unos seres nacen para vivir, otros para trabajar, otros para mirar la vida. Yo tenía un pequeño y ruin papel de espectadora. Imposible salirme de él. Imposible libertarme" (I thought, *It's useless to race if we always have to travel the same incomprehensible road of our personality. Some creatures were born to live, others to work, others to watch life. I had a small, miserable role as spectator. Impossible to get out of it. Impossible to free myself*) (Laforet 163, [184]). It is then that she breaks down and cries, surrounded by the "indiferencia de la calle" ("indifference of the street") (Laforet 163, [184]). In these tears, Martín Gaite reads Andrea's "aceptación del papel de espectador, al que Carmen Laforet la tenía destinada desde el principio" (acceptance of the role of spectator, which Carmen Laforet had her destined for since the start) (96). It is then that she returns to her house near dawn observing the diverse street life of the early morning hours and declaring herself to be "un elemento más, pequeño y perdido en ella [la calle de Aribau]" ("one more element on it [Calle de Aribau], small and lost") (Laforet 164, [184]). Doubtless, despite the apparent similarities, she is expressing something quite distinct from George Sand, who remarked, upon dressing as a man in the streets of Paris, that "[n]o one knew me, no one looked at me [...] I was an atom lost in that immense crowd" (quoted in Wilson 52).²⁸ Her anonymity does not offer adventure or euphoria; rather,

---

28 Walter Benjamin describes the Parisian physiologies as attempts "to give people a friendly picture of one another," a challenge when neighbors and passersby know something of the true nature of those around them but perhaps possible in a crowded urban environment that favors broad sketches of types of people over intimate knowledge of the individuals that make up the teaming masses (70). Post-Civil War, "having a picture" of those around you is particularly threatening and perhaps difficult—the flâneur writing poetry about the strangers flowing through

she feels trapped. Still, where Andrea feels trapped by her personality, her way of perceiving the world around her, it is what structures her life and brings her moments of escape.[29]

As an atom or element in a larger structure, Andrea comes up against the frequently brutal realities of those who surround her. Her uncles' wartime activities, her aunt's relationship with her boss, Juan's frustrated artistic efforts, Román's pathological manipulation, Gloria's secret nighttime gambling, Ena's mother's long-ago disillusionment while in thrall to Román—all of these intrigues are revealed to Andrea, and she becomes caught up in many of them before being whisked away from the family home to Madrid at the close of the novel. I argue that Andrea's experience is not just mediated through images but also through objects and people, smells and sounds, and that this composite experience is a psychological and corporeal one. She recounts the many cold and tepid showers she takes throughout the novel in her attempts to shift some aspect of her experience, recognizing her affective states as partially physical. Yet she is trapped by her hunger, by her family, by her poverty. Her chills, headaches, and mood swings further drive home the physicality of her interaction with the city.

Andrea is also always being watched: she comes to feel the ways in which she is an object in other people's worlds. Early on in Andrea's time at the university, Ena and her friends watch her from afar as she walks into a rainstorm seemingly unaware of her surroundings and caught off guard by the downpour; later Ena recounts her amusement at this scene, typical of Andrea's initial naivete in her new surroundings. When she thinks she has found a moment of beauty and peace behind the cathedral, Gerardo chides her for being out alone. The kitchen maid tells her she knows when Andrea sneaks up the stairs outside of Román's apartment. Angustias knows that she goes for prohibited walks. Juan forbids her from locking her bedroom door. She cannot observe without being watched; she is the always-surveilled spectator, but she is also always the object in others' self-centered worlds as they are objects in hers. Early in the novel, Román

---

the streets cannot be said to have much in common with the producers of Francoist propaganda who attempted to define the proper Spanish (certainly not Catalan) society, family, and individual.

29 Dawn Smith-Sherwood's essay "Las chicas raras de STEM: Recuperating #WomensPlace in Spanish Literary and Scientific Histories" considers Andrea's spectatorship or observation as part of her rareza and cites her "seemingly scientific demeanor" before going on to reflect on real-life women whose scientific activity was what made them strange. In *A Laboratory of Her Own: Women and Science in Spanish Culture*, ed. Victoria L. Ketz, Dawn Smith-Sherwood, and Debra Faszer-McMahon (Nashville, TN: Vanderbilt University Press, 2021), 38.

tells her what he thinks makes his room less disturbing than the apartment where the rest of the family lives: "Aquí las cosas se encuentran bien, o por lo menos eso es lo que yo procuro... A mí me gustan las cosas. [...] Abajo no saben tratarlas. Parece que el aire está lleno siempre de gritos... y eso es culpa de las cosas, que están asfixiadas, doloridas, cargadas de tristeza" ("Things are comfortable here, or at least that's what I'm trying to achieve... I like things. [...] Downstairs they don't know how to treat them. It seems that the air is always filled with shouting... and the things are responsible for that, they're asphyxiated, grief-stricken, heavy with sadness") (Laforet 32, [26]). I suggest that this might describe Andrea's relation to both people and objects in the novel. The mistreated people and objects around her fixate her. The relation that she constructs that is life-sustaining for her, her oblique attachment, is an aesthetic one: she sees her disturbing surroundings, home and street, as objects that feed or starve her, sustain or threaten her.

It is no surprise that she first felt sympathetically toward Gloria when seeing her pose naked for Juan: it is a scene not just of vulnerability but one in which Gloria's experience is specifically aestheticized (see Laforet 30). Later in the novel, after Gloria has confided in her about the details of her relationship with Juan, the two women admire one another's feet (see Laforet 180). She is eventually able to see her own experience this way, becoming in a manner of speaking an object for herself. When Gloria tells her that Ena is Román's lover, she leaves the house and walks through Barcelona, wondering if she has gone mad from hunger. She stands at the port and imagines:

> Desde alguna cubierta de barco, tal vez, unos nórdicos ojos azules me verían como minúscula pincelada de una estampa extranjera... Yo, una muchacha española, de cabellos oscuros, parada un momento en un muelle del puerto de Barcelona. Dentro de unos instantes la vida seguiría y me haría desplazar hasta algún otro punto. Me encontraría con mi cuerpo enmarcado en otra decoración. (Laforet 184)

> (From some deck, perhaps, Nordic blue eyes would see me as a tiny brushstroke on a foreign print... I, a Spanish girl with dark hair, standing for a moment on a dock in the port of Barcelona. In a few seconds, life would move on, displacing me to some other point. I'd find myself framed by another print.) (209)

She has glimpses of herself, of her own body, as though she were able to see herself, perhaps even her self-centered world, from afar. Where Uexküll points out that a single species cannot know the Umwelt of another species, it is also true that it cannot know its own Umwelt from outside. Andrea's documentation of her experience may be understood as a struggle to do just that; she seeks out objects and experiences that might shift her world without having the perspective to know what would best allow for her survival. Uexküll recognized that cities changed humans' interactions with their environments, and I argue that complex constructions like gender roles do the same: they foreclose and make nearly imperceptible stimuli and entire external objects that might allow for survival in other ways. Following the scene at the docks, Andrea goes to a bar where she orders beer, cheese, and almonds, her head aching, imagining, yearning that the place where she sits will shift and take her away to open up "nuevamente los horizontes" ("horizons [...] once again") (184, [209–10]). Eventually, however, she finds herself pulled back to her house as though by "un hilo invisible" ("an invisible thread") (184, [210]). Andrea's Umwelt is clearly not a happy one, but she manages to survive and does so more or less on her own terms, eating out rather than with her family, befriending Ena while dismissing young men.

I think it is not an accident that Andrea's aesthetic mode of perception and the novel's proliferation of details that do not seem to add up to a clear psychological portrait are what construct the prototypical chica rara's self-centered world. Laforet looks to allow her protagonist to perceive her world as it is constructed by stimuli and by the need to survive outside of narrativized gender roles. There are plenty of secrets and small mysteries that are uncovered over the course of the novel, but part of its strangeness lies in the discovery that no one of those narratives will explain Andrea's family to her or explain Andrea to herself. The chaos of feelings and sensations that develop along the way make up the real secret experience of the novel, invoking all of the senses in countless small moments: "un olor a porquería de gato," "la fruta seca fue para mí un descubrimiento," "me abrió los dedos, para ver la confusa red de rayas de la palma," "un panorama de azoteas y tejados," "chirridos de pájaros" ("the stink of cat," "dried fruit was a discovery for me," "[she] opened my fingers in order to see the confused net of lines on my palm," "a panorama of flat roofs and tiled roofs," "the chirping of birds") (Laforet 18 [9], 93 [101], 119 [131], 146 [164], 196 [223]). Andrea's record of those moments—which she sometimes is able to view as aesthetically sustaining ones—reveal that potential stimuli for feeling as she does, and as she might, exist on every scale. As Congdon says of smells, "en sí no comunican nada, pero al entrar en contacto con el sistema olfativo, empieza inmediatamente un proceso de 'sense-making'" (in themselves they do not communicate anything, but upon coming into contact with the olfactory system, they immediate begin a process of sense making) (147).

If at the end of the book we read Andrea's "escape" to Madrid as simply the acceptance of the role that has been carved out for her during that horrific year, then the closing words of the novel are chilling. We might then believe that her trip to a new city is no more an escape than her year in Barcelona has been, particularly if her identity carries with it all of the marks imposed on her by a family, a city, and a nation rather unhinged. I suggest that in fact her way of taking in the world around her, her creation of a first-person text reflecting that engagement, points toward what will in fact allow for her survival in the future. What we are left with is the hint of a secret language of resistance, one that balks at patriarchal control and is the evocative language of inquietude that I would argue forms the first draft of a language that can describe "el mundo que <u>domina secretamente</u> la vida." Even if Laforet never successfully pulled off her betrayal of the male-dominated literary tradition and her erasure or setting aside of the masculine, I propose that we read in this early project her concern with the constraints imposed on women's language and experience but also evidence of resistance against these constraints and an implacable drive to let us know that something else lies in wait, quietly shaping the course of women's lives.

Conclusion

Looking at Andrea's perception and taking in of the environment, we might say that she perceives what she needs to grow up as a young woman. But she also demonstrates a drive toward inhabiting space differently, orienting herself around objects differently. She breaks rules about acceptable ways of being in public and private and, in doing so, she becomes a disconcerting young woman. Her strange behavior points to a mode of perception that is hidden from her family and presented obliquely to readers. In many moments we cannot say what drives her. Andrea is not just a chica rara by the standards of 1940s Spain: she is an unsettling protagonist with unclear motivations today. But her aestheticizing view of everything from the dirty bathroom—"La locura sonreía en los grifos torcidos" ("Madness smiled from the bent faucets")—to the city street shifts her relation to the objects around her (Laforet 17, [8]).

Felt experience and perception seem to contravene social narratives of gender in *Nada*, as Andrea returns to and finds comfort or self-expression in supposedly dangerous spaces. Andrea's opacity pits a narrative of gender that would make sense of a coherent femininity against a sensory, perceptive experience of gender that evades sense making and develops through psycho-corporeal interactions with our self-centered worlds. When that experience runs up against our expectations drawn from gendered narratives, the resulting collision reads as strangeness, rareza. We might think about strange young women as not just forming oblique attachments to objects but as perceiving objects obliquely, in a way necessary to the survival of their strange femininities. This strangeness becomes apparent when we pay attention to the misalignment between gender narratives (akin to expectations of childhood innocence) and the experiences and movements through space that young women first perceive as possibilities and then are drawn to as a matter of survival.

CHAPTER FOUR

Difference and Desire after Darwin: Animal *Rareza* and *Perto do coração selvagem*

> We thus learn that man is descended from a hairy quadruped, furnished with a tail and pointed ears, probably arboreal in its habits, and an inhabitant of the Old World.
> —Charles Darwin, *The Descent of Man*[1]

Evolving animality

The afterlives of Darwin's theory of evolution are many and varied, and terms such as *evolution, natural selection,* and *survival of the fittest* have been employed in the service of any number of nonscientific causes.[2] The popularity of this Darwinian lexicon and the significant purchase of evolutionary ideas in the popular imagination to this day make the constellation of ideas surrounding Darwin's work even more deeply entrenched, and distorted, in their popular forms than the scientific currents explored in other chapters. The implication of Darwin's research that perhaps most unsettled contemporary thought when he published and in subsequent decades was the assertion, recognized though implicit in *The Origin of Species* and explicit in *The Descent of Man*, that humans evolved from animals. But, in work more directly in conversation with this study, Darwin also wrote on binary and nonbinary sexual difference as well as sexual selection and penned *The Expression of the Emotions in Man and Animals*. His writing taken as a whole had the effect of drawing attention to the mutability of the human and

---

1 Charles Darwin, *The Descent of Man, and Selection in Relation to Sex*, rev. ed. [1871] (Princeton, NJ: Princeton University Press, 1981), 389.

2 "Survival of the fittest" was in fact coined by Herbert Spencer after reading Darwin and later used by Darwin himself. He reflected on the usefulness of the term in letters to Alfred Russell Wallace available online as part of the Darwin Correspondence Project: see Darwin Correspondence Project, "Letter no. 5145," accessed March 2, 2023, www.darwinproject.ac.uk/DCP-LETT-5145.

the possibility of relation with those animals or people previously held to be utterly foreign; such loosening of the limits of the species also raised questions about the limits of the self and ways of relating to others. Much like species-level questions sparked concerns about individual humans in Uexküll's writing and the reception of his work, Darwinism provoked questions about the actions and choice of individual people. Evolution as popularly imagined left the human species open and vulnerable to change.

Aspects of Darwin's theory were hotly debated even decades after his books were published, and references to Darwinism and evolution made consistent appearances in popular culture around the world long after his death in 1882. Examining philosophical genealogies of sexual difference, desire in sexual selection, and the possibility of narrating the human species, I ask what is gendered about the human animal in a Darwinian world. And how do the *chicas raras* pick up on those currents of change? Because Darwin's writing has had a more pronounced reception and his ideas more public afterlives than some of the ideas I explored in earlier chapters, I look to some of the ways other scholars have understood his influence on literature and the popular imagination, and I look at some examples of unscientific uses of Darwinian vocabulary in popular Brazilian culture. While lay readers interested in Uexküll's Umwelt might have had to turn to the *Revista de Occidente* and potential magnetizers might have purchased specialist spiritualist publications, Darwin was on the pages of every kind of text.

It is in this context of heightened attention to the porous boundaries of the human species that I turn to Clarice Lispector's earliest novel. Published in 1942, *Perto do coração selvagem* has an experimental prose style that has encouraged a number of reflections on unstable bodily forms and material dissolution and communion. Critics have picked up on feral or animalistic strains in its protagonist, Joana—strains often expressed in terms of unexpected feelings. Much like in *Personas en la sala*, hatred, love, happiness, affection, and boredom all show up, or fail to appear, in unpredictable ways. Rather than crossing into masculinity, Joana's strange femininity departs directly from the recognizably human into animal terrain. In this final chapter, I am interested in connecting the affective strangeness of Lispector's text to reconfigurations of humanness that trouble the acts of sensing and saying. In *Perto* we see narrative and sense making perturbed in the experiences of a young women. Specifically, I trace the ways that Joana's nonhumanness indicates lines of relation that point outside of her species—a sort of thinking made possible by Darwin—and simultaneously and inextricably indicates lines of relation outside of the narrative of binary gender difference. Here I revisit Darwin's writing on sexual difference and selection, seeing it not as enshrining a binary as the driving force of variation but as pointing to sensory and affective feelings that promote the creative production of difference. I ask how femininity—imagined as animal, in Darwin's view of the animal—suggests new forms of gendered affection. And I ask how the human when understood as related to and open to other animal species produces an experience of gender.

Clarice Lispector

If Norah Lange had to contend with capturing the imagination of the Buenos Aires elite of her time, Lispector must have felt even wider circles in thrall to her. Benjamin Moser opens his biography, *Why This World*, by comparing Lispector to the Sphynx.[3] A page later, he relates the words of intellectuals struggling to describe Lispector's physical and intellectual pull, often by comparing her to other famous women (such as Marlene Dietrich and Virginia Woolf). But where Lange favored public performance, Lispector was so renowned for her reticence that even the most basic facts of her biography were uncertain. Moser relates the hazy mythology that replaced such facts:

> "Clarice Lispector" was once thought to be a pseudonym, and her original name was not known until after her death. Where exactly she was born and how old she was were also unclear. Her nationality was questioned and the identity of her native language was obscure. One authority will testify that she was right-wing and another will hint that she was a Communist. One will insist that she was a pious Catholic, though she was actually a Jew. Rumor will sometimes have it that she was a lesbian, though at one point rumor also had it that she was, in fact, a man. (3)

Moser responds to this uncertainty with a narrative of his own—one that returns frequently to Lispector's youth and the years leading up to her birth. Though Lispector left Ukraine with her family when she was still an infant, fleeing pogroms, Moser places a great deal of importance on her impoverished origins and the violence her family suffered before she was born and at the time of her birth. Basing his account largely on writings by Clarice's sister, Elisa, Moser relates that their mother was raped by soldiers

---

3 Benjamin Moser, *Why This World: A Biography of Clarice Lispector* (New York: Oxford University Press, 2009). Earlier biographical sketches of the author can be found in Teresa Cristina Montero Ferreira's *Eu seu uma pergunta* (Rio de Janeiro: Rocco, 1999) and Nádia Battella Gotlib's *Clarice: Uma vida que se conta* (São Paulo: Editora Ática, 1995).

and contracted syphilis, which would eventually paralyze her and lead to her death at the age of forty-two in Brazil (see 27, 61). While Clarice was born unharmed by the disease, this violence and her mother's sickness loom large in this biographical account. Moser quotes a passage from 1968 in which Clarice alludes to her own birth:

> "I was prepared for birth in such a beautiful way. My mother was already sick, and a common superstition had it that pregnancy would cure a woman of her illness. So I was deliberately created: with love and hope. Except that I didn't cure my mother. And to this day that guilt weighs on me: they made me for a specific mission, and I let them down." (Quoted in Moser 28)

As signaled by my interest in Darwin, the idea of alternate genealogies will be important to my reading of *Perto*, and the one suggested here is a sort of alternative affective genealogy that explains how love and hope bore guilt. It is a different story from the one Lispector tells of Joana, but we will nevertheless see Lispector's protagonist engaged in her own struggle with how to feel and how to understand herself as a human in relation to other humans.

Moser is also attentive to the echoes of Lispector's personality in her characters. Reading *Perto*, he identifies the animal-like Joana as being similar to the beast-like or feline Clarice (see Moser 56). Moreover, he cites this "embrace of an animal nature" and "complete refusal of any anthropocentric morality" as the inevitable outcome of the violence surrounding her very young life: "Given the savage circumstances of Clarice's early life, she could hardly have reached any other conclusion than that life is not human and has no 'human value'" (Moser 56–57). Whether or not she or anyone else who survived the pogroms or the Holocaust could in fact have reached another conclusion about human life, Lispector's portrayal of human–animal continuity, alongside the material and affective strangeness she inscribes in her work, would seem to be much more than the inevitable product of an experience of genocidal violence.

As to the political and social formation of gender roles in the Brazil that Lispector was living and writing in, we see phenomena similar to those we have observed in other national contexts: the social roles assigned to women were contracting rather than expanding; at the same time, women were cited by politicians as important ciphers of national health.[4] In "From Working

---

4 Lispector is rarely read as reflecting on her homeland. For an analysis of her writing as an exploration of the inner life of the nation, and specifically of race in Brazil, see Lucia Villares, *Examining Whiteness: Reading Clarice Lispector through Bessie Head and Toni Morrison* (London: Legenda, 2011).

Mothers to Housewives: Gender and Brazilian Populism from Getúlio Vargas to Juscelino Kubitschek," Joel Wolfe notes:

> Vargas's [1930-1945, 1951-1954] focus on the poor usually emphasized women's status as workers, and so his gendered policies reflected concerns about the status of working women. Kubitschek [1956-1961], on the other hand, attempted to transform workers into consumers as a form of political incorporation. His policies shifted the emphasis from women as workers to women as housewives, even though the majority of Brazilian women continued to work outside the home.[5]

Women would lead strikes and protests from 1945 through the early 1950s, though these too were impetus for male politicians "to attempt to return to a nostalgic state of allegedly traditional gender roles by domesticating women workers and creating high-paying industrial jobs for their husbands" (Wolfe 101). The domestication of women, whether as workers or housewives, contrasted with not only Lispector's violent family history but with the daily experience of most Brazilian women outside of the upper classes. Even for the most privileged, "domestication" implied limits rather than greater freedoms, and, in the service of the nation, inscribed economic, social, and political violence in the figure of the woman. A violence that, as we will see, Lispector's Joana makes visible.

When *Perto* opens, Joana is a young girl. Her mother has died and her father raises her until his own death. Any exploratory and wondrous childhood scenes end there, and Joana is sent to live with her aunt, who condemns her unusual behavior, seems unnerved by the child, and calls her a viper, *uma víbora fria* (Lispector 51). The novel includes childhood and adulthood scenes of Joana interacting with her male teacher and his wife, in a strange triangulated relationship not unlike the one in *Memorias de Leticia Valle*. In *Perto*, however, the strange girl grows into a strange woman and marries a man, Otávio. The remainder of the book sketches out their relationship, Otávio's renewed relationship with an ex-lover, Lídia, who becomes pregnant, Joana's interaction with Lídia, and finally her own affair. With its scant plot, the novel is filled with narrative descriptions that seem to dip into Joana's own consciousness, illustrating her interactions with the material world and with animals and humans punctuated by reflections on the nature of feelings, love, desire, and beauty. In what follows, I look at

---

5 Joel Wolfe, "From Working Mothers to Housewives: Gender and Brazilian Populism from Getúlio Vargas to Juscelino Kubitschek," in *Gender and Populism in Latin America: Passionate Politics*, ed. Karen Kampwirth (University Park: Penn State University Press, 2010), 92-93.

several aspects of how Darwinism was scientifically and popularly received in Brazil; at the questions regarding human–animal relations, desire, and difference in his writings; and at the philosophical and scholarly lines of inquiry that show Darwinism to be a cultural concept as much as it is a scientific one. With that context in mind, I return to Joana and Lispector's rendering of her strange desirous way of being as both a component of her gender and a reflection of the openness of the human species.

The reception of Darwinism in Brazil

A origem das espécies was translated from the French edition into Portuguese by Joaquim Dá Mesquita Paul and published by Portuguese press Lello & Irmão around 1910.[6] *O pensamento vivo de Darwin*, by Julian Huxley, translator unknown, was published in São Paulo in 1944.[7] In *Evolucionismo no Brasil: Ciência e educação nos museus, 1870-1915*, Regina Cândida Ellero Gualtieri notes that scholars have focused on the welcoming reception given to Darwinism in Latin American social debates, though less attention has been paid to its reception and incorporation by Latin American scientists.[8] While Gualtieri notes that some scholars have declared that Brazilian scientists did not even awaken to the possibilities of Darwinism for their work until the mid-twentieth century, she finds evidence of debates over evolutionary theory occurring in natural history museums, which she fleshes out using museum publications, bulletins, journals, and more (see Gualtieri 16). The museum was at once a site for the development of scientific ideas and for their diffusion to the public. Gualtieri asserts that Darwinism was particularly attractive to Brazilians because of its potential as a metaphor, or even roadmap, for social change: "De fato, idéias como a seleção natural e a luta pela vida de Darwin, o recapitulacionismo de Haeckel e a lei da diferenciação progressiva de Spencer eram muito atraentes no Brasil do final do século, que estava tentando se transformar, se modernizar" (In fact, ideas like Darwin's natural selection and struggle for existence, Haeckel's recapitulation theory, and Spencer's law of progressive differentiation were

---

6 For more on the problematic introduction of Darwin in Portuguese, see Felipe A. P. L. Costa's "Lendo Darwin em português" in *Observatório da Imprensa* 802 (2014): observatoriodaimprensa.com.br/armazem-literario/_ed802_lendo_darwin_em_portugues/.

7 For more on Darwin in Brazil, see Josie A. P Silva and Marcos C. D. Neves, *Arte e ciência: Um encontro interdisciplinar* (Maringá: Massoni, 2010); Neves and Silva, *Evoluções e revoluções: O mundo em transição* (Maringá: Massoni, 2010).

8 See Regina Cândida Ellero Gualtieri, *Evolucionismo no Brasil: Ciência e educação nos museus, 1870-1915* (São Paulo: Editora Livraria da Física, 2009), 15.

very attractive in fin de siècle Brazil, which was striving to transform itself and modernize) (13). She describes the reception of Darwinism and related theories as facilitating new ways of seeing the world. "A maneira de perceber o mundo alterou-se de forma significativa; o meio natural e a sociedade passaram a ser compreendidos como ambientes em constante transformação e não apenas como domínios de permanência e previsibilidade" (The way of perceiving the world shifted significantly; the natural environment and society came to be understood as existing in constant transformation and not simply as realms of permanence and predictability) (Gualtieri 11). That changed outlook did not just offer political and social possibilities: "a incorporação do ser humano no reino animal também recebeu críticas vigorosas, pois era mais um golpe na visão antropocêntrica do mundo" (the incorporation of human beings in the animal kingdom was also harshly criticized as it was another blow against an anthropocentric view of the world) (Gualtieri 23). I suggest that this destabilizing shift effected not just new political and social understandings on the communal or national level but also changes to the lived and felt experiences of individuals, due to widespread awareness of the basic tenets of Darwinism, further spread by how individuals were now conceived of and treated by institutions and the state.

Drawing on *Life and Letters of Charles Darwin*, published in 1887, Cezar Zillig's *Dear Mr. Darwin: A intimidade da correspondência entre Fritz Müller e Charles Darwin* fleshes out the life story of Fritz Müller, a German scientist who immigrated to Brazil in 1852 and lived out his life there; Müller was also associated with the Museu Nacional, as Gualtieri points out, and is frequently cited in discussions of Darwinism in Brazil (see Gualtieri 16).[9] Müller first read *The Origin* in 1860 and dedicated his research to areas that could corroborate Darwin's claims. Müller and Darwin corresponded from 1865 to 1882, exchanging sketches, observations, plant bulbs, photos of themselves, and more. Müller would publish his own short pro-Darwin book, *Für Darwin*, in 1864 (see Zillig 3). Müller's observations are also cited in Darwin's *The Expression of the Emotions*. Zillig refers to a "prototipo da Internet" that reached Brazil, at least through Müller if not others: it consisted of a network of correspondence among scientists, and he cites Hildebrand, Alex Agassiz, Ernst Haeckel, Weismann, Milne Edwards, Max Schultze, Hooker, C. Spence Bate, Bates, Asa Gray, and Meyer (see Zillig 60–61).

In another study on the reception of Darwinism in Brazilian institutions and the public, Karoline Carula analyzes a series of public conferences held

---

9 See Cezar Zillig, *Dear Mr. Darwin: A intimidade da correspondência entre Fritz Müller e Charles Darwin* (São Paulo: 43 SA Gráfica e Editora, 1997).

in the late nineteenth century—"As Conferências Populares da Glória"—on Darwinism and other scientific topics and traces the ensuing public debate in periodicals and eventually novels.[10] She notes that the "conferências populares" were in fact likely received by a markedly upper-class audience and were intended to focus on academic themes rather than issues thought to be of interest to a broad swath of the public (see Carula 44-47). While those conferences came to an end in 1880—and the studies outlined here, like most on the reception of Darwinism, similarly wrap up around the beginning of the twentieth century—looking to less academic settings for the diffusion of discourses in the decades that follow turns up continued evidence of evolutionary theory taking hold in the popular imagination in diverse and creative ways.

Darwinism, perhaps more than any other contemporary theory, was not only swept into the popular imagination but also extensively referred to by name. Mentions of Darwin and Darwinism abound in publications of all sorts with varying degrees of scientific rigor. From 1930 to the mid-1940s, the newspaper *O Cruzeiro* registers the appearance of Darwin in widely diverse settings: articles on magnetism and the mystery of death; tips for your garden; the caption of a photo of piglets competing for milk; an ad for Havelock Ellis's *A seleção sexual no homem*; a story called "A esposa perfeita" (The perfect wife) in which the woman's father writes a book refuting Darwin (marking theirs as "uma família de idiotas!" [a family of idiots!]); and an article titled "Glamourize Suas Pernas!" (Glamorize your legs!) illustrated with photos of Hollywood stars whose striking legs can be explained by "leis de Lamarck e Darwin" (laws of Lamarck and Darwin).[11] Readers need not be erudite to speak of Darwin, but they would be idiots to dismiss him. This diffusion of Darwin-esque—if not strictly Darwinian—ideas speaks to how compelling the broad strokes of his theory were, and how inescapable. The relation between humans and animals, the question of survival, and reflections on female beauty were all tinged with Darwin's influence. I now look behind these themes at the anxieties and possibilities they contained and may have transferred to individual and social experiences of gender.

---

10 See Karoline Carula, *A tribuna da ciência: As Conferências Populares da Glória e as discussões do darwinismo na imprensa carioca (1873-1880)* (São Paulo: Annablume, 2009).
11 Scanned versions of all issues of *O Cruzeiro* are accessible via the digitized archives of Brazil's Biblioteca Nacional Digital: bndigital.bn.gov.br/.

Reading Darwin in literature and culture

I argue for the importance of Darwinism—the term standing in here for all that can be seen to emerge directly from his writing and from the narratives that arose around it—not only where it explicitly appears as a referent but also as a source of creative tension and narrative production around questions of life, the human and the animal, and sexual difference. To frame this approach, I turn first to Gillian Beer, whose foundational readings of Darwin in relation to metaphor, creativity, and narrative suggest the porousness of scientific and nonscientific thought and reflect on the role of language in both.

In "Darwin in South America: Geology, Imagination and Encounter," Beer brings out the centrality of pleasurable imagining in Darwin's writing, seeing it as crucial to understanding how he built his scientific concepts. She also draws attention to Darwin's empathy, which, according to her, allowed him to focus on the relations between lives.[12] Beer's reflections on Darwinian empathy, metaphoric language, thought experiments, imagination, and the scientific-modernist oceanic community all provide intriguing ways into the scientific-artistic bramble of his writing and subsequent literature, and she suggests that the affective experience of scientific imagining and writing slips into public discourse on scientific discovery, silently shaping not just what we think we know about the world but how we feel about it. In *Darwin's Plots: Evolutionary Narrative in Darwin, George Eliot and Nineteenth-Century Fiction*, Beer explores Darwin's literary reading habits to understand how he went about conceiving of and shaping scientific ideas. She finds evidence of his struggle to rein in metaphoric language and restrain his semantic tendency to let single words and phrases develop multiple meanings, as detailing more precise and limited definitions became necessary to explain and defend his theories.[13] Beer argues that Darwin's relation to materialism and the manifestation of that point of view in his texts reflects not just scientific conviction but rather understandings and narratives of the world that he derived from his readings of Thomas Hardy, among others (see Beer, *Darwin's Plots* 36–37). Beer's writing is a good reminder that influences on how we narrativize the world—and how we experience it—are everywhere. What is more, this is not a one-way flow of influence from exalted scientific disciplines downward and outward; language

---

12 See Gillian Beer, "Darwin in South America: Geology, Imagination and Encounter," in *Science and the Creative Imagination in Latin America*, ed. Evelyn Fishburn and Eduardo Ortiz (London: Institute for the Study of the Americas, 2005), 13–23.

13 See Beer, *Darwin's Plots: Evolutionary Narrative in Darwin, George Eliot and Nineteenth-Century Fiction* (Cambridge: Cambridge University Press, 2009), 33–34.

is persistently untransparent and resistant—at the very least in Beer's reading of Darwin—to even narrative itself. Patience A. Schell and Travis Landry have both argued for Darwin's imbrication with social questions, in the contexts of Chile and Spain, respectively. Schell makes the case for Darwin, and naturalists more generally, as carrying out their work through professional and social networks that depend deeply on personal connections and collaboration (Zillig's work on Darwin's correspondence with Müller in Brazil provides one example of such a relationship). These social relationships extend the import of scientific work beyond the page or even the museum. Landry looks at Darwin's case for female choice in sexual selection in connection to women as portrayed in the Spanish realist novel. In doing so, he takes a careful approach to scientific discourse and literary representation, writing, "Darwin does not fall on the side of either literature or science but rather collapses the two in a creative unity where our engagement with the material world cannot be separated from responses of representation" (27). Building on these readings of Darwin as embedded in social and cultural currents that then developed their own Darwinian layers, I look at some of the central concerns of his publications that resurface in my reading of *Perto*.

What Darwin wrote

Despite these precedents for understanding Darwin in relation to global social, cultural, and literary contexts, his work might seem an unusual pairing with a modernist author often read alongside James Joyce (by Hélène Cixous, among others), Katherine Mansfield (for whom Lispector expressed a predilection [see Moser 143-44]), or Virginia Woolf—modernists whose experiments with language might be at ease alongside discourses of particles and waves (and indeed questions of material continuity and discontinuity will surface here yet again).[14] But Darwin's lasting grip on the popular imagination suggests a real and lasting shift in how humans experienced

---

14 Regarding questions of influence and the Anglophone modernist tradition in which Lispector is often placed, she explicitly rejected the suggestion of any Joycean influence on her work, pointing out that the title and epigraph citing *Portrait of the Artist as a Young Man* were suggested to her by Lúcio Cardoso and that she did not read Joyce until after her book had been written (Moser 124-25). Lispector shared her own reflections on the avant-garde and experimental writing in a lecture she gave repeatedly, "Literatura de vanguarda no Brasil" (Avant-garde literature in Brazil); see Nádia Battella Gotlib, "Clarice Lispector the Conference Speaker: The Vanguard and the Right to Narrate," in *After Clarice: Reading Lispector's Legacy in the Twenty-First Century*, ed. Adriana X. Jacobs and Claire Williams (Cambridge: Legenda, 2022), 105-18.

their humanness, and, most decidedly, in how they talked about it. And if Darwinism became a less-than-rigorous reference—one that could be employed in the admiration of women's legs—that is not to say that it was an empty one. Rather, I argue that the flexible uses of Darwinism that developed since the publication and dissemination of *On the Origin of Species* and *The Descent of Man* (as well as his 1872 *The Expression of the Emotions in Man and Animals*) suggest that the influence of his texts was wide ranging and deep. It is worth sketching out here some of the plotlines that, unfurling and twisting into the twentieth century, would so captivate international audiences.

In *On the Origin of Species by Means of Natural Selection, or the Preservation of Favoured Races in the Struggle for Life*, Darwin primarily introduces the concept of the struggle for life as giving rise to natural selection, the mechanism for gradual inherited change through evolution:

> Dei o nome de seleção natural ou de persistência do mais apto à conservação das diferenças e das variações individuais favoráveis e à eliminação das variações nocivas. As variações insignificantes, isto é, que não são nem úteis nem nocivas ao indivíduo, não são certamente afetadas pela seleção natural e permanecem no estado de elementos variáveis, como as que podemos observar em certas espécies polimorfas.[15]

> (This preservation of favourable variations and the rejection of injurious variations, I call Natural Selection. Variations neither useful nor injurious would not be affected by natural selection, and would be left a fluctuating element, as perhaps we see in the species called polymorphic.)[16]

Natural selection, in contrast to the artificial selection that occurs with the domestication of animals, "pode atuar sobre todos os órgãos interiores, sobre a menor diferença de organização, sobre todo o mecanismo vital. O homem tem apenas um fim: escolher para vantagem de si próprio; a natureza, ao contrário, escolhe para vantagem do próprio ser" ("can act on every internal organ, on every shade of constitutional difference, on the whole machinery of life. Man selects only for his own good; Nature only for that of the being which she tends") (Darwin, *Origin* [97], 84). It is here that Darwin introduces sexual selection, which will be much more fully

---

15 *A origem das espécies, no meio da seleção natural ou a luta pela existência na natureza*, trans. Joaquim Dá Mesquita Paul (Porto: Lello & Irmão, 1910[?]), 94. I cite the pagination of a 2003 e-book that reproduces Paul's translation: http://ecologia.ib.usp.br/ffa/arquivos/abril/darwin1.pdf.
16 Charles Darwin, *The Origin of Species by Means of Natural Selection or The Preservation of Favoured Races in the Struggle for Life* [1859] (New York: Bantam, 2008), 82.

fleshed out in *The Descent of Man*. Predicting certain critiques, he addresses the incompleteness of the geological record extensively—why we do not see each intermediary step—as well as the apparent absence of organs in intermediate or transitional states. He states that external conditions, habit, and use/disuse may all lead to variation (which supposes the inheritance of acquired characteristics) (see Darwin, *Origin* 168). In the face of the stunning diversity of animal life on earth, he states: "Creio que todos os animais derivam de quatro ou cinco formas primitivas no máximo, e todas as plantas de um número igual ou mesmo menor" ("I believe that animals have descended from at most only four or five progenitors, and plants from an equal or lesser number") (Darwin, *Origin* [549], 472). He takes great pains to state the many mechanisms and facts of which he and other scientists remain ignorant and is careful to address how these gaps do or largely do not alter his approach. Where did Darwin imagine Darwinism would take humans? "Entrevejo num futuro afastado caminhos abertos a pesquisas muito mais importantes ainda," he wrote. "A psicologia será solidamente estabelecida sobre a base tão bem definida já por M. Herbert Spencer, isto é, sobre a aquisição necessariamente gradual de todas as faculdades e de todas as aptidões mentais, o que lançará uma viva luz sobre a origem do homem e sua história" ("In the distant future I see open fields for far more important researches. Psychology will be based on a new foundation, that of the necessary acquirement of each mental power and capacity by gradation. Light will be thrown on the origin of man and his history") (Darwin, *Origin* [553], 476-77). Indeed, light had already been thrown on the origin of man, though Darwin waited several years to expound on that topic in *The Descent of Man, and Selection in Relation to Sex*.

The Descent of Man sets out the concept of sexual selection, which explains adaptations that otherwise seem not to benefit the species as conferring reproductive advantages and spells out the case of natural selection for humans. The very first chapter is titled "The Evidence of the Descent of Man from Some Lower Form." The chapters that follow expand on how this came about, and they lead Darwin into reflections on the development of intellectual and moral faculties, as well as "On the Races of Man" (chapter 7).[17] Though after the publication of *The Origin of Species* the descent of man from animals was understood to form part of Darwin's theory, he explicitly states it in

---

17 Racist notions of evolution, with some underpinnings in Darwin and with some external importations, surely overlapped with racist ideas of national evolution: Villares notes in the case of Brazil that "whitening, although not an explicit policy, as under the First Republic, remained as a desired ideal. *Morenidade* [brownness] was tolerated, even celebrated, because of the non-articulated notion that the Brazilian population was, in the course of time, becoming white" (32).

this later book, wanting to harness and present all possible evidence, aware of how weighty a contribution to scientific and popular discourse it was (see Darwin, *Descent* 389). In his conclusion, he recapitulates his argument that humans are descended from a lower form and have evolved through natural selection, and notes that "muitos caracteres de escassa importância fisiológica, ou também de notável importância, foram alcançados através da seleção sexual" ("many characters of slight physiological importance, some indeed of considerable importance, have been gained through sexual selection") (Darwin, *Descent* 387).[18] The concept of sexual selection and its connection to beauty and desire continues to prove fruitful for philosophers and theorists today. In his chapter on "Principles of Sexual Selection," Darwin explains that male "ornaments," like colorful plumage and songs, exist only to attract females so they may procreate, which "implica poderes de discriminação e gosto por parte da fêmea" ("implies discrimination and taste on the part of the female") ([252], 259). He admits that "em vários pontos se torna um pouco incerto o modo preciso de como age a seleção sexual" ("the precise manner in which sexual selection acts is somewhat uncertain") ([252], 259). As we will see below, philosophical theorizations of beauty, desire, and choice have developed this originally Darwinian idea. Travis Landry points out that Darwin was aware that what he observed in the animal world was not always apparent or acceptable in Victorian human society, and this is a tension in his work, but he still "extrapolates from nature and assumes that what is true for animals will also be so for humans" (51).[19]

The Expression of the Emotions in Man and Animals again shows continuities between humans and nonhumans. In it Darwin contemplates how the body, with special attention to the face, expresses emotion, considering individual and inherited habits and reflexes in humans and nonhuman animals.[20]

---

18 While Brazil's Biblioteca Nacional includes in its holdings a 1933 translation of *Descent*, *A descendencia do homem e a seleção sexual*, trans. Zoran Ninitch (Rio de Janeiro: Ed. Marisa, 1933), here I cite the following more recently published translation: *A origem do homem e a seleção sexual*, trans. Attílio Cancian and Eduardo Nunes Fonseca (n.p., Brazil: Hemus, 1982), 699.

19 Landry, in *Darwin, Sexual Selection, and the Spanish Novel*, focuses on sexual selection and female choice in relation to the *cuestión de la mujer* (woman question) coupled with a reading of Spanish novels.

20 See Darwin, *The Expression of Emotion in Man and Animals* [1872] (New York: D. Appleton & Co., 1899). As this work does not appear to have appeared in Brazil in Portuguese until later, I have cited only the English publication. However, Darwin's reflections on emotions are clearly tied to his other theories and may well have entered Brazil both implicitly in Darwin's other writings and through the presence of his thinking and work in museums, public forums, and elsewhere.

While Darwin's suppositions regarding bodily habits—on everything from the "obliquity of the eyebrows under suffering" to the "cause of the contraction of the muscles round the eyes during screaming"—are anecdotal and generally consider human and nonhuman cases separately, his parallel examples of inherited habits in humans and inherited habits in nonhuman animals, for example, show that the same mechanisms are at work in both groups (Darwin, *Emotions*, chaps. 6 and 7). In his introduction, he writes about expressions in humans, such as their hair standing on end in fear or baring their teeth in anger, that he feels only make sense if we accept "that man once existed in a much lower and animal-like condition" (Darwin, *Emotions* 34). And, indeed, the structure of the entire book is predicated on the belief that working through the physical and emotional experiences of humans and nonhumans side by side represents a reasonable and worthwhile social and scientific endeavor. In his conclusion, he explicitly speculates on where and why in our descent from apes weeping developed as an expression of emotion (see Darwin, *Emotions* 591). He even tentatively suggests that dogs' propensity to bark might be owed to their extensive contact with "so loquacious an animal as man" (Darwin, *Emotions* 582). Not only are the same physical-affective processes at work in humans and nonhumans with regard to inheritance, habit, and mimicry, but the two groups continue to interact with and influence one another. This continued porosity of the human and nonhuman species will play an important role in Lispector's writing.

While Darwin was writing decades before the publication of *Perto*, the reverberations of Darwinism continued to be felt throughout the first half of the twentieth century. This was as true in the scientific world as it was in the arts, philosophy, and popular culture. Peter J. Bowler, citing Julian Huxley's use of the term "the eclipse of Darwinism," explains that while evolution was widely accepted in the scientific community at the turn of the century, the mechanisms driving evolution were hotly debated, selection theory faced stiff critique, and Darwinism's "death" was predicted.[21] Older theories of Lamarckism—the heritability of acquired characteristics—and orthogenesis—evolution toward a given end—were revived to oppose Darwinian selection, and so too was emerging genetic research stemming from Mendel's earlier work roped in to fight the anti-Darwin fight (see Bowler 234). Proponents of these conflicting theories did not, however, band together in a united front, and Darwinian selection remained at the center of the debate throughout the decades, never expiring on its oft-mentioned deathbed.

---

21 Peter J. Bowler, *Evolution: The History of an Idea* (Berkeley: University of California Press, 1984), 233.

Whether due to the continued scientific debate, the circulation of reflections on social Darwinism, or the pull of theories of selection and descent on the popular imagination, Darwin remained a referent in nearly all fields of discourse for decades. The evident attraction of Darwinian thought is apparent to this day, as the idea of humans as linked with nonhuman animals through both lineage and a shared world emerges in conversations about animality, life and death in the Anthropocene, and, as for Elizabeth Grosz, sexual difference.

The metaphorical possibilities and narrative uncertainty that Beer detects in Darwin come to serve Grosz in her 2011 work *Becoming Undone: Darwinian Reflections on Life, Politics, and Art*. In it, we see a remote intellectual genealogy drawn out, brought to the fore, and made to bear theoretical weight. I pause here to look at the scientific-philosophical story she develops in which she creatively traces the results of a Darwinian paradigm through Bergson and Deleuze, finally showing how a return to Darwin's writing on sexual difference might provide useful insights into Irigaray. Grosz's work combines an intellectual genealogy (Darwin-Bergson-Deleuze) with an innovative pairing of thinkers who seem to have very different concerns (Irigaray-Darwin). With this jump from Darwin to Irigaray, Grosz demonstrates the unexplored potential of a framing that was not present in the later work and quite likely not at the fore of its author's mind. What for Grosz is a suggestive and fortuitous pairing represents an analytical method fairly unconcerned with matters of influence, even of the diffuse, ether-imbuing sort. While I am interested in the contemporaneity of scientific debates with the literary texts I read, this productively pushes at the boundaries of how Darwinism might be understood—and, for me, how it might be read in Lispector's novel.

Grosz begins her discussion of a new kind of feminism by signaling a move away from a definition of freedom as "freedom from" (that would seek to loosen repressive systems and proffer rights) and toward one of "freedom to" (Grosz 61-62). She critiques feminism that relies on fixed subjects through ideas of identity or intersectionality, arguing that oppression is not a system or structure (not even a complex one that could conceive of overlapping and interacting patriarchal, racist, homophobic oppressions) but rather the *patterns* that emerge from acts of every scale (see 97). She advocates for a feminism that multiplies (Deleuzian) difference and produces agency and invention by recognizing the new acts that can emerge under the same conditions of those that are currently constituted as oppressive patterns. Grosz's project is to corral Darwin to support Irigaray's idea of sexual difference as the motor of all difference. This difference would be able to feed into new patterns allowing for a feminist *freedom to*.

In order to understand Irigaray's insistence on sexual difference as the site for the production of Deleuzian difference, Grosz picks upon Darwin's sexual selection, which he elaborates in *The Descent of Man*. She emphasizes that sexual selection is separate from, and sometimes even at odds with, natural selection. Natural selection works on a species-wide level to increase fitness, while sexual selection operates at the level of individuals privileging those who are able to attain mates. This gives rise to any number of traits that may not necessarily correspond with fitness, but that focus instead on nonfunctional, nonadaptive matters of appeal, aesthetics, pleasure, creativity, abundance, variety, and, fundamentally, attraction, making sexual selection a matter of "bodily intensification" (Grosz 118). As sexual selection relies on competition (generally male) and discernment (generally female), the latter allows for sexual selection to be a creative force producing ornamental or frivolous change (see Grosz 160). Grosz is also interested in how sexual selection generally drives the (for her always two) sexes to appear more and more distinct—in other words, it is an engine for the multiplication of difference: "sexual selection functions to deflect natural selection through its extravagant and excessive pleasures, its inventions and intensifications of new relations, new forms of attraction, and new modes of artfulness. Sexual selection is arguably the greatest invention of natural selection" (165). For Grosz, Irigaray and Darwin complement, strengthen, and complicate one another. Sexual difference allows us to understand that "the natural cultivates culture" rather than the other way around (Grosz 168). The two very distant thinkers "have each come to a point of commonness in which different bodies, divided along lines of sex, become the means for new natural and cultural relations, the road to new forms of politics and new forms of life" (Grosz 168). Grosz seems unbothered by giving credit for multiplicitous difference to sexual binarism, but I believe that desire and creative proliferation in Darwin, which feed her theorization, need not depend on divisions "along lines of sex." Instead, we might think about the body-in-evolution as a desiring, discerning body, and the human animal as one who desires and discerns, in part, through a matrix of gendered feeling, one which includes masculinity and femininity and more, variously fragmented and arrayed.

As we saw above, Darwin himself was doubtless fascinated by the mechanism of sexual selection: he devotes four chapters of *Descent* to the secondary sexual characteristics of birds. He argues strongly in favor of sexual selection acting on humans and not just nonhuman animals. But before turning to Lispector's novel, I would like to highlight how readily Darwin ascribes taste, choice, and desire to all animals. Though females are the ones doing the choosing, readers would be unlikely to come away from *Descent* thinking that males do not possess such feelings and preferences.[22] For an explanation of how male humans at least develop such capabilities, we might turn to Darwin's reflections on intellectual and moral capacities, which both develop thanks to natural selection—moral sense being trickier to explain but resting on social instincts in combination with man's intellectual acuity and reflections on the past and future (see *Descent* 392). It is understandable that males would develop the same ability for aesthetic taste and desire (or simply the capability of choosing that which is "least distasteful") that female animals, according to Darwin, possess (*Descent* 273). In Darwin's narrative, males additionally become faster, stronger, cleverer, more robust, and more attractive—which while centering certain abilities as masculine also speaks to the sorts of aesthetic shifts that can occur as a result of choice and discernment. If males, too, can evolve to desire and choose and prefer, then the sexual bifurcation that Grosz returns to seems to me less important than the conceptual innovation of creative species-wide change driven by feelings.

Darwinian implications for a strange protagonist

The broad strokes that trail behind Darwin's writing include the idea that humans are animals, that human and nonhuman animals might function similarly not just in their biology but in their social and affective lives, that humans and nonhumans might influence one another, and that desire and choice can produce newness. On the basis of these insights, rather than anthropomorphizing animals—or simply understanding humans as more animal-like or beastly than we might have wanted to admit—we instead can engage the limit of our knowledge of animals to understand the limit of our knowledge of other humans. Lispector's novel pushes at those limits. *The Expression of the Emotions in Man and Animals* might be considered disappointing in its inability to do more than speculate broadly about nearly inane specificities—the shape of the eyebrow of a distressed person—but, seen another way, Darwin's book gazes upon humans just as it does upon animals, with an estranging effect in both cases. Whereas Santiago Ramón y Cajal writes in "Las sensaciones de las hormigas"[23] that "como en todas las especies animales, el mundo exterior percibido por la hormiga es un mundo aparte,

---

22 Though it is also true that *man* stands in for all humans generally in his writing. US abolitionist and women's rights activist Antoinette Louisa Brown Blackwell, writing *The Sexes throughout Nature* in 1875, would critique the superiority of men in Darwin's text, calling males and females "true equivalents." Brown Blackwell, *The Sexes throughout Nature* (New York: G. P. Putnam's Sons, 1875).

23 Santiago Ramón y Cajal, "Las sensaciones de las hormigas," *Archivos de Neurobiología* 2, no. 4 (1921).

específico, fundamentalmente diverso del nuestro, salvo la comunidad de ciertas propiedades geométricas y de determinadas emanaciones materiales" (as in all animal species, the external world perceived by the ant is a world apart, specific and fundamentally different from ours, except for the commonality of certain geometrical properties and certain material emanations) what Darwin's take on the emotions leads us to question is the givenness of our own world as constructed through our physical sensations and affective engagement with it (Ramón y Cajal 15–16).

Moreover, the human species is open and unfinished; Darwin is clear that humans are situated within a process of nonteleological evolutionary change, not at an endpoint. And given humans' continuity with other animal species as well as mutual influence and shared mechanisms, a thorough understanding of human experience, including gender, might not be best derived from an examination of only human lives or through entrenched narratives of human experience. Human experiences coded as animal may touch on those experiences that narrative has not been able to address. Both the openness of the human and specifically its openness to animality serve to open up the possibilities of human felt experience (sensorial as well as affective), both in the sense that things could be otherwise, could move evolutionarily in another direction, and in the sense that in the current moment things are other than how we may narrate them to be: Darwinian evolution is in progress, in a present tense that dismantles our ability to talk about ourselves.

On an evolutionary scale, an individual's choices and actions are not important, but the way Darwin writes about sexual selection (by females, of attractive and competitive males) does seem to foreground the preferences of each individual bird. And while Darwin was concerned with species, his readers quickly shifted their focus to individuals, all the way up to today's tongue-in-cheek Darwin Awards. Thus, at an individual level, Darwinism's openness to change might also affect how we see difference and deviance, since they hold the possibility of the future direction of the species. Even if we understand that some difference renders an individual more or less fit, deviation in itself is possibility—possibility that is in the process of being tested out. Joana, for all her strangeness, is described as apt to survive—disturbingly fit, as it were. On top of this, sexual selection hints at the multiplication of difference and eventual lasting change as being based on feelings, desire, and choice.

Women as already animals: reading Lispector

Animality and the animal in Lispector are most frequently examined in light of *A paixão segundo G. H.* or the several of her short stories that contain explicit animal appearances.[24] In this study, I am more interested in the appearance of the nonhuman animal in what is otherwise apparently human. While this strain of animal investigation has spread through critical theory, I would like to identify a possible genealogy of animality, via Darwin and Lispector, that has questioned the sanctity of the human and that has particularly gendered inflections. Woman as feline, as serpentine, as animal may seem like a tired trope, but I argue that, paired with Darwinian and evolutionist concerns, this theme suggests anxieties about the borders between self and other, about how humans relate among themselves, and about a threat to the existing relational order that is contained and often concealed in strange femininities.[25]

Women are not alone in being described in threateningly nonhuman terms. Those who are poor, non-white, those displaying marginalized sexualities—all are at risk of being cast as "uncivilized" or "less than human." Those categories slip quickly into the category of animal, and so I ask: What happens when evolutionary theory not only inserts the human into a genealogy of the animal but as a result inserts animality as a natural feature of humanity? How are those marginalized identities viewed and experienced in a Darwinian age?

Perto do coração selvagem, Lispector's first book and in some ways one of her most stylistically traditional, is often critically overlooked—particularly when scholars seek to reflect on the role of the animal in Lispector's oeuvre. In the 325-page issue of *Espéculo: Revista de Estudios Literarios* put out by the Universidad Complutense de Madrid in 2013 and devoted entirely to Lispector, *Perto* receives far less attention and fewer even passing mentions

---

24 See, for example, Jutta Ittner, "Who's Looking? The Animal Gaze in the Fiction of Brigitte Kronauer and Clarice Lispector," in *Figuring Animals: Essays on Animal Images in Art, Literature, Philosophy, and Popular Culture*, ed. Mary Sanders Pollock and Catherine Rainwater (New York: Palgrave, 2005), 99–118.

25 In his chapter "Women and Animals," Mark Bernstein reads the historical denigration of women in animal terms as a sign that women are especially poised to offer a new, feminist mode of relating across species to nonhuman animals (see *Without a Tear: Our Tragic Relationship with Animals* [Chicago: University of Illinois Press, 2004], 161–88). Lori Gruen, in an earlier ecofeminist text, argues that "the categories 'woman' and 'animal' serve the same symbolic function in patriarchal society. Their construction as dominated, submissive 'other' in theoretical discourse (whether explicitly so stated or implied) has sustained human male dominance. The role of women and animals in postindustrial society is to serve/be served up; women and animals are the used" ("Dismantling Oppression: An Analysis of the Connection Between Women and Animals," in *Ecofeminism*, ed. Greta Gaard [Philadelphia: Temple University Press, 1993], 61).

than later books such as *Água viva*.²⁶ However, critics have pointed out some of the novel's structural quirks, including how childhood is treated throughout, and how the narrative, or rather non-narrative, style favors moments of reflection and striking realization whether attributed to the narrator or the protagonist: "El relato no sigue un desarrollo cronológico, sino que se estructura a partir de breves momentos epifánicos" (The text does not develop chronologically; instead, it is structured around brief epiphanic moments).²⁷ To further understand how those epiphanic moments come about, that same scholar, Andrea Jeftanovic, analyzes the irruption of childhood in *Perto* as "bloques de devenir niño" (blocks of becoming-child) and reflects on the becomings in the novel, referring to the feminine in Lispector as "lo inacabado, siempre a punto de transformarse" (what is unfinished, always about to transform) (259). *Perto* might indeed be considered an exploration of a child–woman–animal network that is manifested in the body: "El cuerpo para Joana es su gran instrumento cognitivo; a partir de él se moviliza un conjunto de sensaciones que motiva experiencias de descubrimiento y extrañamiento" (The body for Joana is her great cognitive instrument; a set of sensations are mobilized through it that drive experiences of discovery and estrangement) (Jeftanovic 259). I would propose thinking of her body not as a cognitive instrument but as a feeling manifestation of the species, reacting to and communicating with other bodies, and becoming its present animal self.

Jutta Ittner, reading Lispector's *A paixão segundo G. H.*, cites John Berger to reflect on how humans and animals do or do not see one another: "In his essay, 'Why Look at Animals,' John Berger undertakes to approach the elusive animal 'seer' by trying to distinguish between the human and the animal gaze. Between two men the inevitable abyss can usually be bridged: 'Language allows men to reckon with each other as with themselves'" (Ittner 108).²⁸ In this sort of account, animals are removed and humans

---

26 Joaquín María Aguirre, ed., special issue, *Espéculo: Revista de Estudios Literarios*, no. 51 (2013). The phrase "agua/água viva" appears 143 times as compared to twenty-two total mentions of "perto do coração" and "cerca del corazón." In a brief 2006 article in the same journal, "Duas senhoras-meninas transgressors: *Nada* de Carmen Laforet e *Perto do Coração Selvagem* de Clarice Lispector," Lélia Almeida identifies Joana as a *chica rara* in the style of Laforet's Andrea (*Espéculo: Revista de Estudios Literarios* 34 [2007]).

27 Andrea Jeftanovic, "*Perto do coração selvagem* de Clarice Lispector: La infancia como temporalidad y espacio existencial," *Revista Iberoamericana* 73, nos. 218–19 (2007): 253.

28 Ittner also explores the role of the epiphanic in Lispector, common to modernist writers such as Joyce. For more on the language of epiphany as well as reflections summing up how the ways that Lispector and *Perto* in particular have been

huddle together within the species: but what of that which language *disallows* or simply does not reach across the abyss? In Lispector, the abyss becomes an interval that is as much internal to our experience of ourselves and the world we touch as it is external, "between men." Darwin reminded readers not only of how little they had previously known about their animal selves, but, again and again, of how much they were still ignorant of. For all the pages Darwin could fill with explanatory language, the gap between humans and their experience of themselves as human animals remains the thrilling, befuddling shocker in his oeuvre. Joana does not gaze upon the earthworm and wonder what it is: she gazes upon her husband and wonders what it is.

In a less traditional line of literary criticism, one that raises the question of sex or gender in relation to language, Hélène Cixous read Lispector and engages her texts in her own creative and philosophical work. She returns to Lispector again and again while reflecting on sexual difference. Though Lispector's writing may seem capacious enough to have something to say about almost anything, it is rather hard to pin down what it might have to say about sex and gender. The markers of animality and of childhood can seem more prominent than those of femininity or womanhood, and so the fact that Cixous discerns something in these texts of utmost relevant to sexual difference is intriguing. Her "Cuentos de la diferencia sexual" expounds on the topic with extensive, creative citation of Lispector alongside Jacques Derrida.[29] When Cixous reads Lispector's "The Message," for example, she sees not femininity but "slightly unusual sexes, for example new sexes; sometimes the new sex is a word, sometimes the sex begins to speak."[30] The proliferation and multiplication of language in Lispector thought of as

understood as *écriture féminine*, see chapter 2 of Cláudia Nina's *A palavra usurpada: Exílio e nomadismo na obra de Clarice Lispector* (Porto Alegre: EDIPUCRS, 2003).

29 Hélène Cixous, "Cuentos de la diferencia sexual," trans. Mara Negrón, *Lectora* 21 (2015): 209-31.

30 Cixous, "'Mamae, disse ele,' or Joyce's Second Hand," trans. Eric Prenowitz, in *Stigmata: Escaping Texts* (London: Routledge, 1998), 100-128. On "The Message," Cixous writes:

> Here we are with this text *The Message*, a bit in the same situation, hesitating or feeling uncertainty and the origin of uncertainty, which is the mystery of sexual differences, ever since the beginning of the text. And what's more the text is unabashed, this is not hidden, it is incessantly reinscribed, re-edited, it is constantly a question of sex, and at the same time in a slightly unexpected way, not entirely classical. When the word sex appears, neat and clean, it is not always in a form or a place that is obvious and familiar to us. There are words which make sex, brutally. Not only is sexual opposition or sexual difference or sexual indifferentiation in the text on every page, but what's more there are

sexual difference may in fact go some way toward explaining the gender of her protagonists: aesthetic discernment drives the elaboration of linguistic and syntactical difference in her works, giving rise to textual worlds in which the ordinary arrangements and materials for gendered life appear reworked. Mara Negrón's essay "Cuerpo: Los límites de lo narrable o 'casi siempre mujeres'" further explores Cixous's approach to the intersection of women, writing, and sexual difference.[31] In Negrón's reading, definition—which might be said to be the basis of narrative and theory—becomes "definir indefiniendo" (defining in undefining) and "jugar con el tiempo de la definición" (playing with the time of definition) (*De la animalidad* 159).

We might think of this as it relates to Darwinian indefinitiveness of the human species (indeed, of all species) and the time of evolution as it unfolds in the present and reworks the present as part of a continual process. When Cixous refers to the impossibility of *defining* a feminine/female practice of writing, Negrón notes that that impossibility is what makes writing possible.[32] Cixous's writing, with its plays on words and intentional semantic instability, writing that is itself desirous and affective—Beer might have described Darwin's writing in a similar way—is a practice in the non-narrative multiplication of difference: "No se trata pues en esos textos de hacer discurso y si [sic] de hacer sentir por la escritura al lector la imposibilidad de teorizar la diferencia sexual" (In these texts, it is not a question of creating narrative discourse but of making the reader feel through the writing the impossibility of theorizing sexual difference) (Negrón, "Más allá" 298). *Perto do coração selvagem* might be said to be a text that takes up the impossibility of theorizing, or even narrating, talking about, gendered lives.

Regarding the question of narrating life, in a chapter titled "In My Core I Have the Strange Impression That I Don't Belong to the Human Species: Clarice Lispector's *Água Viva* as Life Writing?" Elizabeth Friis notes the phrase in the text, "Quero ser bio."[33] In a footnote, she elaborates:

slightly unusual sexes, for example new sexes; sometimes the new sex is a word, sometimes the sex begins to speak. (121)

31 Negrón, *De la animalidad no hay salida: Ensayos sobre animalidad, cuerpo y ciudad* (San Juan: La Editorial Universidad de Puerto Rico, 2009).

32 Negrón, "Más allá del saber: La inocencia de Hélène Cixous y la pasión de Clarice Lispector," *Nuevo Texto Crítico* 14–15 (1995): 298.

33 Elizabeth Friis, "In My Core I Have the Strange Impression That I Don't Belong to the Human Species: Clarice Lispector's *Água Viva* as Life Writing?" in *Narrating Life: Experiments with Human and Animal Bodies in Literature, Science and Art*, ed. Stefan Herbrechter and Elizabeth Friis (Boston: Rodopi, 2016), 33–54.

When Lispector uses the word "bios," she is of course not using it in the sense given to it by Agamben in *Homo sacer* (1998). In Lispector, "bio" designates "All that is living"—thus including for instance completely "unqualified" life such as electricity. We shall see later that her *bios* more likely resembles Braidotti's *zo*, "bare life" simply not being a negative category in Lispector. (34n5)

Friis uses this question of life to address life writing. Here, I would recall the question of energy as it relates to matter raised in chapter 1:[34] I suggest that we can understand life in *Perto* as arising from the stuff that humans are made of—Lispector refers repeatedly to *matéria-prima*—which points to continuity between bodies as well as to existing in a state of change that echoes open-ended evolutionary change. This state of being, materially and in flux, is, in Lispector, particular to women.

"O movimento explicava a forma": Joana's desire

Reading *Perto* not only demands that we consider the protagonist's relation to desire that presses at the limits of the human species, it also takes us back through the other categories constructing gender explored throughout these chapters: Joana runs up against and through the materiality of things, which becomes visible in the narration, she notes that her perceptions have the power to bring things into being, her relations with other creatures and with objects reciprocally remake the world. Her desire and her gender are intertwined with these experiences—and the possibility and limits of narrative are always nearby. Indeed, the novel itself, with its sparse plot and multiplying reflections and elaborations, challenges us to ask what fits in a story and what escapes the confines of plot. Here, no material is extraneous, and yet much of the book pulls away from narrative, suggesting that when we limit our understanding of lived experience to readily accessible, easily readable plotlines, we are missing out on the bulk of what, in undefining, defines lives.

The book opens with the sounds of young Joana's father's typewriter, the clock, and the silence: "entre o relógio, a máquina e o silêncio havia uma orelha à escuta, grande, cor-de-rosa e morta. Os três sons estavam ligados pela luz do dia e pelo ranger das folhinhas da árvore que se esfregavam umas nas outras radiantes" ("[a]midst the clock, the typewriter and the silence

---

34 I would also recall from chapter 2 the protagonist's desire in *Personas* to see those she loved dead. The dead body may be a form of the material body, or *bio*, that Lispector writes of—a corpse, but still vital.

there was an ear listening, large, pink and dead. The three sounds were connected by the daylight and the squeaking of the tree's little leaves rubbing against one another radiant") (Lispector 13, [3]). Sounds linked by light: this scrambled version of ordinary sense perception introduces the way that Joana will experience the world outside of herself and how she will take it in. This perception allows the young protagonist to imagine, and simultaneously know, what must be happening in the world beyond the limits of her body: that in the earth outside the window "uma ou outra minhoca se espreguiçava antes de ser comida pela galinha que as pessoas iam comer" ("a worm or two was having a stretch before being eaten by the hen that the people were going to eat") (Lispector 13, [3]). This food chain does not seem to be violent as much as it seems to suggest an order of things informed by potential, eventual, and intimate contact. Hearing sounds that allow her to imagine the worm, the hen, and the human is what structures Joana's world. Her struggle is to close the gap with what she knows to exist. The narrator notes as much when Joana looks at her father hoping to attract his attention: "Nada veio porém. Nada. Difícil aspirar as pessoas como o aspirador de pó" ("But nothing came. Nothing. It's hard to suck in people like the vacuum cleaner does") (Lispector 14, [4]). Her mere looking does not have the power over people that it has to reveal to her an entire sensory world: there is a gap that will continue to appear throughout her life. Her desire to bridge that gap and create contact with other bodies recalls the labor of magnetizers, discussed in chapter 2, to influence or commune with others, living or dead.

One of Joana's secrets, formative for her un-narrativized experience—and perhaps *the* secret of her existence—stems from an experience that she does not, as a child, allow herself to tell even her father. She walks with her hands extended in front of her until she runs into a piece of furniture:

> Entre ela e os objetos havia alguma coisa mas quando agarrava essa coisa na mão, como a uma mosca, e depois espiava [...] só encontrava a própria mão, rósea e desapontada. [...] Esse era um de seus segredos [...] *que não conseguia pegar "a coisa"*. Tudo o que mais valia exatamente ela não podia contar. Só falava tolices com as pessoas. (Lispector 15–16; emphasis mine)

> (Between her and objects there was something, but whenever she caught that something in her hand, like a fly, and then peeked at it [...] she only found her own hand, rosy pink and disappointed. [...] That was one of her secrets [...] *that she never managed to catch "the thing."* Precisely the things that really mattered she couldn't say. She only talked nonsense to people.) (6)

She experiences a gap, she can neither "aspirar as pessoas" nor "pegar 'a coisa,'" and, perhaps most important, she cannot speak of it. There is no language for this distance imposed between her and people, between her and things. One way to understand Joana's desire would be to say she wishes to close that gap: later, speaking of the stars and the rain, she will implore, "Meu Deus, pelo menos comunicai-me com elas, fazei realidade meu desejo de beijá-las" ("Dear God, at least allow me to communicate with them, satisfy my desire to kiss them"), and she confesses "eu quero ser estrela" ("I want to be a star") (Lispector 66, 67, [58]). This desire arcs out of the species, out of the animal, and into the organic universe around her. We might recall the writing of Arthur Eddington and others that reminded us that we are indeed made of the stuff of stars. But, for Joana, the distance between that truth and her human reality is stark and often painful: indeed in one of her epiphanic moments, Joana grasps that

> o movimento explicava a forma!—*e na sucessão também se encontrava a dor porque o corpo era mais lento que o movimento de continuidade ininterrupta.* A imaginação apreendia e possuía o futuro do presente, enquanto o corpo restava no começo do caminho, vivendo em outro ritmo, cego à experiência do espírito... Através dessas percepções—*por meio delas Joana fazia existir alguma coisa*—ela se comunicava a uma alegria suficiente em si mesma. (Lispector 44; emphasis mine)

> (movement explained form—*and pain was also to be found in succession because the body was slower than the movement of uninterrupted continuity.* The imagination grasped and possessed the future of the present, while the body was there at the beginning of the road, living at another pace, blind to the experiences of the spirit... Through these perceptions—*by means of them Joana made something exist*—she communed with a joy that was enough in itself.) (36)

Joana makes things exist: we may again think of magnetism and the occult, and the capacity to bring things into being through thinking them, manifesting them in ethereal currents that run through the air. But we may also think of scientific discovery as working in this way: Darwin making humans animal by thinking of them as such. Cognizant of this potential, a young Joana tells stories to her classmates to test out her power, to make them see things (much like Leticia's storytelling in *Memorias*) (see Lispector 145). In the passage above, she has made something exist by virtue of the realization that movement explains form. I would argue that what she brings into being is not the movement, the form, nor the potential truth of that statement; her perception of that reality brings into being a way for her to be in the world, in her body, moving through space and time. And what does it mean for movement to explain form? And for the body to painfully lag behind that continuity? For Darwin, the form of the species captures a moment in an uninterrupted continuity of movement powered by variation and adaptation. Still, reading Darwin, even as he insists that change is happening even when he cannot point to the fossil record or to organs in intermediate states to prove it, it can be easy to imagine change as steps, rather than movement. The body is too slow, and narrative too fast: we are living in and through something we cannot feel and that language struggles to express.

Perto presents a number of continuities for us to pay attention to. We may read them in light of evolutionary continuity through change within species as well as in light of shared relationships across species. In passing, the narrator tells us of the life and death of the woman with the voice (who shows Joana an apartment for rent). The woman's death is described as follows: "A uma vida tão bela deve ter-se seguido uma morte bela também. Certamente hoje é grãos de terra. Olha para cima, para o céu, durante todo o tempo. Às vezes chove, ela fica cheia e redonda nos seus grãos. Depois vai secando com o estio e qualquer vento a dispersa. Ela é eterna agora" ("Such a fine life must have been followed by a fine death too. She is no doubt grains of earth today. She gazes up at the sky, the whole time. Sometimes it rains and she becomes full and round in her grains. Then the heat dries her out and any old wind disperses her. She is eternal now") (Lispector 78, [70]). This eternal continuity through beauty, here with the earth, is present in the most mundane episodes in Joana's life, and she makes it visible to others. Moreover, it leads out of the human into animals and the natural world: Joana pets a pregnant dog when Otávio first sees her: "E havia qualquer coisa no seu olhar, nas suas mãos apalpando o corpo da cachorra que a ligava diretamente à realidade desnudando-a. Como se ambas formassem um só bloco, sem descontinuidade. A mulher e a cadela ali estavam, vivas e nuas, com algo de feroz na comunhão" ("And there was something in her gaze, in her hands patting the body of the dog that connected her directly to reality laying her bare. As if the two of them formed a single continuous block. There they were, the woman and the dog, alive and naked, with something ferocious in the communion") (Lispector 90, [82]). The woman–dog block is the reality that Joana, with her gaze, her hands, and the dog's body, reveals. It is also the reality that Joana desires. When she speaks to Otávio, recounting that she threw a book at an old man who disgusted her, we get one of the moments that prompts her to express what she wants and what traps her: "'Só depois de viver mais ou melhor, conseguirei a desvalorização do humano', dizia-lhe Joana às vezes. 'Humano—eu. Humano—os homens individualmente separados'" ("'Only after I've lived more or better, will I manage to depreciate what is human,' Joana sometimes told him. 'Human—me. Human—mankind separated into individuals'") (Lispector 93, [84]). Despite her aunt's critique of her serpentine nature, despite her reflection being that of "uma gata selvagem" ("a wildcat") in the mirror, despite even her communion with the dog she strokes, Joana is human (Lispector 81, [73]). The separation that marks humans, that is human, is a shortcoming that she recognizes and must live with while experiencing the ways in which it is not true for her. We will see how her humanness in continuity with animality and other matter becomes a question of femininity.

Darwinism can be understood as providing an alternate genealogy for the human family tree. One idea to consider in *Perto* is how Lispector proposes alternate genealogies for Joana. Both of Joana's parents die when she is young, her aunt is decidedly unaffectionate and uninfluential in her life, and instead we see other connections grow around her: her teacher and his wife; Otávio and Lídia, his lover; her own lover and his ex-lover; the dog she once pets; even the objects she touches.

When Joana is a child, her father picks her up and, the narrator notes, "Anda tão solta a criança, tão magrinha e precoce... Respira apressado, balança a cabeça. Um ovinho, é isso, um ovinho vivo. O que vai ser de Joana?" ("The child was running wild, so thin and precocious... He sighed quickly, shaking his head. A little egg, that was it, a little egg. What would become of Joana?") (Lispector 17, [8]). A page later, adult Joana reflects on the violent, evil force she contains, the "fera" ("wild beast") the "animal perfeito" ("perfect animal") inside of her (Lispector 18, [9]). She seems to grow up along an alternate evolutionary track: from living egg to wild animal, she is constantly aware of the feelings that bring her close to things and a sense of lack. Joana does not inherit the traits of her mother and father; her life traces an alternate genealogy. Her father talking with his friend says, "Eu mesmo prefiro que esse broto aí não a repita. E nem a mim, por Deus... Felizmente tenho a impressão de que Joana vai seguir seu próprio caminho" ("I really hope the little one there doesn't repeat her. Or me, for God's sake... Fortunately I get the impression that Joana is going to follow her own path") (Lispector 28, [20]). Her path is surely a strange one and one that is rooted in her bodily experience: "Y foi tão corpo que foi puro espírito" ("And she was so body that she was pure spirit"); "'Joana... Joana...' chamava-se ela docemente. E seu corpo mal respondia devagar, baixinho: Joana" ("'Joana... Joana...' she called herself softly. And her body barely answered slowly, quietly: 'Joana'") (Lispector 97, 100, [88], [91]). For Darwin, the body proves to be the link with other species. Joana's body is what contains the truth of her genealogy; she is her own fossil record, and the other women she meets—along with the realizations she has about her body and the limits of human bodies writ large—define her just as much as ancestors or inheritance might.

Still a young child, Joana relates to her teacher and his wife in a way reminiscent of *Memorias de Leticia Valle*: the older man struggles to relate to Joana, and while the wife interrupts their communication, Joana recognizes pain in that woman who smiles at her and calls her the teacher's "amiguinha" (Lispector 56). Joana competes with this woman, but there is no violent interpretation and inscription of social norms on their way of relating as there is for Leticia. Instead, she exits awkwardly and the scene dissolves: "O que acontecia? Tudo recuava... E de súbito o ambiente destacou-se na sua consciência com um grito, avultou com todos os detalhes submergindo as pessoas numa grande vaga..." ("What was going on? Everything was receding... And suddenly the setting stood out in her awareness with a scream, loomed up in all its detail submerging the people in a big wave...") (Lispector 59, [51]). Much later, she goes to visit her old teacher, whose wife has by now left him: "E, apesar da repulsa que a outra ainda lhe inspirava, numa reminiscência, Joana descobrira surpresa que não só então, mas talvez sempre, se sentira unida a ela, como se ambas tivessem algo secreto e mau em comum" ("And, in spite of the repulsion that the wife still inspired in her, recollecting, Joana realized with surprise that not only then, but perhaps always, she had felt united with her, as if they both had something secret and evil in common") (Lispector 115, [105]). The dark secret, or rather feeling as if there were such a secret, creates a line of affective relation between the two women. (Leticia's unspeakable secret, her *inaudito* life, similarly structures her world. The protagonist of *Personas en la sala* imagines that the women she watches are keeping secrets.) And this relationship between women, passing through an unspoken zone of contact, might be said to suggest an alternate genealogy, another way for desire to shape Joana's life.

In a rather abrupt turn reflecting the unexpected paths of desire in the novel, Joana meets a man on the street and has an affair with him in the house where he lives with his ex-lover. When she sees him approach: "Estavam cortadas as veias que a ligavam às coisas vividas, reunidas num só bloco longínquo, exigindo uma continuação lógica, mas velhas, mortas" ("The veins that connected her to the things she had experienced had been cut, gathered up in a single faraway block, demanding a logical continuation, but old, dead") (Lispector 160, [152]). We see, through Joana's eyes, the materialization of affect in corporeal language. The veins that sustain living things in her world need not be contained in a single body. The ex-lover, Joana, and her teacher's wife form a trio of women, and the narrator asks "O que as ligava afinal? As três graças diabólicas" ("What connected them after all? The three diabolical graces") (Lispector 167, [159]). The relationships between Joana and her husband, Joana and her lover, even Joana and her teacher are unusual enough. Yet we are repeatedly directed to observe the affective flow, the unexpected links, between women: Joana and the teacher's wife, Joana and her lover's ex-lover. Is it affect, matter, gender, species that links them? Joana at one point reflects that "[p]iedade é a minha forma de amor. De ódio e de comunicação" ("[p]ity is my way of loving. Of hating and communicating") (Lispector 22, [13]). Love, hate, and communication all pass through *piedade*; that is how she has named her affection, or maybe her desire. The feelings shared among women create a contemporary lineage that remakes her in the present moment.

Joana's perception of continuity along with her unorthodox ways of relating to humans and things lead her to experience a number of strange feelings. A scene describing her bath at boarding school has her reveling in her young body: she moves it in and out of the water, and she laughs "em leves murmúrios como os da água. Alisa a cintura, os quadris, sua vida" ("in light murmurs like those of the water. She strokes her waist, her hips, her life") (Lispector 64-65, [57]). "Quando emerge da banheira é uma desconhecida que não sabe o que sentir" ("When she emerges from the tub she is a stranger who doesn't know what to feel") (Lispector 66, [57]). The result of estrangement from her own body—that was at the same time her experience of marveling in her own body—is not knowing what to feel. As with other female protagonists in this study, Joana does not seem to feel correctly: happiness, to her, is not an end in itself. She asks her teacher: "Depois que se é feliz o que acontece? O que vem depois? [...] Ser feliz é para conseguir o quê?" ("[O]nce you're happy, what happens? What comes next? [...] Being happy is for what?") (Lispector 29, [21]). Darwin also asked about how emotions operate in humans and, when unable to find explanations, turned to animals. When explaining sexual selection, he described the process as hinging also on inexplicable taste. Both Darwin and Joana observe the human species and find its true motivations and drivers of change somewhat inexplicable.

In another scene demonstrating Joana's apparently inhuman relation to feeling and wanting—to affection—she is sent to live with her aunt after her father dies, and she steals a book. She announces that stealing is only bad if you are afraid, that she will only steal when she wants to. As a result of this incapacity to feel bad or guilty, she is sent to boarding school. The aunt, admitting that she would not have sent her own daughter, Armanda, away for the same infraction, says: "Armanda até roubando, é gente! E essa menina... [...] É uma víbora. É uma víbora fria" ("Armanda, even if she were a thief, is human! But that girl... [...] She's a viper. She's a cold viper") (Lispector

51, [43]). Stealing may not have struck her as wrong, but her aunt is able to communicate that something is wrong with her. She runs to her teacher, who tells her: "Afinal nessa busca de prazer está resumida a vida animal. A vida humana é mais complexa: resume-se na busca do prazer, no seu temor, e sobretudo na insatisfação dos intervalos" ("Animal life boils down to this pursuit of pleasure after all. Human life is more complex: it boils down to the pursuit of pleasure, to the fear of it, and above all to the dissatisfaction of the time in between") (Lispector 52, [44]). The division that the teacher marks between human and animal life will not hold up for Joana—*víbora fria* or *matéria-prima* that she is—but it may indeed be the gap represented by these intervals that structures Joana's guiding experience of feeling. No single emotion will be enough. For as we later read, "Era sempre inútil ter sido feliz ou infeliz. E mesmo ter amado. Nenhuma felicidade ou infelicidade tinha sido tão forte que tivesse transformado os elementos de sua matéria, dando-lhe um caminho único, como deve ser o verdadeiro caminho" ("It was always useless to have been happy or unhappy. And even to have loved. No happiness or unhappiness had been so strong that it had transformed the elements of her matter, giving her a single path, as the true path must be") (Lispector 100–101, [91–92]). And it is the draw toward that material transformation—that happiness and unhappiness cannot effect—that shapes Joana's sensory, affective, corporeal experience. Still later, *alegria* returns with a different effect: "A alegria cortou-lhe o coração, feroz, iluminou-lhe o corpo" ("Happiness pierced her heart, ferocious, lit her body") (Lispector 62, [54]). Perhaps this provides an answer to the *why?* of emotions for Joana: happiness, joy, is a return to the body. What does it get you? That illumination of the body, which simultaneously appears as a material limit, lines drawn around it, and a connection, through the species, to other bodies.

And while there is pain in experiencing the limits of her body, Joana's perceptions—how she will see herself in the mirror—make something else of that human situation:

> Se o brilho das estrelas dói em mim, se é possível essa comunicação distante, é que alguma coisa quase semelhante a uma estrela tremula dentro de mim. Eis-me de volta ao corpo. Voltar ao meu corpo. Quando me surpreendo ao fundo do espelho assusto-me. Mal posso acreditar que tenho limites, que sou recortada e definida. Sinto-me espalhada no ar, pensando dentro das criaturas, vivendo nas coisas além de mim mesma. (Lispector 67–68)

> (If the twinkling of the stars pains me, if this distant communication is possible, it is because something almost like a star quivers within

me. Here I am back at the body. Return to my body. When I surprise myself in the depths of the mirror I get a fright. I can hardly believe that I have limits, that I am cut out and defined. I feel scattered in the air, thinking inside other beings, living in things beyond myself.) (59)

Again, she is returned to her body, and the limits of the body and of the human are consistently an imposition and a surprise. She feels herself to be thinking and living in other creatures and things. She is, even, connected to the stars. But her body as reflected in a mirror—and likely by society, in the eyes of other humans—begs to differ. And so she lives out both realities, one that she senses and one that she observes, feeling both of them as they shape her life.

In another scene, she faces not a mirror but Otávio next to her in bed. She wonders who he is, knowing he is a man, male, her husband, and that more fundamentally "[h]avia dois corpos limitados sobre a cama" ("[t]here were two delimited bodies on the bed") (Lispector 133, [124]). There is seemingly a conflict between the narrator's insistence on the "corpo limitado" that marks humans and Joana's repeated experience that such a thing has little to do with her. If those bodies with limits are humans, what is it to be a woman?

> Sim, sim, aí estava a verdade: elas existiam mais do que os outros, eram o símbolo da coisa na própria coisa. E a mulher era o mistério em si mesmo, descobriu. Havia em todas elas uma qualidade de matéria-prima, alguma coisa que podia vir a definir-se mas que jamais se realizava, porque sua essência mesma era a de "tornar-se". Através dela exatamente não se unia o passado ao futuro e a todos os tempos? (Lispector 141)

> (Yes, yes, there was the truth: they existed more than other people, they were the symbol of the thing in the thing itself. And woman was mystery in itself, she discovered. There was in all of them a quality of raw material, something that one day might define itself but which was never realized, because its real essence was "becoming." Wasn't it precisely through this that the past was united with the future and with all times?) (133)

What is it to be the symbol of the thing in the thing itself? Having to live as the manifestation of a social idea of femininity—while still having a body? The social control of women's bodies heightens awareness of their materiality and their animality. Indeed, Lispector returns us to the *matéria-prima* of women that is always in formation. The union of past and future in the body itself is something of a Darwinian image, one that casts individuals in an inextricable relation to the human species and to other species in a material relationship that unfolds over time.

Are women in a place to manipulate the symbol while it manipulates them? Is Joana special in being able to change the air around her so that she can do so (as in the passage below)? Or does she simply make this process visible? All women, we read, are matter in transformation; they are the movement that undefining defines form. And is Joana a woman? She is "um corpo vivendo, nada mais" ("a body living, nothing more") (Lispector 188, [181]). Later, the narrator will say she is not a woman, and yet:

> Não era mulher, ela existia e o que havia dentro dela eram movimentos erguendo-a sempre em transição. Talvez tivesse alguma vez modificado com sua força selvagem o ar ao seu redor e ninguém nunca o perceberia, talvez tivesse inventado com sua respiração uma nova matéria e não o sabia, apenas sentia o que jamais sua pequena cabeça de mulher poderia compreender. (Lispector 200)

> (She wasn't a woman, she existed and what she had inside her were movements lifting her always in transition. Maybe at some point she had modified with her wild force the air around her and no one would ever notice, maybe she had invented with her breathing new matter and didn't know it, merely feeling what her tiny woman's mind could never comprehend.) (193)

What is it to be not a woman with "a pequena cabeça da mulher"? And to simultaneously live with that quotidian reference to women with their silly empty little heads? To know and feel the imposition of that quotidian sense of identity and simultaneously sense one's own matter in transformation, in movement, feeling its way toward another way of being, if one that will only be available to the future of the species? That is, perhaps, a good definition of femininity, of what it is to feel like a woman.

Thus we have in *Perto* both the gap, the interval, experiences of constant estrangement, and yet also connection, contact, and potential transformation. Human bodies are the link to the future of the species and also exist in the state of not having arrived: there is no arrival, there is only the space in between. And so the estranging interval is the same place where that contact outside of the body, outside of gender, outside of the species, takes place. For Joana, some aspect of being a woman is to live in that species gap, to feel and experience that interval, and to feel its movement, its drive toward mutability, as what confers form on the body and on daily experience. Wanting, desire, as Darwin describes it with regard to sexual selection, is both of the body and of the species:

the body is always in a cross-body relationship with other members of the species and other species outside of it. Joana's desire might be for the continuous experience of herself as not strictly a woman, not strictly human—for a shift to living in movement, the movement of the species, rather than living in the resultant forms that do not, on ordinary time scales, themselves shift but instead make us imagine gender as defined, able to be captured in social roles and prescriptions.

Conclusion

From Darwin's legacy, we understand that difference and deviation may be understood as variation, as a portal for potential change, and that imperceptible change is indeed happening in the present moment; it is at work in the human species, which is open and mutable, part of a continuous animal genealogy. Darwin's heavily descriptive language resists narrative and definition, allows for multiplying meanings, and insists on acknowledging gaps in knowledge. Desire can drive change through the species, and any estrangement in encountering our animal relations can be quickly turned back to reflect the strangeness of our fellow humans.

Joana is indeed a strange human animal; gender seems to fall away readily from her. But she is also a woman. And some measure of her strangeness may arise from how unmarked by femininity Lispector allows her to be. Alternate genealogies—whether that means understanding Joana as serpentine or catlike, or seeing her true family as the groupings of women she comes into contact with—are a way of recognizing that influence and meaningful reorientations to patterns of living and feeling can come from unexpected places. Whereas Lídia gets pregnant, Joana does not: her multiplication of difference through desire creates its own genealogy. Lispector shows us how materiality and unexpected relationships multiply around Joana, creating new paths for the evolution of her strange femininity. Not only does Lispector show it, but she shows us that Joana senses it. This is Joana's version of feeling femininity strangely; her perception of and affective orientation toward her world show us that narratives surrounding desire, familial relations, reproduction, and the construction of bodies can give way to other experiences.

We see Joana's gender constructed through desire and her desire through gender: the possibilities of what, whom, how we can desire run into, and sometimes right through, gendered expectations and norms, and our experience of that desire in turn shapes our felt experience of gender. Darwin offered readers a new way of thinking about desire by connecting it to sexual selection in all species, now understood to be open and changing. Not only can desire have real consequences for all members of the species but the possible ways in which we can desire are opened up. What were previously perceived as human limits are now just a temporary if slow-moving blur.

Conclusion

When I began reading popular science texts alongside novels, I may have imagined that each would tell me a story about how something like materiality or perception works. However, what I found, not just in the literature but in the science as well, was evidence of feelings: excitement and anxiety about the implications of developing research, anger at other scientists, concern over how humans inhabit the world and affect one another. These affectively charged texts, and the rhetoric and metaphors that detach from scientific writing and take on a life of their own in the popular imagination, are as much about imagined possibilities as they are about observed realities. I soon realized that Rosa Chacel's, Norah Lange's, Carmen Laforet's, and Clarice Lispector's novels also offered non-narrative approaches to the felt experience of gender. All of these novels offer ways of making sense of the world through feelings, and I realized that both the science and the literature were pushing me away from a focus on narrative, in search of a different way to talk about gender. That approach has felt as strange as it has productive. In this conclusion, I suggest future avenues for research in the spirit of the encounter between the scientific imaginary and literary renderings of gender that I have explored here. I also reflect on the difficulties of tracking down and creating room for non-narrative, felt experiences of gender in literature and elsewhere, especially while experiencing and observing oppressive attitudes toward gender on and off the page.

Teresa de Lauretis has defined subjectivity as ambi-valent: one valence "is that of subjection to determined social (but not only social) constraints. The other is that of the capacity for self-determination, self-defense, resistance to oppression and to the forces of the external world, but also resistance to and self-defense from forces that act in the internal world."[1] The diverse

---

1 Teresa de Lauretis and Patricia White, *Figures of Resistance: Essays in Feminist Theory* (Urbana: University of Illinois Press, 2007), 220.

scientific writing I have examined is concerned in various ways with the relationship between the external and the internal worlds, and I would like, in conclusion, to reflect on how that subjection and capacity meet up in the experience that is gender, which blurs the internal-external divide.

As for subjection, there may be hegemonic ways of experiencing the materiality, relation, perception, and desire that construct gender; there are certainly hegemonic ways of narrating gendered experience in those categories. I read the scientific writing I have examined here as dislodging old narratives and suggesting new discursive material that can and has been subsumed in new narratives, in part. Yet some of that material—metaphors, recurring imagery, expressive language, textual excitement and concern—does not get taken up by narratives that tell us how gender is or ought to be. The creative potential of that leftover material may suggest new ways of feeling in the world. I see this process as occurring constantly and not just with science: there is new non-narrative material—or diffuse, disjointed narrative—emerging all the time that may let us feel in new ways.

Is this part of a feminist plot—or a real feminist desire—to abolish gender? No, in that the mutability that I note is already happening, has happened, will happen, whether we like it or not, and may continue to work within gender, and in many cases within a gender binary. I am indeed attracted by the idea of more and new possibilities running through and skirting gender, by a more capacious femininity and an expanse of nonbinary experience. I think that change in that direction might occur through how we discuss and think about gender. With this proliferation of scientific imagery and literary insight into the staggering complexity of how gender is felt and experienced, I offer not a blueprint for change, for dissolving the gender binary or somehow leaving behind gender all together, but a way of understanding gender that views it as constantly shifting and open to change from unexpected directions. This allows us to reflect on how fortuitous and indeed strange it is that with the anxiety over uncontrollable outside influence, evidenced by magnetism, and with the strict patrolling of women's roles and bodies, female mediums had the ability to push at corporeal limits. This mode of reading leads us to consider what is lost or foreclosed when women's unusual experiences are coded as mystical rather than viewed through a scientific lens.

And if the view I have presented of the construction of gender as a felt experience is sufficiently complex and nuanced, it bears asking, yet again: Why femininity, if the patriarchy and toxic masculinity—and even more broadly, gender—affect everyone? In *Perto do coração selvagem*, the narrator reflects that "a visão consistia em surpreender o símbolo das coisas nas próprias coisas" ("vision consisted of surprising the symbol of the thing in the thing itself") before later calling women the symbol of the thing in the thing itself (46, [38], see 141). Along similar lines, I would like to think about women as feeling femininity as a symbol within and throughout their gender. Given the potential for resistance to a patriarchal system that they come to symbolize and embody—containing as they do both the effects of such a system and indicators of its potential fault lines—they are subjected to more societal control, allowed to exercise less autonomy, and made to feel less agency, and the processes defining and undefining their gender are starker, easier to see, often more violent, and perhaps more nuanced because power and control are artful. And women suffer in myriad material ways in this regime of symbolic meaning: they have less money, less access, less freedom, experience more violence, more distractions, more exhaustion—and these effects are multiplied for women of intersecting marginalized identities.

So what might it mean to "surprise" that symbol? What way of looking, of reading, would allow us to spot it, and simultaneously spot the ways that it comes into being, the feelings that flow into it and unfold from it? My proposed methodological response here has had to do with reading science and reading women—both as a form of resistance.

Reading women, taking their work seriously, taking their work creatively and not proscriptively, is, to me, a feminist and political act. It can, I believe, mobilize affects and frames of reference that may form part of activist praxis—which is simply one way that we cross out of the internal world into the external one. It may also provide moments of deeply personal reflection, and perhaps a reminder that we are made up of more than the inescapably large-scale gendered impositions that we face. This desire to read women's writing and embrace its complexity, even opacity, has provided the impetus to turn to novels that have been largely overlooked, such as *Personas en la sala*, and to return to those whose critical readings seem by now well rehearsed, such as *Nada*.

As for reading science, I propose that the methodological tack I have set out is one that could be extended today to proliferating technologies: What, for example, becomes of gender online? Who is the quantum *chica rara*? How do current biomedical technologies shape gendered possibilities? Alternatively, there is work to be done recuperating nontextual cultural manifestations of early twentieth-century scientific ideas, be that in films, visual arts, fiber arts, public events, or other creative work happening off the page. The drive behind my examination of scientific discourse has specifically been oriented toward considering gender as constructed through a substrate of experience that is difficult to perceive and harder still to speak of—the question of perception and sensing being itself central to scientific discourse. It is a creative and narrative challenge to understand gender as felt and made within every interaction and brush with the material world, which includes moments of patriarchal, heterosexist, and transphobic violence, of exclusion, of aggression—multiplied as various intersecting modes of oppression meet—but also includes moments of confusion, happiness, hunger, delight, and the chaos of feelings that emerge in these novels. By contemplating some of the scientific quandaries that arise when attempting to describe aspects of the world we do not ordinarily perceive—a world that can be simultaneously atomic *and* magnetic *and* perceptual *and* evolutionary—we may get a sense of the manifold ways in which gender is constructed and the need for many vocabularies to describe it.

Indeed, I hope to have provided new vocabulary and frames of reference for approaching gender and sexuality—a timely proposition as the academic, popular, and activist uses of *queer* are tested and pushed, perhaps to their limits, and as virulent transphobia seeks to confine gender in the most limiting and violent of ways. *Rareza*, without a perfect correlate in English, may provide a fruitful linguistic path for thinking further about gender as inherently unsettled, strange, marked by violence, quotidian, and unbounded.

I finally wish to address a question of scale—if this science as a whole underscores any one point it is that what does not meet the eye does indeed inform our bodies and selves. What, then, is the interface between the kind of "invisible forces of perceptions and feelings" version of gender I have described and the experience of gender shaped by unavoidable and highly visible occurrences such as catcalls, harassment, and gender-based violence? When a man meows at me on the street, am I returned to the openness of the species, suggesting the possibility of an alternate genealogy of difference attuned not to humanness but to animality, so that I might feel the ridiculousness of the human patriarchal construction of gender that makes my body and psyche publicly available and vulnerable as the site of contestation over power and social norms? Maybe... If we think of the gender-based structures and patterns that we recognize and perceive with relative ease, is it not yet more powerful to imagine them as atomically constructed, as magnetic, as embedded in us through our senses or through a species-wide relationship? I suggest that it is. And might vibratory theory, for example, help us to conceive of and speak of the psycho-corporeal feeling of being a woman in public? Might magnetism as much as the concept of the gaze help us come to terms with visceral differences between public and private? I think so.

Thus it is not only that this scientific discourse awakened the public to new possibilities for understanding the world in the first decades of the twentieth century, or that it can as a result provide us with nuanced reading tools for opaque and rich literature from that period: decades later, we might still ask how these paradigms, and those that would follow, affect our experience and understanding of gender—as well as how they might serve as productive sources for affect theory, queer theory, or feminist theory. Literature by and about those women who are called strange may continue to be one of the most fruitful places to look for renewed conceptions of how we come to feel as we do in the world. Early on in *Memorias de Leticia Valle*, Leticia wonders: "¿Es qué podré llegar alguna vez a entender las cosas como los otros? Eso sería el mayor castigo que pudiera esperarme" (Might I someday be able to understand things like others do? That would be the worst punishment that could await me) (20). It is my hope that my methodology, arising from a science-infused approach to rareza, spurs ways of understanding things, and understanding gender, that I cannot begin to imagine.

Works Cited

Agamben, Giorgio. *The Open: Man and Animal*. Translated by Kevin Attell. Stanford: Stanford University Press, 2004.
Aguirre, Joaquín María, ed. Special issue, *Espéculo: Revista de Estudios Literarios*, no. 51 (2013).
Ahmed, Sara. *Queer Phenomenology: Orientations, Objects, Others*. Durham, NC: Duke University Press, 2006.
Almeida, Lélia. "Duas senhoras-meninas transgressors: *Nada* de Carmen Laforet e *Perto do Coração Selvagem* de Clarice Lispector." *Espéculo: Revista de Estudios Literarios*, no. 34 (2006).
Altisent, Marta E. "Images of Barcelona." In *A Companion to the Twentieth-Century Spanish Novel*, edited by Marta E. Altisent, 137–57. Woodbridge: Tamesis, 2008.
Arkinstall, Christine. *Spanish Female Writers and the Freethinking Press, 1879–1926*. Toronto: University of Toronto Press, 2014.
Baeza Salvador, Armando. *Ciencia popular: Los misterios de la ciencia (magnetismo animal, sonambulismo, hipnotismo, espiritismo, etc., etc.)*. Barcelona: Ramón Molinas, 19??.
Barad, Karen. *Meeting the Universe Halfway: Quantum Physics and the Entanglement of Matter and Meaning*. Durham, NC: Duke University Press, 2007.
———. "Nature's Queer Performativity." *Kvinder, Køn & Forskning (Women, Gender, and Research)* 1–2 (2012): 25–53.
Bataille, Georges. *Erotism: Death and Sensuality*. Translated by Mary Dalwood. San Francisco: City Light Books, 1986.
Beer, Gillian. "Darwin in South America: Geology, Imagination and Encounter." In *Science and the Creative Imagination in Latin America*, edited by Evelyn Fishburn and Eduardo Ortiz, 13–23. London: Institute for the Study of the Americas, 2005.
———. *Darwin's Plots: Evolutionary Narrative in Darwin, George Eliot and Nineteenth-Century Fiction*. Cambridge: Cambridge University Press, 2009.
———. "Wave Theory and the Rise of Literary Modernism." In *Open Fields: Science in Cultural Encounter*, 295–320. Oxford: Clarendon Press, 1996.
Benavides Lucas, Manuel. *De la ameba al monstruo propicio: Raíces naturalistas del pensamiento de Ortega y Gasset*. Madrid: University Autónoma de Madrid, 1988.
Benjamin, Walter. *The Writer of Modern Life: Essays on Charles Baudelaire*. Edited by Michael W. Jennings and translated by Howard Eiland et al. Cambridge, MA: Harvard University Press, 2006.

Bennett, Jane. "Of Material Sympathies, Paracelsus, and Whitman." In *Material Ecocriticism*, edited by Serenella Iovino and Serpil Oppermann, 239–52. Bloomington: Indiana University Press, 2014.

———. *Vibrant Matter: A Political Ecology of Things*. Durham, NC: Duke University Press, 2010.

Bergmann, Emilie L. *Women, Culture and Politics in Latin America: Seminar on Feminism and Culture in Latin America*. Berkeley: University of California Press, 1992.

Bernstein, Mark. *Without a Tear: Our Tragic Relationship with Animals*. Chicago: University of Illinois Press, 2004.

Bianchi, Susana. "Los espiritistas argentinos (1880–1910): Religión, ciencia y política." In *Ocultismo y espiritismo en la Argentina*, edited by Robert S. Aruj, Susana Bianchi, and Daniel J. Santamaría, 89–127. Buenos Aires: Centro Editor de América Latina, 1992.

Blackman, Lisa. *Immaterial Bodies: Affect, Embodiment, Mediation*. London: Sage, 2013.

Bloom, Paul. *Against Empathy: The Case for Rational Compassion*. New York: Ecco, 2016.

Bogen, James, "Theory and Observation in Science." *The Stanford Encyclopedia of Philosophy*. Edited by Edward N. Zalta. 2017. plato.stanford.edu/archives/sum2017/entries/science-theory-observation/.

Boll, Marcel. *Qué es: La energía, el vacío, el calor, la luz, el color, el sonido, la electricidad, el magnetismo, la afinidad, el azar*. Buenos Aires: Ed. Pleamar, 1948.

Bowler, Peter J. *Evolution: The History of an Idea*. Berkeley: University of California Press, 1984.

Brennan, Teresa. *The Transmission of Affect*. Ithaca, NY: Cornell University Press, 2004.

Brown, J. Andrew. *Test Tube Envy: Science and Power in Argentine Narrative*. Lewisburg: Bucknell University Press, 2005.

Brown Blackwell, Antoinette Louisa. *The Sexes throughout Nature*. New York: G. P. Putnam's Sons, 1875.

Büchner, Ludwig. *Force and Matter: Empirico-Philosophical Studies, Intelligibly Rendered*. Translated and edited by J. Frederick Collingwood. London: Trübner and Co., 1864.

———. *Fuerza y materia: Estudios populares de historia y filosofía naturales*. Translated by A. Avilés. 8th ed. Barcelona: La Revista Blanca, 1925[?].

Butler, Judith. *Gender Trouble: Feminism and the Subversion of Identity*. New York: Routledge Classics, 2006.

———. "Imitation and Gender Insubordination." In *The Lesbian and Gay Studies Reader*, edited by Henry Abelove, Michele Aina Barale, and David M. Halperin, 307–20. New York: Routledge, 1993.

———. *The Psychic Life of Power: Theories in Subjection*. Stanford: Stanford University Press, 1997.

Caballé, Anna, and Israel Rolón Barada. *Carmen Laforet: Una mujer en fuga*. Barcelona: RBA, 2010.

Cabrera, Blas. *El magnetismo de la materia*. Buenos Aires: Institución Cultural Española, 1944.

———. "La Teoría de la Relatividad." Sociedad de Oceanografía de Guipúzcoa. 1921. Biblioteca Nacional de España, Madrid.

———. "¿Qué es la materia?" Curso de conferencias desarrollado en la Escuela Especial de Ingenieros Agrónomos. Sesión inaugural. 1934. Biblioteca Nacional de España, Madrid.

Carula, Karoline. *A tribuna da ciência: As Conferências Populares da Glória e as discussões do darwinismo na imprensa carioca (1873-1880)*. São Paulo: Annablume, 2009.

Cavanaugh, Cecelia. *New Lenses for Lorca: Literature, Art, and Science in the Edad de Plata*. Lewisburg, PA: Bucknell University Press, 2013.

Chacel, Rosa. "Esquema de los problemas prácticos y actuales del amor." *Revista de Occidente* 31, no. 92 (1931): 129-80.

———. *Memorias de Leticia Valle*. [1945]. Barcelona: Bruguera, 1980.

Chalita, Carlos. *El origen del magnetismo*. Buenos Aires: Casilla de Correo, 1948.

Cixous, Hélène. "Cuentos de la diferencia sexual." Translated by Mara Negrón. *Lectora* 21 (2015): 209-31.

———. "'Mamae, disse ele,' or Joyce's Second Hand." Translated by Eric Prenowitz. In *Stigmata: Escaping Texts*, 100-128. London: Routledge, 1998.

Cleminson, Richard, and Francisco Vázquez García. *Hermaphroditism, Medical Science and Sexual Identity in Spain, 1850-1960*. Cardiff: University of Wales Press, 2009.

———. *"Los Invisibles": A History of Male Homosexuality in Spain 1850-1939*. Cardiff: University of Wales Press, 2007.

Congdon, Renee. "Olores y sonidos de la postguerra española: Un análisis sensorial de *Nada* de Carmen Laforet." In *Carmen Laforet: Después de "Nada", mucho*, edited by Mark Del Mastro and Caragh Wells, 135-59. Valencia: Albatros Ediciones, 2022.

Cornejo Parriego, Rosalía. *Entre mujeres: Política de la amistad y el deseo en la narrativa española contemporánea*. Madrid: Biblioteca Nueva, 2007.

Costa, Felipe A. P. L. "Lendo Darwin em português." *Observatório da Imprensa* 802 (2014): observatoriodaimprensa.com.br/armazem-literario/_ed802_lendo_darwin_em_portugues/.

Culver, Charles A. *Teoria y aplicaciones de electricidad y magnetismo*. Translated by H. Ciancaglini. Buenos Aires: Arbó, 1949.

Cura, Mercedes del, and Rafael Huertas. "Medicina y sexualidad infantil en la España de los años treinta del siglo XX: La aportación del psicoanálisis a la pedagogía sexual." In *La sexualidad en la España contemporánea (1800-1950)*, edited by Jean-Louis Guereña, 189-203. Cádiz: Universidad de Cádiz, 2011.

D'Ambrosio Servodidio, Mirella. "Spatiality in *Nada*." *Anales de la Narrativa Española Contemporánea* 5 (1980): 57-72.

Darwin, Charles. *A origem das espécies, no meio da seleção natural ou a luta pela existência na natureza*. Translated by Joaquim Dá Mesquita Paul. Porto: Lello & Irmão, 1910[?]. http://ecologia.ib.usp.br/ffa/arquivos/abril/darwin1.pdf.

———. *A origem do homem e a seleção sexual*. Translated by Attílio Cancian and Eduardo Nunes Fonseca. N.p., Brazil: Hemus, 1982.

———. *The Descent of Man, and Selection in Relation to Sex*. [1871]. Rev. ed. Princeton, NJ: Princeton University Press, 1981.

———. *The Expression of Emotion in Man and Animals*. [1872]. New York: D. Appleton & Co., 1899.

———. *The Origin of Species by Means of Natural Selection or The Preservation of Favoured Races in the Struggle for Life*. [1859]. New York: Bantam, 2008.

Domínguez, Nora. "Literary Constructions and Gender Performance in the Novels of Norah Lange." Translated by Anny Brooksbank and Catherine Davis. In *Latin American Women's Writing: Feminist Readings in Theory and Crisis*, edited by Anny Brooksbank Jones and Catherine Davis, 30–45. Oxford: Clarendon Press, 1996.

Dror, Otniel. "Seeing the Blush: Feeling Emotions." In *Histories of Scientific Observation*, edited by Lorraine Daston and Elizabeth Lunbeck, 326–48. Chicago: University of Chicago Press, 2011.

Eastman, Max. *The Literary Mind: Its Place in an Age of Science*. New York: Scribner, 1931.

Eddington, Arthur. "La ciencia y el mundo invisible." *Revista de Occidente* 87 (1930): 324–70.

———. *Estrellas y átomos*. Translated by Juan Cabrera y Felipe. Madrid: Revista de Occidente, 1928.

———. "Science and the Unseen World." Google Play. Pickle Partners Publishing, 2019.

———. *Stars and Atoms*. Oxford: Oxford University Press, 1927.

Enke, A. Finn. *Transfeminist Perspectives in and beyond Transgender and Gender Studies*. Philadelphia: Temple University Press, 2012.

Enns, Anthony, and Shelley Trower, eds. *Vibratory Modernism*. Basingstoke: Palgrave Macmillan, 2013.

Ferreira, Teresa Cristina Montero. *Eu seu uma pergunta*. Rio de Janeiro: Rocco, 1999.

Filho, Adonis. "Perto do coração selvagem." *O Jornal*, December 31, 1943, 7.

Fishburn, Evelyn, and Eduardo L. Ortiz, eds. *Science and the Creative Imagination in Latin America*. London: Institute for the Study of the Americas, 2005.

Flatley, Jonathan. *Affective Mapping: Melancholia and the Politics of Modernism*. Cambridge, MA: Harvard University Press, 2008.

Friis, Elizabeth. "In My Core I Have the Strange Impression That I Don't Belong to the Human Species: Clarice Lispector's *Água Viva* as Life Writing?" In *Narrating Life: Experiments with Human and Animal Bodies in Literature, Science and Art*, edited by Stefan Herbrechter and Elizabeth Friis, 33–54. Boston: Rodopi, 2016.

Garay, José. *La física en preguntas y respuestas: Óptica, magnetismo, electricidad*. Buenos Aires: Progreso y Cultura, 1942.

Gasparini, Sandra. "Dos mujeres que aterran: Magnetizadoras y asesinas en los umbrales de dos géneros modernos." Paper presented at the IV Jornadas de Reflexión: Monstruos y Monstruosidades 2010, organized by the Instituto de Estudios Interdisciplinarios de Género de la U.B.A. October 21, 22, and 23, 2010.

Glick, Thomas F. *Einstein in Spain: Relativity and the Recovery of Science*. Princeton, NJ: Princeton University Press, 1988.

Gotlib, Nádia Battella. *Clarice: Uma vida que se conta*. São Paulo: Editora Ática, 1995.

———. "Clarice Lispector the Conference Speaker: The Vanguard and the Right to Narrate." In *After Clarice: Reading Lispector's Legacy in the Twenty-First Century*, edited by Adriana X. Jacobs and Claire Williams, 105–18. Cambridge: Legenda, 2022.

Grace, Daphne. *Beyond Bodies: Gender, Literature and the Enigma of Consciousness*. Amsterdam: Editions Rodopi, 2014.

Grammático, Karin. "Populist Continuities in 'Revolutionary' Perónism? A Comparative Analysis of the Gender Discourses of the First Perónism (1946-1955) and the Montoneros." Translated by Karen Kampwirth. In *Gender and Populism in Latin America: Passionate Politics*, edited by Karen Kampwirth and Kurt Weyland, 122-39. University Park: Penn State University Press, 2010.

Greiner, Rae. "Thinking of Me Thinking of You: Sympathy versus Empathy in the Realist Novel." *Victorian Studies* 53, no. 3 (2011): 417-26.

Grosz, Elizabeth. *Becoming Undone: Darwinian Reflections on Life, Politics, and Art*. Durham, NC: Duke University Press, 2011.

Gruen, Lori. "Dismantling Oppression: An Analysis of the Connection Between Women and Animals." In *Ecofeminism*, edited by Greta Gaard, 60-90. Philadelphia: Temple University Press, 1993.

Gualtieri, Regina Cândida Ellero. *Evolucionismo no Brasil: Ciência e educação nos museus, 1870-1915*. São Paulo: Editora Livraria da Física, 2009.

Haeckel, Ernst. *El monismo como nexo entre la religión y la ciencia: Profesión de fe de un naturalista*. Translated by M. Pino G. Madrid: Fernando Cao y Domingo de Val, 1893.

———. *La evolución y el trasformismo*. Madrid: Imprenta Rollo, 1886.

———. *Monism as Connecting Religion and Science: A Man of Science*. Translated by J. Gilchrist. Project Gutenberg, 2005. www.gutenberg.org/ebooks/9199.

Hallstead-Dabove, Susan. "Disease and Immorality: The Problem of Fashionable Dress in Buenos Aires (1862-1880)." *Latin American Literary Review* 37, no. 73 (2009): 90-117.

Hayles, N. Katherine. "Speculative Aesthetics." *Speculations: A Journal of Speculative Realism* 5 (2014): 158-79.

Henry, Holly. *Virginia Woolf and the Discourse of Science: The Aesthetics of Astronomy*. Cambridge: Cambridge University Press, 2003.

Hilgevoord, Jan, and Jos Uffink. "The Uncertainty Principle." *The Stanford Encyclopedia of Philosophy*. 2016. Edited by Edward N. Zalta. plato.stanford.edu/archives/win2016/entries/qt-uncertainty/.

Hurtado de Mendoza, Diego. "Las teorías de la relatividad y la filosofía en la Argentina (1915-1925)." In *La ciencia en la Argentina entre siglos: Textos, contextos e instituciones*, edited by Marcelo Montserrat and Jens Andermann, 35-51. Buenos Aires: Manantial, 2000.

Ittner, Jutta. "Who's Looking? The Animal Gaze in the Fiction of Brigitte Kronauer and Clarice Lispector." In *Figuring Animals: Essays on Animal Images in Art, Literature, Philosophy, and Popular Culture*, edited by Mary Sanders Pollock and Catherine Rainwater, 99-118. New York: Palgrave, 2005.

Jagot, Paul C. *Método científico de magnetismo, hipnotismo, sugestión, tomo III: Cómo hacer reaccionar la actividad nerviosa sobre los órganos enfermos*. Translated by Pedro Labrousse. Buenos Aires: Editorial Tor, 1963[?].

———. *Método científico moderno de magnetismo, hipnotismo, sugestión*. Buenos Aires: Editorial Tor, 1938.

———. *Método práctico y científico de magnetismo, hipnótismo, sugestión: Curso práctico de experimentación al alcance de todos*. Translated by José Pérez Guerrero. Buenos Aires: Joaquin Gil, 1941.

Jeftanovic, Andrea. "*Perto do coração selvagem* de Clarice Lispector: La infancia como temporalidad y espacio existencial." *Revista Iberoamericana* 73, nos. 218–19 (2007): 253–66.

Kampwirth, Karen, and Kurt Weyland, eds. *Gender and Populism in Latin America: Passionate Politics*. University Park: Penn State University Press, 2010.

Katz, David. *El mundo de las sensaciones táctiles*. Translated by Manuel García Morente. Madrid: Revista de Occidente, 1930.

———. *The World of Touch*. Translated by Lester E. Krueger. New York: Psychology Press, 1989.

Kebadze, Nino. *Romance and Exemplarity in Post-War Spanish Women's Narratives: Fictions of Surrender*. Woodbridge: Tamesis, 2009.

Kirkpatrick, Susan. *Mujer, modernismo y vanguardia en España: 1898–1931*. Translated by Jaqueline Cruz. Madrid: Cátedra, 2003.

Kroker, Arthur. *Body Drift: Butler, Hayles, Haraway*. Minneapolis: University of Minnesota Press, 2012.

Labanyi, Jo. "Resemanticizing Feminine Surrender: Cross-Gender Identifications in the Writings of Spanish Female Fascist Activists." In *Women's Narrative and Film in 20th-Century Spain*, edited by Ofelia Ferrán and Kathleen Glenn, 75–92. London: Routledge, 2002.

Laforet, Carmen. *Nada*. [1945]. New York: The Modern Library, 2008.

———. *Nada*. Translated by Edith Grossman. New York: The Modern Library, 2008.

Laforet, Carmen, and Ramón J. Sender. *Puedo contar contigo: Correspondencia*. Edited by Israel Rolón Barada. Barcelona: Ediciones Destino, 2003.

Landry, Travis. *Darwin, Sexual Selection, and the Spanish Novel*. Seattle: University of Washington Press, 2012.

Lange, Norah. *People in the Room*. Translated by Charlotte Whittle. Sheffield: And Other Stories, 2018.

———. *Personas en la sala*. [1950]. Madrid: Ediciones Barataria, 2011.

Laso Prieto, José María. "El exilio científico español." *Ábaco* 42 (2004): 49–59.

Lauretis, Teresa de, and Patricia White. *Figures of Resistance: Essays in Feminist Theory*. Urbana: University of Illinois Press, 2007.

Lemon, Harvey B., and Michael Ference. *Física experimental analítica: Magnetismo y electricidad*. Buenos Aires: Espasa Calpe, 1947.

Lispector, Clarice. *Near to the Wild Heart*. Translated by Alison Entrekin. New York: New Directions, 2012.

———. *Perto do coração selvagem*. [1943]. Rio de Janeiro: Rocco, 1998.

Lorde, Audre. "Uses of the Erotic: The Erotic as Power." In *Sister Outsider: Essays and Speeches*, 53–59. Berkeley, CA: Crossing Press, 1984.

Mangini, Shirley. "Women, Eros, and Culture: The Essays of Rosa Chacel." In *Spanish Woman Writers and the Essay: Gender, Politics, and the Self*, edited by Kathleen M. Glenn and Mercedes Mazquiarán de Rodríguez, 127–43. Columbia: University of Missouri Press, 1998.

Marco, Valeria de. "*Nada*: El espacio transparente y opaco a la vez." *Revista Hispánica Moderna* 49, no. 1 (1996): 59–75.

Martín Gaite, Carmen. *Desde la ventana: Enfoque femenino de la literatura española*. Madrid: Espasa-Calpe, 1987.

———. *Usos amorosos de la postguerra española*. [1987]. Barcelona: Anagrama, 2011.
Massumi, Brian. *Politics of Affect*. Cambridge: Polity, 2015.
Mateo, María A. *Retrato de Rosa Chacel*. Barcelona: Círculo de Lectores, 1993.
Mauss, Marcel. *A General Theory of Magic*. Translated by Robert Brain. London: Routledge, 1972.
———. *Magia y sacrificio en la historia de las religiones*. Translated by Henri Hubert. Buenos Aires: Lautaro, 1946.
Medina Doménech, Rosa María. "Ideas para perder la inocencia sobre los textos de ciencia." In *Interacciones ciencia y género: Discursos y prácticas científicas de mujeres*, edited by María José Barral, Carmen Magallón, Consuelo Miqueo, and María Dolores Sánchez, 103–27. Barcelona: Icaria, 1999.
Miguel, María E. *Norah Lange: Una biografía*. Buenos Aires: Planeta, 1991.
Molloy, Sylvia. *At Face Value: Autobiographical Writing in Spanish America*. Cambridge: Cambridge University Press, 1991.
Moser, Benjamin. *Why This World: A Biography of Clarice Lispector*. New York: Oxford University Press, 2009.
Murphy, Katherine. "Monstrosity and the Modernist Consciousness: Pío Baroja versus Rosa Chacel." *Anales de la Literatura Española Contemporánea* 35, no. 1 (2010): 141–75.
———. "Spanish Modernism in Context: Failed Heroism and Cross-Cultural Encounters in Pío Baroja and Joseph Conrad." *Bulletin of Spanish Studies* 97, no. 5 (2020): 807–29.
———. "Unspeakable Relations: Eroticism and the Seduction of Reason in Rosa Chacel's *Memorias de Leticia Valle*." *Journal of Iberian and Latin American Studies* 16, no. 1 (2010): 51–72.
Nagel, Thomas. "What Is It Like to Be a Bat?" *The Philosophical Review* 83, no. 4 (1974): 435–50.
Negrón, Mara. *De la animalidad no hay salida: Ensayos sobre animalidad, cuerpo y ciudad*. San Juan: La Editorial Universidad de Puerto Rico, 2009.
———. "Más allá del saber: La inocencia de Hélène Cixous y la pasión de Clarice Lispector." *Nuevo Texto Crítico* 7, nos. 14–15 (1995): 295–305.
Neves, Marcos C. D., and Josie A. P. Silva. *Evoluções e revoluções: O mundo em transição*. Maringá: Massoni, 2010.
Nina, Cláudia. *A palavra usurpada: Exílio e nomadismo na obra de Clarice Lispector*. Porto Alegre: EDIPUCRS, 2003.
Nouzeilles, Gabriela. *Ficciones somáticas: Naturalismo, nacionalismo y políticas médicas del cuerpo (Argentina 1880–1910)*. Rosario: Beatriz Viterbo Editora, 2000.
O'Byrne, Patricia. "Popular Fiction in Postwar Spain: The Soothing, Subversive *Novela Rosa*." *Journal of Romance Studies* 8, no. 2 (2008): 37–57.
———. *Post-War Spanish Women Novelists and the Recuperation of Historical Memory*. Woodbridge: Tamesis, 2014.
Ochoa, Debra J. "Critiques of the 'Novela Rosa': Martín Gaite, Almodóvar, and Etxebarría." *Letras Femeninas* 32, no. 1 (2006): 189–203.
Ortega, Teófilo. "El espejo y el camino." *Revista del Ateneo* 54 (1930): 127–30.
Ortiz, Eduardo L. "A Convergence of Interests: Einstein's Visit to Argentina in 1925." *Ibero-Amerikanisches Archiv* 21, nos. 1–2 (1995): 67–126.

Otis, Laura. *Membranes: Metaphors of Invasion in Nineteenth-Century Literature, Science, and Politics*. Baltimore: The Johns Hopkins University Press, 1999.

Pérez-Magallón, Jesús. "Leticia Valle o la indeterminación genérica." *Anales de la Literatura Española Contemporánea* 28, no. 1 (2003): 139–59.

Polinntzieu, Q. G. *Magia blanca moderna, ó sea magnetismo, hipnotismo, sugestión y espiritismo*. Barcelona / Buenos Aires / Mexico City: Maucci, 1899.

Protevi, John. *Political Affect: Connecting the Social and the Somatic*. Minneapolis: University of Minnesota Press, 2009.

Ramón y Cajal, Santiago. "Las sensaciones de las hormigas." *Archivos de Neurobiología* 2, no. 4 (1921): n.p.

Reichenbach, Hans. *Átomo y cosmos: Concepción física actual del universo*. Translated by Javier Cabrera. Madrid: Revista de Occidente, 1931.

———. *Atom and Cosmos: The World of Modern Physics*. [1933]. Translated by Edward Allen. New York: Macmillan, 1957.

Richardson, Sarah. *Sex Itself: The Search for Male and Female in the Human Genome*. Chicago: University of Chicago Press, 2013.

Rivero, Alicia. "Heisenberg's Uncertainty Principle in Contemporary Spanish American Fiction." In *Science and the Creative Imagination in Latin America*, edited by Evelyn Fishburn and Eduardo Ortiz, 129–50. London: Institute for the Study of the Americas, 2005.

Rodriguez, Julia. *Civilizing Argentina: Science, Medicine, and the Modern State*. Chapel Hill: University of North Carolina Press, 2006.

Rosales, Elisa. "*Memorias de Leticia Valle*: Rosa Chacel o el deletreo de lo inaudito." *Hispania* 83, no. 2 (2000): 222–31.

Rovelli, Carlo. *Reality Is Not What It Seems: The Journey to Quantum Gravity*. Translated by Simon Carnell and Erica Segre. New York: Riverhead Books, 2017.

Ruggiero, Kristin. *Modernity in the Flesh: Medicine, Law, and Society in Turn-of-the-Century Argentina*. Stanford: Stanford University Press, 2004.

Sala y Villaret, Pedro. *Materia, forma y fuerza: Diseño de una filosofía*. Madrid: José Cruzado, 1891.

Santamaría, Daniel J. "Razones y sinrazones del ocultismo." In *Ocultismo y espiritismo en la Argentina*, edited by Robert S. Aruj, Susana Bianchi, and Santamaría, 7–45. Buenos Aires: Centro Editor de América Latina, 1992.

Sarlo, Beatriz. *La imaginación técnica: Sueños modernos de la cultura argentina*. Buenos Aires: Ediciones Nueva Visión, 1992.

Scarlett, Elizabeth A. *Under Construction: The Body in Spanish Novels*. Charlottesville: University Press of Virginia, 1994.

Scheler, Max. *Esencia y formas de la simpatía*. Translated by José Gaos. Buenos Aires: Losada, 1942.

Schell, Patience A. *The Sociable Sciences: Darwin and His Contemporaries in Chile*. New York: Palgrave Macmillan, 2013.

Schopenhauer, Arthur. *Las ciencias ocultas: Magnetismo animal, el destino del indivuduo, ensayo sobre las apariciones de espíritus*. Buenos Aires: Kier, 1946.

Schuller, Kyla. "The Microbial Self: Sensation and Sympoeisis." *Resilience: A Journal of the Environmental Humanities* 5, no. 3 (2018): 51–67.

Scrivner, Lee. *Becoming Insomniac: How Sleeplessness Alarmed Modernity*. Basingstoke: Palgrave Macmillan, 2014.

Sedgwick, Eve Kosofsky. "Queer and Now." In *Tendencies*, 1–19. London: Routledge, 1994.
Sierra, Marta. *Gendered Spaces in Argentine Women's Literature*. New York: Palgrave Macmillan, 2012.
———. "Oblique Views: Artistic Doubling, Ironic Mirroring and Photomontage in the Works of Norah Lange and Norah Borges." *Revista Canadiense de Estudios Hispánicos* 29, no. 3 (2005): 564–84.
Silva, Josie A. P., and Marcos C. D. Neves. *Arte e ciência: Um encontro interdisciplinar*. Maringá: Massoni, 2010.
Smith-Sherwood, Dawn. "Las chicas raras de STEM: Recuperating #WomensPlace in Spanish Literary and Scientific Histories." In *A Laboratory of Her Own: Women and Science in Spanish Culture*, edited by Victoria L. Ketz, Dawn Smith-Sherwood, and Debra Faszer-McMahon, 33–51. Nashville, TN: Vanderbilt University Press, 2021.
Stockton, Kathryn Bond. *The Queer Child, or Growing Sideways in the Twentieth Century*. Durham, NC: Duke University Press, 2009.
Stueber, Karsten. "Empathy." *The Stanford Encyclopedia of Philosophy*. Edited by Edward N. Zalta. 2017. plato.stanford.edu/archives/spr2017/entries/empathy/.
Swanson, Larry W., and Lyndel King, Eric Himmel, Eric A. Newman, Alfonso Araque, and Janet Dubinsky. *The Beautiful Brain: The Drawings of Santiago Ramón y Cajal*. New York: Abrams Books, 2018.
Thibaud, Jean. *Vida y transmutaciones de los átomos*. Translated by Xavier Zubiri. Buenos Aires: Espasa-Calpe, 1942.
Uexküll, Jakob von. *Cartas biológicas a una dama*. [1925]. Translated by Manuel G. Morente. 2nd edition. Madrid: Revista de Occidente, 1945.
———. *Ideas para una concepción biológica del mundo*. [1922]. Translated by R. M. Tenreiro. 2nd edition. Buenos Aires / Madrid: Espasa-Calpe, 1934.
———. "La biología de la ostra jacobea." *Revista de Occidente* 9 (1924): 297–331.
———. *Meditaciones biológicas: La teoría de la significación*. Translated by José M. Sacristán. Madrid: Revista de Occidente, 1942.
———. *Teoría de la vida*. Madrid: Editorial Summa, 1944.
Unruh, Vicky. *Performing Women and Modern Literary Culture in Latin America*. Austin: University of Texas Press, 2006.
Villares, Lucia. *Examining Whiteness: Reading Clarice Lispector through Bessie Head and Toni Morrison*. London: Legenda, 2011.
Weyl, Hermann. *¿Qué es la materia?* Translated by Blas Cabrera. Madrid: Revista de Occidente, 1925.
Wiegman, Robyn. "The Times We're In: Queer Feminist Criticism and the 'Reparative' Turn." *Feminist Theory* 15, no. 1 (2014): 4–25.
Wilson, Elizabeth. *The Sphinx in the City: Urban Life, the Control of Disorder, and Women*. Berkeley: University of California Press, 1991.
Wolfe, Joel. "From Working Mothers to Housewives: Gender and Brazilian Populism from Getúlio Vargas to Juscelino Kubitschek." In *Gender and Populism in Latin America: Passionate Politics*, edited by Karen Kampwirth, 91–108. University Park: Penn State University Press, 2010.
Zillig, Cezar. *Dear Mr. Darwin: A intimidade da correspondência entre Fritz Müller e Charles Darwin*. São Paulo: 43 SA Gráfica e Editora, 1997.

Index

affect theory 3, 5, 9, 47–50
Agamben, Giorgio 105, 113, 118, 161
Agassiz, Alex 145
Ahmed, Sara, *Queer Phenomenology* 6
Altisent, Marta E. 109n5
Arkinstall, Christine 83–85n27

Baeza Salvador, Armando 80
Bataille, Georges 41
Beer, Gillian 8, 16, 47n36, 147
Bellot, Gabrielle 75–76n16
Benjamin, Walter 127n24, 133n28
Bennett, Jane 6, 7
Bergson, Henri 153
Bernstein, Mark 157n25
Bianchi, Susana 78, 84
Blackman, Lisa, *Immaterial Bodies* 9
Bloom, Paul 86–87
Borges, Jorge Luis 67, 68
Borges, Norah 22–23, 67, 94n38
Bowler, Peter J. 152
Braidotti, Rosi 161
Brennan, Teresa 6
  The Transmission of Affect 6n10
Büchner, Ludwig 27–28
Burgos, Carmen de 38
Butler, Judith 4, 121

Caballé, Anna 111
Cabrera, Blas 76–77n17
Cabrera y Felipe, Juan 35
Carnell, Simon 66n5
Carula, Karoline 145–146
Chacel, Rosa 12, 38, 41–42, 66, 173
  Memorias de Leticia Valle 2, 11, 13–14, 20n2–22, 38, 39, 40–62, 67, 102, 143, 163, 166
  trope of "little girlness" 43–44, 52–53
chicas raras 2, 3, 15–17, 51, 106–107, 122–123, 140
  online 175
Cixous, Hélène 148, 159–160
Cleminson, Richard 37, 38–39
Congdon, Renee 108–109n4
contagion 40–51, 87n31, 97n39
Cornejo Parriego, Rosalía 51, 52
Cruz, Jacqueline 10n18
Cura, Mercedes del 39
Cvetkovich, Ann, *Depression: A Public Feeling* 6

Darwin, Charles 3, 8, 12, 16–17, 117, 139–172
  The Descent of Man 139, 149–150, 154
  The Origin of the Species 139, 149–151
  selection theory 152–153
de Beauvoir, Simone 4
Deleuze, Gilles 153, 154
Domingo Soler, Amalia 83–84, 85
Domínguez, Nora 70–71, 90
Dror, Otniel 87–88

Eastman, Max 3–4
  The Literary Mind 3
Eddington, Arthur 29–36, 113n13, 163
Edelman, Lee 52
Einstein, Albert 75–76n16
empathy 85–91
Enke, Finn 4
Enns, Anthony 72n11

Entrenkin, Alison 1n1
Ernst, Max 22

Flatley, Jonathan 10n18
Franco, Francisco 109
Freud, Sigmund 14, 23, 38
Friis, Elizabeth 160–161

García Morente, Manuel 32
gender 173–177
   alternate genealogy 17, 142–143, 165, 171–172
   childhood sexuality 39–40, 43, 47–57, 159
   chromosomal difference 37, 38
   constructed and performative 4, 17–18, 47–51, 51–52, 69–70, 110, 161–162, 173–174, 174
   eroticism 41–43
   felt experience 5–6, 11, 36, 44, 60–61, 103, 107–108, 121, 137, 173–177
   gendered survival 15, 51, 105–106, 111, 124–125
   hermaphroditism 37–38
   intersexuality 37–38
   online 175
   performativity 14–15
   queerness 2–3, 13, 14, 45–46, 56, 123–124
   scientific research on sexual difference 37–40
   sexual binarism 154
   signifiers 45–46, 51–52
   see also women
Girondo, Oliverio 67–68
Glick, Thomas F. 75–76n16
González Lanuza, Eduardo 67
Grace, Daphne, *Beyond Bodies* 66n5
Greiner, Rae 86
Grossman, Edith 2n2
Grosz, Elizabeth 8, 16, 53n40, 153–155
   Becoming Undone 153
Gruen, Lori 157n25
Gualtieri, Regina Cándida Ellero 144–145

Haeckel, Ernst 25–27, 29, 34n20, 35–36, 116–117n14, 144–145

El monismo como nexo 25–26
Hardy, Thomas 147
Hayles, N. Katherine 36, 44n34
Heisenberg, Werner, uncertainty principle 31n16, 34n21, 112n10
Helmholtz, Hermann von, Law of Conservation of Energy 26
Henry, Holly, *Virginia Woolf and the Discourse of Science* 10n18
Hernández, Felisberto 71
Hidalgo, Alberto 68
Huertas, Rafael 39
Huidobro, Vicente 68
human species 168, 171–172
   alternate genealogy 165, 171–172, 176
   animality 140, 155–159, 176–177
   constant transformation 145, 168–169
   felt experience 156, 168
   mutability 140, 156, 170–171, 174
   self-determination 173
Huxley, Julian 144, 152
hypnotism 63, 77, 81

Irigaray, Luce 8, 153–154
Ittner, Jutta 158–159n28

Jagot, Paul 14, 63–64, 77n18, 81–83
James, William 88
Jeftanovic, Andrea 158
Joyce, James 10n18, 23–24, 148n14

Katz, David 32, 33, 80
Kebadze, Nino 110
Kirkpatrick, Susan 10n18
Kroker, Arthur 44n33
Kubitschek, Juscelino 142–143

Laforet, Carmen 12, 173
   Nada 2, 11, 12, 15–16, 106–138, 175
Landry, Travis 16, 148, 151
Lange, Norah 12, 14, 67–71, 89n35, 141, 173
   45 días y 30 marineros 63n2, 93
   gendered gaze 91–103
   Personas en la sala 2n2, 11, 12, 14, 64–71, 91–103, 123–124, 126, 140, 161n34, 166

writing and performing gender 67-71, 72-73
Lauretis, Teresa de 173
Lavoisier, Antoine, Law of Conservation of Matter 26
Lipps, Theodor 86
Lispector, Clarice 10n18, 12, 173
   A paixão segundo G. H. 156-157, 158
   Perto do coração selvagem 1n1-2, 11, 12, 16, 140-172, 174
literature
   alternative form of sense making 58-59, 60, 67
   analyses of gender 11, 24
   construction of gender 1, 4, 11, 47-51, 103, 140-141
   female gaze 71-74, 102-104
   female protagonists 2, 13
   novela rosa 2, 106-107
   gendered strangeness 2-3, 13, 14, 45-46, 56, 123-124, 140-141, 176-177
   postwar 106-107
   pseudoscientific writing 3, 8, 14, 74-83
   scientific reimagining 19-20
   scientific vocabulary and ideas 1, 3, 7-9, 14, 63-64, 147-148, 173
   self-help 14, 63-64
Lorde, Audre 42-43

magnetism 3, 8, 14-15, 63-64, 76-83, 97, 103-104, 163-164, 174
   electromagnetism 66, 77, 83
   personal and animal 66, 77-78
   pseudoscience and self-help 77-83
Maier, Carol 2n2
Mangini, Shirley 42n29
Marañón, Gregorio 37-38
Marco, Valeria de 109, 127, 128
Marden, Orison Swett 81
Martín Gaite, Carmen 2, 15-16, 106, 107, 122, 133
   Desde la ventana 2
   see also chicas raras
Massumi, Brian 5
Mateo, María A. 22-23
   Retrato de Rosa Chacel 22-23

materiality 11, 24-28, 147, 173
   domestic and street 126-132
   force and form 24-25
   (im)perceptibile matter 29-34, 44
   mutable matter 28-29
   "observer effect" 30-31n16, 50-51, 112n10
   physicality 45n35
   sameness and perception 24-25, 28-29, 44
   sensory perception 24-25, 30-33, 95, 114-115, 162
   solid matter 34-35
   tejido material 28-29
   vibratory theory 33-34, 80-81, 97, 176
   see also monism; vitalism
Mauss, Marcel, *General Theory of Magic* 88-89
Mayer, Julius Robert von, Law of Conservation of Energy 26
Medina Doménech, Rosa María 64n3
Mesmer, Franz 81
miasma theory 97n39
Miguel, María E. 89n35
Milne Edwards, Alphonse 145
mimetic posture 7
Mira, Alberto 38
modernism 3-4, 10n18
   literary 12
Molloy, Sylvia 71
monism 13, 25-27, 35, 116
   inseparability of force and matter 26-27
Moreno, Carola 67
Moser, Benjamin *Why This World* 141-142
movement, theory of 33-34
Müller, Fritz 148
Murphy, Katherine 40, 51-52
   "Spanish Modernism in Context" 10n18
mutability 140, 156, 170-171, 174

Nagel, Thomas 31n17
Negrón, Mara 160
new materialist theory 3, 5
Nouzielles, Gabriela 72n12
novela rosa 2, 106-107, 109-110, 122-123

O'Byrne, Patricia 110
Ocampo, Victoria 22–23, 38, 72
occult literature 8, 14, 74–77, 163
Ochoa, Debra 2
Ortega, Teófilo 112
   Revista del Ateneo 118
Ortega y Gasset, José 15, 53, 111–112, 119–121n19
Ortelli, Roberto 67
Otis, Laura, *Membranes* 7

perception 11, 105–106, 161
   constant transformation 145, 168–169
   self-centered worlds 105–138
Pérez Rubio, Timoteo 22
Permanyer, Lluis 111
Picasso, Pablo 22
Piñero, Francisco 67
Protevi, John, *Political Affect* 6

quantum entanglement 66n5

Ramón y Cajal, Santiago 15, 33–34, 92, 117, 155–156
Reichenbach, Hans 13, 24, 29, 44, 54
   Átomo y cosmos 19, 24
relationality
   observation 48
   role in constructing gender 65–67
Richardson, Sarah 37
Rivero, Alicia 34n21
Rolón Barada, Israel 111
Rosales, Elisa 58
Rovelli, Carlo, *Reality Is Not What It Seems* 66n5

Sala y Villaret, Pedro 34n20, 90
   Materia, forma y fuerza 29, 79–80
Sand, George 133
Santamaria, Daniel 78–79
Sarlo, Beatriz 74–75, 82n23
Scarlett, Elizabeth, *Under Construction* 23
Scheler, Max 42, 89, 113n13
Schell, Patience A. 16, 148
Schuller, Kyla 11n20
Schultze, Max 145

scientific writing *see* literature, scientific vocabulary and ideas
Scrivner, Lee, *Becoming Insomniac* 7
Sedgwick, Eve Kosofsky 15, 117, 121, 124–125
Segre, Erica 66n5
Sender, Ramón 16, 107, 124, 128
Sierra, Marta 70n8, 72, 73, 90, 94n38
Simmel, Georg 42
Smith, Adam 86
somnambulism 77, 81
Spencer, Herbert 139n2, 144–145
   law of progressive differentiation 144–145
spiritism 78–79, 99
   and women 83–85
Stockton, Kathryn Bond 53, 124
   The Queer Child 52
Stueber, Karsten 85
Suleiman, Susan 90
surrealism 23–24
sympathy 85–91
   suggestion 63, 66, 81
   see also contagion; empathy

Thibaud, Jean 28, 31, 111
Titchener, Edward 85
Trower, Shelley 72n11

Uexküll, Jakob von 31–32, 44n34, 111–112, 113–122, 129
   Cartas biológicas a una dama 113–114, 115
   Teoría de la vida 105
   Umwelten (self-centered worlds) 15, 16, 31, 105, 107, 112n10, 113–122, 135–137, 140
Umwelten 3
Unruh, Vicky 65n4, 68–69, 90

Vargas, Getúlio 142–143
Vázquez García, Francisco 37, 38–39
Vergés, Josep 111
vibratory theory 33–34, 80–81, 97, 176
Villares, Lucia 150n17
Vischer, Robert 86
vitalism 25–26, 28

Whittle, Charlotte 2n2, 12
Whitworth, Michael 10
Wiegman, Robyn 121
Wilson, Elizabeth A., *Gut Feminism* 6
Wolfe, Joel 142-143
women 4, 13, 90
    animality 156-158, 168-170
    female gaze 71-74
    femininity 109-110, 169-170, 174
    secret world 107-108, 118-122
    spiritism 83-85
Woolf, Virginia 10n18, 75-76n16, 141, 148
    The Waves 47n36

Zillig, Cezar 145, 148
Zubiri, Xavier 28, 111

Printed and bound by CPI Group (UK) Ltd, Croydon, CR0 4YY
23/05/2024